AMERICAN
HERITAGE

December, 1968 · Volume XX, Number 1

What Are These People Doing?

TO FIND OUT, TURN TO PAGE 101

AMERICAN HERITAGE

The Magazine of History

SENIOR EDITOR
Bruce Catton

EDITOR
Oliver Jensen
MANAGING EDITOR
Robert Lincoln Reynolds
ART DIRECTOR
Murray Belsky
ART EDITOR
Joan Paterson Kerr
ARTICLES EDITOR
E. M. Halliday
ASSOCIATE EDITORS
Robert S. Gallagher   David G. Lowe
Barbara Klaw   John L. Phillips
Douglas Tunstell
COPY EDITOR
Brenda Niemand
EDITORIAL ASSISTANTS
Mary Dawn Earley   Rosemary L. Klein
Mary A. Hawkins   Joanne Shapiro

PUBLISHER
Darby Perry

ADVISORY BOARD
Allan Nevins, *Chairman*
Carl Carmer   Louis C. Jones
Gerald Carson   Alvin M. Josephy, Jr.
Marshall B. Davidson   Howard H. Peckham
John A. Garraty   Francis S. Ronalds
Eric F. Goldman   S. K. Stevens

American Heritage Publishing Co., Inc.

PRESIDENT
James Parton
CHAIRMAN, EDITORIAL COMMITTEE
Joseph J. Thorndike
MANAGING DIRECTOR, BOOK DIVISION
Richard M. Ketchum
SENIOR ART DIRECTOR
Irwin Glusker

AMERICAN HERITAGE is published every two months by American Heritage Publishing Co., Inc., editorial and executive offices, 551 Fifth Avenue, New York, N.Y. 10017. Treasurer, George W. Breitkreuz; Secretary, John C. Taylor III. Correspondence about subscriptions should be sent to American Heritage Subscription Office, 383 West Center Street, Marion, Ohio 43302. Single Copies: $4.25. Annual subscriptions: $16.50 in U.S. and Canada; $17.50 elsewhere. An annual Index is published each spring, priced at $1.00. AMERICAN HERITAGE will consider but assumes no responsibility for unsolicited materials. Title registered U.S. Patent Office. Second-class postage paid at New York, N.Y., and at additional mailing offices.

Sponsored by
American Association for State & Local History · Society of American Historians

CONTENTS   *December, 1968 · Volume XX, Number 1*

CORNPLANTER, CAN YOU SWIM? by Alvin M. Josephy, Jr.   4
'BYE, PHOEBE SNOW, 'BYE, BUFFALO by Oliver Jensen   10
THE BIOGRAPHER AND HIS HERO by Catherine Drinker Bowen   16
WOODEN DELIGHTS by David G. Lowe   18
THE JAY PAPERS II: THE FORGING OF THE NATION
Edited and annotated by Richard B. Morris   24
THE GREAT SEA BATTLE by Peter Padfield
With a portfolio of illustrations   29
HOW HARDING SAVED THE VERSAILLES TREATY
by Robert K. Murray   66
GEORGE WASHINGTON'S MONUMENT   68
"TAKE THE HATRED AWAY, AND YOU HAVE NOTHING LEFT"
by Thomas J. Fleming   74
AN AMERICAN HERITAGE ORIGINAL DOCUMENT
A DAKOTA BOYHOOD by James Earle Fraser   81
THE FLOWERING OF THE SPEAKER'S ART by John L. Phillips   101
A NOTE TO HIPPIES AND FLOWER PEOPLE   112

COVER: This sword was presented in 1813 by the mayor and the Common Council of the City of London to Captain Philip Bowes Vere Broke, master of His Majesty's frigate *Shannon.* On June 1 of that year the *Shannon* had met and bested in single combat the United States frigate *Chesapeake,* ending a string of British naval defeats in the early months of the War of 1812 but producing, in the dying words of the *Chesapeake*'s Captain James Lawrence, one of the enduring rallying cries of American history. A full and handsomely illustrated account of the gallant sea battle begins on page 29. By courtesy of its present owner, the Honorable J. V. B. Saumarez, the sword was photographed by Anthony Howarth at Broke's ancestral home in Suffolk. *Back Cover:* Cornplanter was in vigorous middle age when this lithograph, now owned by the Library of Congress, was made. Even during his lifetime white men were expropriating lands deeded to him and the Senecas by the government. Today the remnants of those lands have been invaded anew, as described in the article beginning on page 4.

In a cemetery high on a promontory overlooking the broad waters of the new Allegheny Reservoir in northwestern Pennsylvania stands a stone monument to a once powerful and celebrated Seneca Indian war chief, The Cornplanter, who fought with the British against the Americans during the Revolution, and then became a loyal friend of the United States and a steadfast protector of American families settling in the wilderness of the upper Ohio River basin. The monument has not been at its present site long. In 1964, amid controversy, anger, and the protests of many Seneca Indians, the United States Army Corps of Engineers moved the memorial shaft, together with what was left of the earthly remains of The Cornplanter and more than 300 of his followers and descendants, from an Indian cemetery ("our Arlington," pleaded a Seneca woman) that was about to be inundated by rising waters behind the engineers' new Kinzua Dam on the Allegheny River.

In the Seneca language, which many of the Indians still speak, *kinzua* means "fish on spear" and refers to a site on the river 198 river miles above Pittsburgh, just south of the New York state line, where the dam

An unhappy descendant surveys Cornplanter's monument, forcibly moved from his "perpetual" grant to a new Indian-white cemetery.

was built. Finished in 1965 at a cost of almost $120,-000,000, it is the largest concrete and earth-fill dam in the eastern United States, almost 1,900 feet long and 179 feet high. It is designed to help control floods, as well as to regulate the flow of water for navigation and for the dilution of polluting waste matter poured into the river by mills above Pittsburgh. Among the dam's important by-products is hydroelectric power, now being exploited by private developers, and the provision of new recreational facilities for the region. Behind the dam is the new Allegheny Reservoir, whose size changes constantly depending on rainfall and the season of the year. At its maximum, in time of severe flood conditions, the lake would extend thirty-five miles upriver to Salamanca, New York, and would have a water surface of more than 21,000 acres. But under ordinary conditions it extends in summer twenty-seven miles, more or less, covers some 12,000 acres, and has a shore line of ninety-one miles. In winter it is a considerably smaller pool, covering a minimum of about 6,600 acres and exposing large areas of mud flats. To the summer vacationer, tourist, and lover of water sports, the reservoir has provided a large new recreation center in the forested mountain country of western New York and Pennsylvania and has already borne out the army engineers' promise that the dam and its lake would result in the development of a relatively untouched part of the Northeast in the

Cornplanter,

The new Kinzua Dam floods the Senecas' ancestral lands —in violation of our oldest Indian treaty. "Lake Perfidy" may even have claimed the bones of their greatest chief

time-honored tradition of American progress.

But there was a cost beyond the cost of the dam, and the raising of a moral question that pricked the conscience of the nation on what has long been an extremely sore point. In creating the Allegheny Reservoir behind Kinzua Dam, the army engineers gutted the Seneca Indians' reservation, drowning approximately 10,000 acres of the Indians' only habitable land, which ran along the Allegheny River, and deliberately breaking an Indian treaty in order to do so. In this instance the violated obligation was the federal government's oldest active treaty, made in 1794 with The Cornplanter's Senecas and five other Indian nations at a time when the new American republic urgently needed their friendship on the turbulent northwest frontier, and resting ever since then on solemn guarantees which were given by President George Washington and which were supposed to endure through the life of the United States itself.

To many non-Indians who were aware of the engineers' treaty-breaking action, it was, as Florida Congressman James Haley of the House Interior and Insular Affairs Committee said on May 18, 1963, "a horrible tragedy, a horribly tragic thing," underscored especially by the fact that the United States was, at the same time, insisting that the rest of the world honor and respect the sacredness of treaties. To the Senecas and to many other American Indians it was,

moreover, another painful reminder that the history of white men's injustices to them had not ended. Indian wars are no more, for the tribes' power to resist with arms has vanished. But their defensive actions still go on, quietly now and with little or no publicity, in courts of law, and the Indians, more often than not, still continue to lose what they are defending. In their sadness they increasingly ask the white man: Why feel guilty and sorry about what happened in the nineteenth century? Pay closer attention to what you are still doing to us.

To the Senecas, the new body of water behind Kinzua Dam is known today as Lake Perfidy. And many a bitter Seneca tells his children and grandchildren that no one knows for sure whose bones lie beneath the transplanted monument above the lake: the way the moving took place, the remains could be those of another Indian from the old cemetery. The great Cornplanter, perhaps, now rests beneath the waters of the reservoir.

From the very beginning, when army lawyers first looked into the problem of acquiring land for the dam and the reservoir, the Corps of Engineers had little concern for the uniqueness of the treaty-secured Seneca position. The corps is a highly efficient and capable expression of the modern technological age, able to build great dams, move mountains, control roaring rivers, and alter any manner of landscape. But to many

can you swim?   By ALVIN M. JOSEPHY, JR.

persons the corps exemplifies, at the same time, the big, self-propelled, faceless juggernauts of the world that grind ahead, seemingly unmoved by the outcries of the people whose lives they affect. As an autocratically tinged bureaucracy and one of the most irresistible lobbies in the nation (relying on the "pork barrel" support of political groups everywhere who sooner or later want public works for their own areas), it befriends the American people in the mass and in the abstract, and makes war on the same people when, as individuals or in small numbers, they get in the way. In 1966 a special study group composed of two colonels and a civilian official of the corps reported that "too often the [engineers'] planning effort is confined to refining the concept and proving the justification for one or a few promising projects. Too few reports contain evidence that adequate consideration was given to alternatives and to all factors pertinent to producing an optimum solution." In the case of the building of Kinzua Dam, an "optimum solution" required that the engineers possess enough of an understanding of, and a concern for, the Senecas' 1794 treaty to deter them from breaking it. The Senecas whom the engineers confronted in the 1950's were descendants of the westernmost of the five confederated Iroquois tribes who for numerous centuries had occupied present-day upper New York state from Lake Champlain to the Genesee River. From east to west they were, in order, the Mohawks, Oneidas, Onondagas, Cayugas, and Senecas. Joined about 1712 by the Tuscaroras, Iroquoian-speaking relatives who had been driven out of North Carolina by the white man, the Iroquois Confederacy became known as the League of the Six Nations. In the mid-1600's, several bands of Senecas had moved southwestward from the Genesee River to the upper Allegheny Valley, and during the next hundred years they established domination over a large area of western New York and Pennsylvania and eastern Ohio, swelling their own numbers and power by absorbing many Indian captives and refugee groups. Both French and English traders were welcomed in the region, but no white settlement was permitted.

George Heron, a steelworker, Navy veteran of World War II, and past president of the Senecas, headed the Indians' difficult relocation program.

Mrs. Harriett Pierce, a descendant of Cornplanter, fought hard—but unsuccessfully—for a suitable piece of land to replace his grant, taken by the dam builders.

Toward the mid-1700's, trouble came for the western Senecas when English and French military groups began to fight for authority over the upper Ohio Valley. The Senecas were caught between the two sides, but when the struggle erupted into the full-fledged French and Indian War, many of the Senecas sided with the French. With the defeat of the latter in 1763, the still-powerful Senecas retired up the Allegheny River to their towns along the New York-Pennsylvania border.

With the coming of the American Revolution, pressure was again exerted on the individual tribes, this time by both the British and the colonists. The Oneidas and some of the Tuscaroras sided with the Americans, many of the Cayugas and Senecas joined Joseph Brant and his Mohawks as allies of the British, and other groups remained neutral.

Under The Cornplanter, whom they elected as their war leader and whom the British commissioned as a captain, the western Senecas from the Genesee and Allegheny valleys conducted raids against American posts and settlements. The Cornplanter, then about forty years old, was already one of the strongest and best known of the Iroquois war chiefs. Born in a Seneca town on the Genesee near present-day Avon, New York, sometime between 1732 and 1740, he was the half-breed son of a prominent Dutch trader from Albany named John Abeel and a Seneca woman. By the time of the Revolution he was the principal war chief and a leading spokesman of the western Senecas.

The Revolution was disastrous for the Iroquois. In retaliation for their raids and for the help the Indians had given the British, American punitive expeditions invaded the countries of the Senecas and other tribes in 1779, burning towns, destroying crops, and driving the people from their homelands. Many of the pro-British Senecas joined Brant at Fort Niagara. In 1780, following the departure of the Americans, some of the

Indians drifted back to their homes. Others formed a large permanent settlement at Buffalo Creek. Cornplanter and the Genesee River Senecas found their country in ruins and moved to the Allegheny River settlements along the New York-Pennsylvania border. There Cornplanter took over the civil leadership of his people from an elderly uncle, Kiasutha.

Under the protection of the British along the Niagara, where English troops and traders remained on American soil until after Jay's Treaty of 1794, the displaced eastern Senecas at Buffalo Creek kept up a bitter hostility to the Americans. And along the Allegheny, Cornplanter and the western Senecas were a threat closer to the Pennsylvania and New York settlements. The danger was acute, for at any time one or all of the disaffected Iroquois groups, under the influence of the British, could join the Ohio country Indians in an all-out, catastrophic war on the settlers.

At this point, Cornplanter was induced to throw in his lot with the Americans, and the Seneca chief's influence was decisive with all the Iroquois. By 1794, when General Anthony Wayne crushed the Ohio tribes with finality at the Battle of Fallen Timbers, Cornplanter had not only immobilized the Senecas and other Iroquois so that they remained out of the conflict, but had overseen the ceding and sale of large areas of Seneca land in western Pennsylvania and New York to the Americans. His actions had been angrily opposed by many Iroquois chiefs, including Red Jacket, a fiery Seneca orator at Buffalo Creek, but Cornplanter had ignored them, saying, "If we do not sell the land, the whites will take it anyway."

The grateful Americans were not unaware of Cornplanter's friendship and the many good services he had rendered them, often at the risk of his life. In December, 1790, he had met President Washington in Philadelphia and had told him that his people were beginning to fear the loss of their own lands to white settlers. On December 29, Washington responded to him in a letter that was to have little meaning to the Army Corps of Engineers when the Senecas presented it to them more than a century and a half later. Washington wrote:

. . . Your great object seems to be the security of your remaining lands, and I have therefore upon this point, meant to be sufficiently strong and clear. That in future you cannot be defrauded of your lands. That you possess the right to sell, and the right of refusing to sell your lands. That therefore the sale of your lands in future, will depend entirely upon yourselves.

At their monthly meeting, four of the sixteen councilors of the Seneca Nation listen to facts and figures demonstrating that they cannot compete with tourist concessions that are federally financed, on the reservoir created by the dam.

In 1791 the state of Pennsylvania, in acknowledgment of Cornplanter's services to American settlers, granted him and his heirs "in perpetuity" three tracts of land, each about a mile square, on the upper Allegheny River in Pennsylvania. One of these, near present-day West Hickory, the chief sold in 1795 to a white friend. Another, at what is now Oil City, he sold to two white men in 1818, but claimed he was paid in worthless money and notes. The third tract, an area known since before the Revolution as The Burnthouse, totalled approximately 908 acres and was on the western bank of the Allegheny about three miles south of the New York state line. It included Cornplanter's own town of Jononhsadegen and two islands in the river. Cornplanter made it his headquarters, settling down there with his followers, who in time built thirty houses for about four hundred people on the grant.

In 1794, discontent arose among many of the Iroquois over increased pressure from the settlers. The Battle of Fallen Timbers had not yet been fought, and the federal government, fearing again that the Iroquois might join the Ohio tribes who in 1790 and 1791 had inflicted serious defeats on American armies, sent Timothy Pickering of Massachusetts as commissioner to meet with the chiefs of the Six Nations at Canandaigua, New York, and establish a lasting peace with them. Pickering's mission was successful: on November 11, 1794, he signed a treaty with fifty-nine sachems and war chiefs, including Cornplanter, Fish Carrier, Red Jacket, Half Town, and Handsome Lake for the Senecas, establishing what was to be a permanent peace between the United States and the different Iroquois tribes.

Article three of the treaty, which was signed by Washington, applied only to the Senecas:

Now the United States acknowledge all the land within the aforementioned boundaries, to be the property of the Sen-

eka nation; and the United States will never claim the same, nor disturb the Seneka nation . . . but it shall remain theirs, until they choose to sell the same to the people of the United States, who have the right to purchase.

These were the words which the engineers, a century and a half later, were to brush aside. The solemn promise was "never," and until the 1950's it gave the Senecas security. In their imagery they made it read, "as long as the grass shall grow and the rivers run," and with that contract they lived in peace.

Cornplanter died on February 18, 1836, and was buried on his grant. That small plot of land in the meantime had taken on added meaning for the Senecas, for there, in 1799, Cornplanter's half-brother, the prophet Ganiodayo, or Handsome Lake, had had the first of his revelations and had preached the Good Message—a set of new religious beliefs and practices—to all the Iroquois. This new religion, which still permeates Iroquois life, has been described as a blending of old Seneca beliefs with an ethical code borrowed largely from the Quakers. Its birth on the Cornplanter grant, from where it spread, endowed the plot with something of the sacredness of a holy shrine. In ensuing years, the burial of Cornplanter and his followers and descendants on the same grounds added to the grant's significance, a fact acknowledged by the state of Pennsylvania in 1866 when it erected the stone monument over Cornplanter's grave.

Under the tutelage of Quakers, who first came to live among the Senecas on the Allegheny River in 1798, the Indians became rapidly acculturated to the white man's way of living. Indians were educated, and Indian men were induced to farm (the Quakers persuaded families to spread out in homesteads along the river, out of sight of each other, so the men would not be embarrassed by being seen in the fields, doing what had traditionally been considered women's work). Beginning in 1803, factional disputes on the Cornplanter grant resulted in a gradual movement by Senecas to new communities higher up on the Allegheny across the New York border, and by 1806 Coldspring, south of present-day Salamanca, had become a new Seneca center.

As a result of various land sales which they continued to make to settlers and land companies, the Senecas' territory eventually dwindled to four, and then three, reservations in western New York. They were the Cattaraugus, close to Lake Erie south of Buffalo; the Tonawanda, slightly northeast of Buffalo; and a long, narrow strip along the Allegheny River, from present-day Vandalia, New York, to the Penn-

sylvania state line. This became known as the Allegany Reservation, its name evolving with a different spelling from that of the river. South of this reservation, across the Pennsylvania line, descendants of Cornplanter still dwelled on his grant, which they had inherited as his heirs.*

In 1848, after the Ogden Land Company had almost managed to swindle the Senecas out of their last holdings in New York by getting drunken, venal, or bogus chiefs to sign papers of sale, a group of young Senecas on the Allegany and Cattaraugus reservations deposed the hereditary chiefs for incompetence and graft and set up a new, republican form of government on those two reservations. Calling themselves the Seneca Nation, they wrote a constitution that separated church and state; provided for a legislative council of eighteen (now sixteen) members and a president and other officers elected annually (now every two years) by all adult males (women now have the vote too); established a judiciary of three "peacemakers" for minor crimes; asked that jurisdiction over serious crimes and major lawsuits be transferred to New York state courts; and detached the two reservations from the League of the Six Nations, which had continued (and still continues, in modified form) to hold together in brotherhood the different Iroquois peoples in the United States and Canada. Today, 120 years later, the Seneca Nation still exists; it has the same form of government, the office of the president rotating every two years between the Allegany and Cattaraugus reservations.

In the middle of the nineteenth century the Erie and Pennsylvania railroads, pushing across New York, bought rights of way from the Senecas and established a junction on the Allegany Reservation. The site grew into a village originally called Hemlock but renamed for Don Jose Salamanca Mayel, a large stockholder in the Erie Railroad. The rights-of-way purchases, plus

New homes (below right) built fo
than the old (left), resulting in les

---

* The Senecas also own, but do not inhabit, a small reservation of some 640 acres near Oil Spring in western New York state.

certain leases granted by the Senecas to private citizens, were confirmed by federal statute in 1875 and 1890, when Congress gave the Allegany Reservation Senecas the right to grant thereafter ninety-nine-year leases to all white homeowners and businesses in Salamanca and in four other white towns established on the reservation. The leases brought ridiculously small returns to the Indians (even today the entire city of Salamanca, with a population of a little more than 9,000, pays the Indians a total of only about $16,000 a year in rent), but all the leases will be renegotiated by 1991, and the new rents will unquestionably be higher.

As the years rolled on, the different Iroquois peoples in New York, surrounded by a sea of whites, were all but forgotten. Living quietly on their reservations, they continued to hunt, fish, and farm, educate their children, and in many cases take jobs in the white man's world. A large number of Allegany Senecas worked in furniture factories or for the railroads in Salamanca. Others followed a path pioneered by the Mohawks and became structural steelworkers, traveling to distant cities for periods of time to help build bridges and skyscrapers. While most of the Iroquois became Christians, many continued to observe the beliefs and practices of Handsome Lake, conducting an annual cycle of ceremonies. These were held in Longhouses, rectangular frame buildings which served as both social and religious centers, as well as meeting places, for the Handsome Lake followers. But even the Christians, still holding themselves apart from the whites around them, continued to have pride in their Indian heritage, and it was said that every Iroquois still had "one foot in the Longhouse."

In the years after World War II, several of the Six Nations were beset by sudden new threats to their reservations. In 1954, when the St. Lawrence Seaway was under construction, its builders wanted to place

relocated Senecas have less ground privacy and a changed way of life.

some of their facilities on the St. Regis Reservation belonging to the Mohawks. The needed land was condemned, and though the Indians received $100,000 in compensation, they were left with the uneasy feeling that one day their entire reservation could be taken from them.

Three years later the Tuscaroras, whose reservation lies near Niagara Falls, were treated even more high-handedly by Robert Moses, chairman of the New York Power Authority. Part of his plan for the giant Niagara Power Project was a pump-storage reservoir to be located on the Tuscaroras' reservation. Their resistance to his original demand for 1,300 acres forced him to scale the reservoir down to 550 acres and to pay the Tuscaroras $886,000 for the land, plus the costs of relocating the nine Indian families who were living on it.

Considering the amount of land and the number of Indian families involved, however, none of these incursions matched the assault which the army engineers made on the Senecas' Allegany Reservation and the Cornplanter grant.

The idea for Kinzua Dam was born in 1928, following disastrous floods in the Ohio Valley. In 1938 and again in 1941, the chief of engineers asked for and received authorization from Congress to build Kinzua and a number of other dams as part of a general program of flood control for the Ohio River basin. The Senecas were not informed by the engineers of their proposal to construct a dam that would inundate a large part of their reservation, and the engineers, in turn, were so unconcerned about the existence of a treaty which they would have to break if they built the dam that they failed to make much of a point of it in their presentation to Congress. To the corps, it seems, land is land, no matter who lives on it. Proceeding on the assumption that the acquisition of land, ultimately, would be the usual matter of paying individual owners, engineers appeared on the Allegany Reservation in 1939 and 1940. The president and the council of the Seneca Nation, thinking that the engineers were making some studies of the river, offered no objection when they began to make surveys along the banks.

Interruptions by Secretary of the Interior Harold Ickes, who wanted Pennsylvania to pay part of the cost of the dam, and then by World War II, temporarily sidetracked the Kinzua project. Through sources other than the Corps of Engineers, however, the Senecas began to learn of the plan for the dam, and by 1955, when the engineers again appeared before the Seneca council to ask permission to continue their surveys on the reservation, the Indians were nervous. The engineers allayed their fears, however, by assuring them that they did not yet know if they wished to

CONTINUED ON PAGE 106

A Cautionary Tale

Back at the turn of the century there was a railroad with an idea that seems strange to our ears today: it wanted to advertise for passengers. It had two things to sell—the shortest main-line route from New York to Buffalo, and the fact that it owned anthracite mines and thus burned hard coal, which makes much less smoke and dust than soft. Casting about for a catchy idea, the officials of the company, the famous Delaware, Lackawanna & Western, hit upon the notion of a lady passenger dressed all in white whose clothes stayed clean upon "the Road of Anthracite." Presently they invented a name, Phoebe Snow; hired a pretty and most ladylike young woman, Mrs. Marion E. Murray, to impersonate her; and made the name and face famous for more than a generation with car cards and doggerel as memorable in their day as Rinso White and Mr. Clean are now. Phoebe appeared by name in 1903, and this was the first of many jingles: *Says Phoebe Snow | About to go | Upon a trip to Buffalo, | "My gown stays white | From morn till night | Upon the Road of Anthracite."*

The old advertising card at right shows how these little messages used to reach an admiring public.

Phoebe and the Lackawanna prospered alike for many years. Mrs. Murray herself appeared in the early motion picture classic *The Great Train Robbery*, which was photographed on the Lackawanna's line to Boonton, New Jersey. Around 1907 she left the railroad for the stage, but other ladies posed for the drawings until the First World War created a coal shortage and forced the Lackawanna to burn bituminous. Another Phoebe appeared briefly in 1930 to celebrate the line's new electric commuting services, and again in the Second World War to plug for the war effort: *"Our first job now," says Phoebe Snow, | "Is getting troops to Tokyo! | Civilian travel won't be fun | Until these westward trips are done."*

A new rhyme scheme, a bad one, and the beginning of excuses for the service—but there was one more fine moment when in 1949 President William White of the Lackawanna named his crack luxury flyer *The Phoebe Snow*. For the christening the original Phoebe, now Mrs. R. V. Gorsch, came out of retirement. The train was a great success, making the daytime run to Buffalo in eight hours from the terminal at Hoboken, a short ferry ride from Manhattan. Then, in 1960, the once-proud railroad merged with its old competitor, the Erie, and the new entity, called the Erie-Lackawanna, chipping away at the passenger service, discontinued the train in 1962. White, as chairman of the board, started up the famous flyer again the next

Lackawanna Railroad

'Bye, Phoebe Snow,
What a way
But if you'll travel
Eschew the

A coach or sleigh
Was once the way
Of reaching Home
On Christmas Day.
Now - Phoebe's right -
You'll expedite
The trip by Road
Of Anthracite.

bye Buffalo.
t was to go!
ome this Yule,
Road of Diesel Fuel.

year, but instead of going to Buffalo, it branched off the combined lines to end at Chicago (which rhymes very badly with "Phoebe Snow"). This service ended for good on November 27, 1966. Mrs. Gorsch outlived the train by only eight months and died at eighty-five, just before the opening of a fine Phoebe Snow exhibition arranged in her honor by the New Jersey Historical Society, which included the advertising cards shown here from the collection of Thomas T. Taber.

Studying the ancient jingles, AMERICAN HERITAGE, ever mindful of Progress, decided to look into how Miss Snow might travel to Buffalo today. Patient waiting on the telephone finally disgorged the reluctant information that there is still one lone train to Buffalo, on such of the combined Erie and Lackawanna lines as survive; it runs only because the Interstate Commerce Commission has not given permission for its abandonment, but that sleepy watchdog has clearly never seen the operation with which the railroad is discouraging even the hardiest of travellers.

Believing in first-hand information, our own re-creation of Phoebe Snow, Mrs. John Phillips, a member of our staff, dressed herself all in white and about midnight headed via the Holland Tunnel (the ferry has been abandoned) for Hoboken, driven by an unwilling cabdriver who could scarcely find the terminal. Mrs. Phillips, her photographer, and entourage were, to judge by the ticket clerk's surprise, the first paying passengers in some days. She was told that the train would leave at 12:15 A.M., consisted of a single day coach, and would require eleven hours to make the trip that used to take eight. As one trainman explained it, various waits make the longer schedule possible, lest faster service encourage too many riders. But the company was not entirely heartless. It provided no diner, but it did stop the car at Binghamton, New York, at sunrise so that passengers might savor the station snack bar. Dawn did not sharpen the new Phoebe's appetite, but it brought magnificent scenery and a high trestle over the great falls of the Genesee River. Crawling thereafter through flatlands to Buffalo, the lonely successor to so many great trains eventually put down a bone-tired traveller—her dress now a tattletale gray —a few miles short of the city because, it appears, the railroad has sold the old station and drops its passengers, if any, in a distant industrial wasteland. This final discouragement (Are you listening, I.C.C.?) has one advantage, however; it is near the airport. Our pictures of the modern trip appear on the next four pages with revised jingles that—unlike the service— are no worse than the originals.   —Oliver Jensen

Miss Phoebe Snow
Has stopped to show
Her ticket at
The Gate, you know.
The Guard, polite,
Declares it right.
Of course—
It's Road of
Anthracite.

Lackawanna Railroad

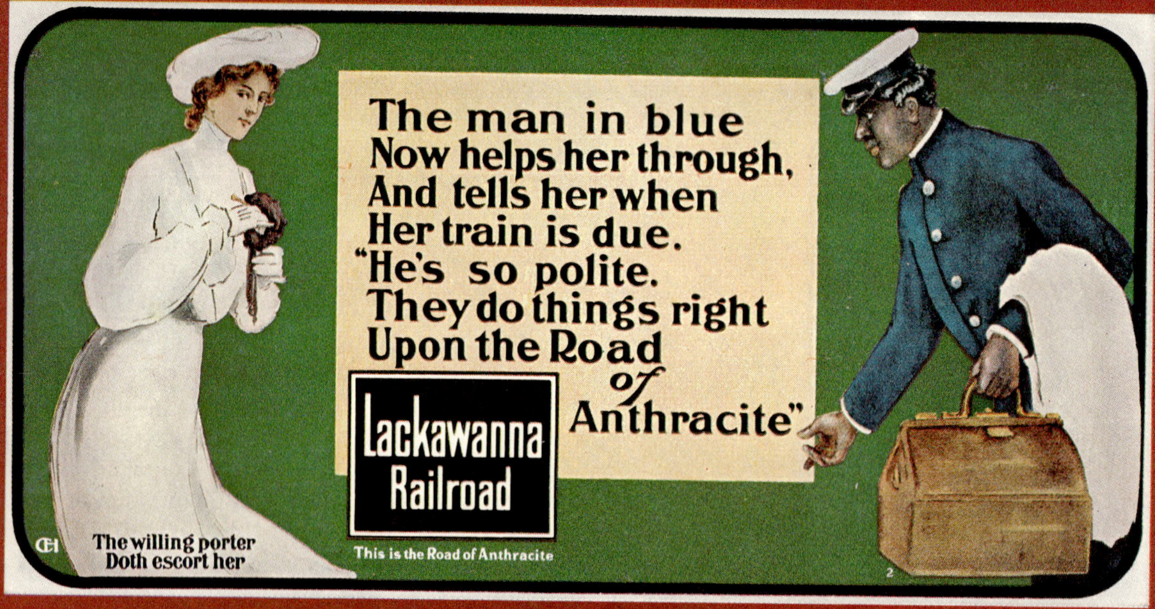

The man in blue
Now helps her through,
And tells her when
Her train is due.
"He's so polite.
They do things right
Upon the Road
of
Anthracite"

Lackawanna Railroad

The willing porter
Doth escort her

This is the Road of Anthracite

Each passing look
At nook or brook
Unfolds a fly-
ing picture book
Of landscape bright,
Or mountain height,
Beside the Road
of
Anthracite.

Lackawanna Railroad

the Road of Anthracite

Mt. Pocono
Delights Miss Snow.

This sad tableau
Shows our Miss Snow
Waiting alone
For the midnight slow.
There's just one train,
Run with disdain,
Through Phoebe's for-
mer rail domain.

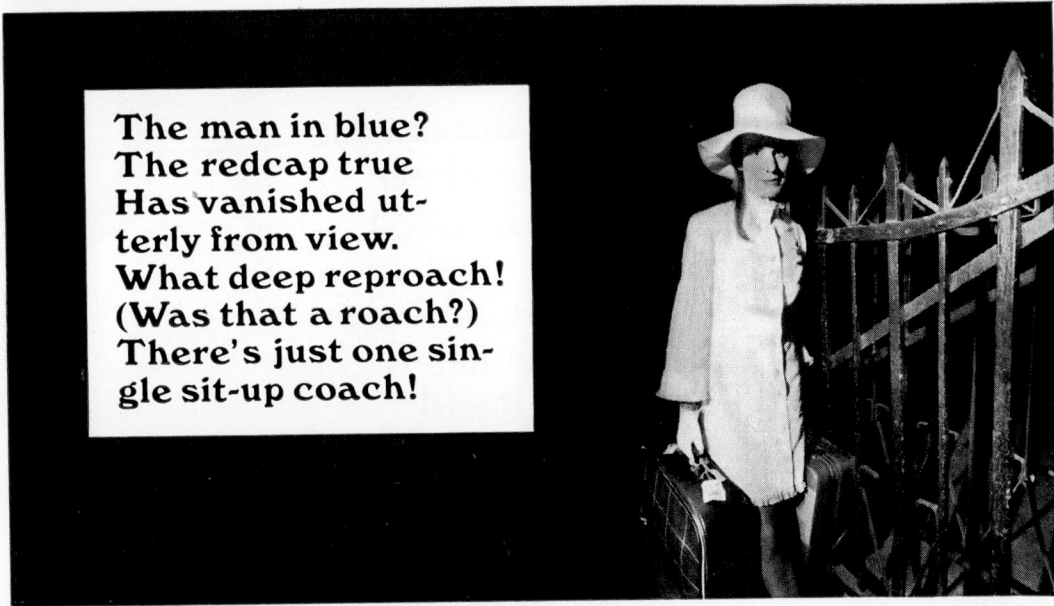

The man in blue?
The redcap true
Has vanished ut-
terly from view.
What deep reproach!
(Was that a roach?)
There's just one sin-
gle sit-up coach!

O landscape bright,
O mountain height!
How can she see
Them in the night?
But dawn does come,
Toward Binghamton.
The passengers?
How many?—One.

A cosey seat
A dainty treat
Make Phoebe's
Happiness complete
With linen white
And silver bright

Lackawanna Railroad

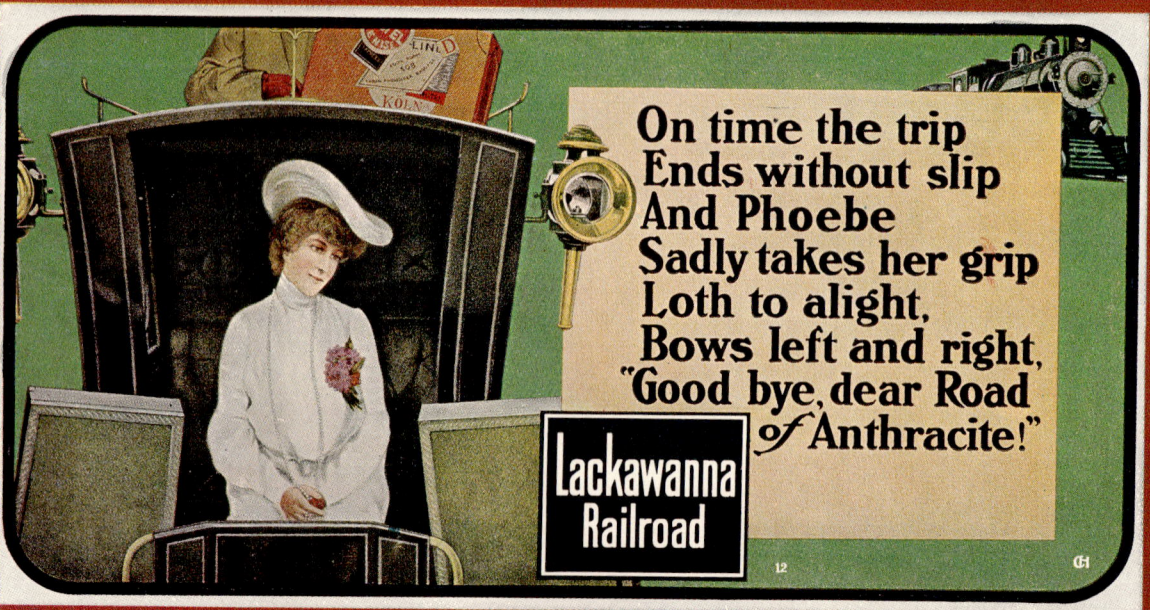

Upon the Road
Of Anthracite.

Miss Snow draws near
The cab to cheer
The level-headed
Engineer,
Whose watchful sight
Makes safe her flight
Upon the Road
of Anthracite.

Lackawanna Railroad

On time the trip
Ends without slip
And Phoebe
Sadly takes her grip
Loth to alight,
Bows left and right,
"Good bye, dear Road
of Anthracite!"

Lackawanna Railroad

Her dainty treat
(Oh, great defeat!)
Is taken at
A "snack-bar" seat.
Her appetite,
At five, is slight—
She lost it sit-
ting up all night.

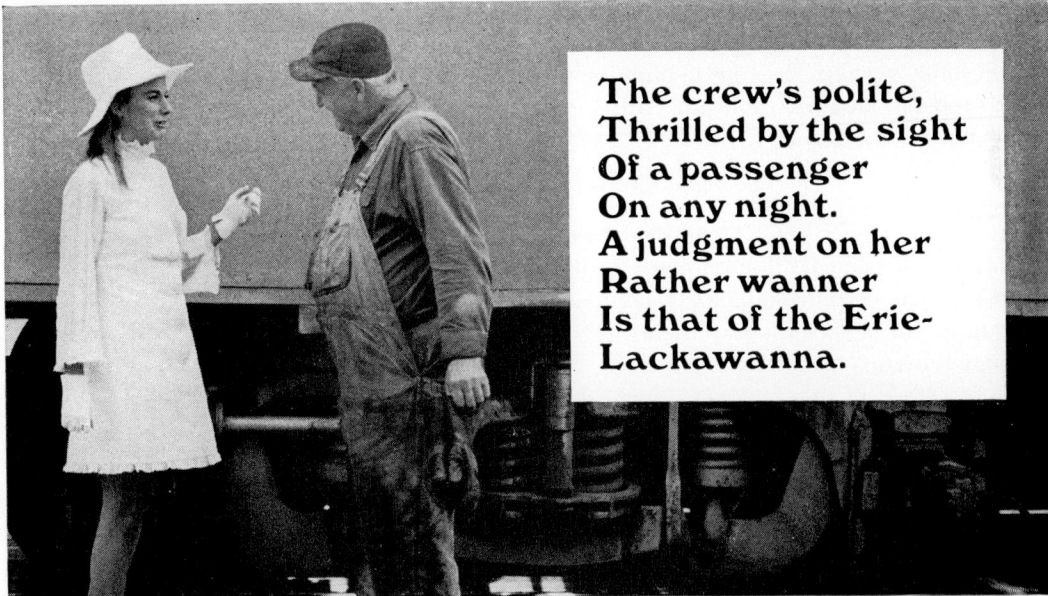

The crew's polite,
Thrilled by the sight
Of a passenger
On any night.
A judgment on her
Rather wanner
Is that of the Erie-
Lackawanna.

Miss Snow that night,
As she took flight,
Forsaking Road
Of Anthracite,
Cried, "I.C.C.!
Why can't you see
The way they're sab-
otaging me?"

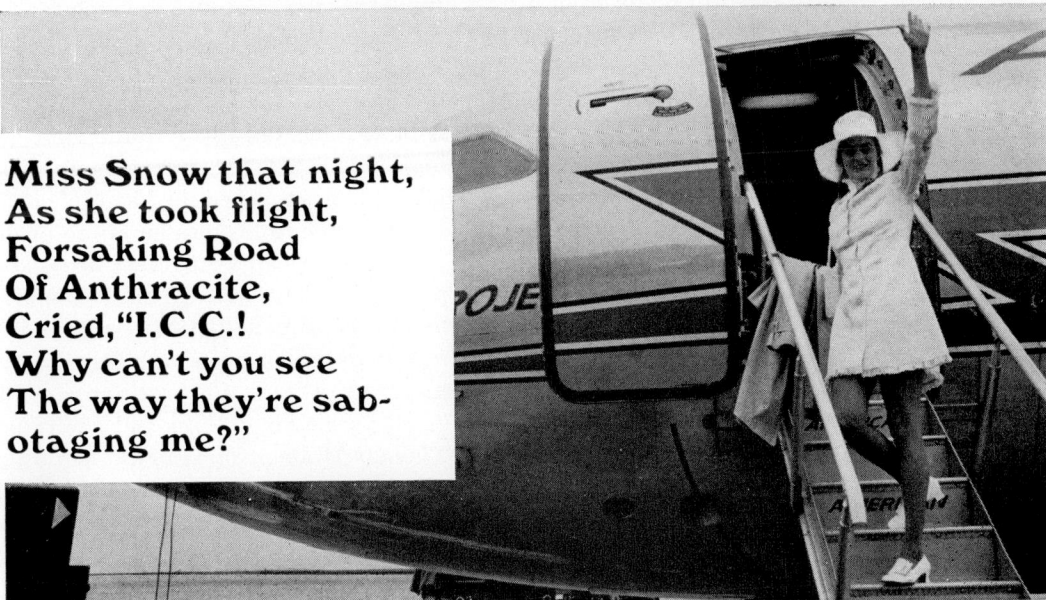

By CATHERINE DRINKER BOWEN

The Biographer and His Hero

"One should write only about what one loves." Ernest Renan, the biographer and historian, said it in the last century; and for this writer at least it is profoundly true, the more impressive because in Renan's lifetime he withstood prolonged literary attacks. If so tough-fibered an author confessed that he loved his subjects, why might not the rest of us do the same? For a considerable time it was unfashionable to admire one's biographical hero; the debunking period lasted a full generation. Lytton Strachey started it, and on the whole it was a healthy movement, a reaction against the laudatory familial biography of the nineteenth century. But Strachey was a brilliantly talented writer; his imitators and followers did not have his genius, and the art of biography suffered. We outgrew the fashion, perhaps because debunking is easy and what is too easy does not hold up. Anthony Trollope said, "There is no way of writing well and also of writing easily." But the stigma remained; a book was not true unless it was malicious.

Since the debunking era, biography has gone through no more literary fashions. Indeed, to the general surprise it has become immensely popular. One of the advantages of being a biographer is this freedom from changing literary modes. People want to read the authentic record of other people's lives and they do not want the story clothed in fashionable obscurity, imagery, symbolism. The modern biographer, if he chooses, can write as John Aubrey wrote two centuries ago in his *Brief Lives,* or as Isaac D'Israeli wrote in his *The Literary Character; or, The History of Men of Genius*—provided that the modern writer is equally talented. He can use facts, dates, explanatory parentheses. He can proceed from point to point, from incident to incident with no apology for being old-fashioned, outmoded. The biographer is not required to declare that life is a cruel and total absurdity, nor to follow his hero inevitably downhill to drugs, casual sex, and a drearily inconspicuous suicide.

This is not to imply that the biographer invariably approaches his work with love in his heart. There are many considerations besides love that may give the biographer his initial inspiration. I asked Hilda Prescott in England why she chose Queen Mary Tudor to write about. No subject could be more difficult. In that ill-starred life, tragedy followed tragedy; Mary's life was one long defeat. She loved her Spanish husband and was not beloved; she yearned for children to the point of imagining herself pregnant; her deepest instincts were denied outlet and she ended by earning in history the epithet of Bloody Mary. Miss Prescott looked me in the eye and said, "I chose Mary Tudor because I thought she would make money for me."

One thinks of the traditional advice given the girl about to choose a husband; "Money first, love will follow." Surely it had been that way with Miss Prescott; a tragic story has not been more compassionately told. But it is indeed true that the biographer does not fall in love with his hero at first sight and remain infatuated. Love comes slowly, after deep acquaintance and many arguments back and forth, though one can judge this only by one's own experience. With Edward Coke, for instance, I had a struggle that could have ended in divorce. Here was a brave man, but he was also stubborn, vain, disagreeable, and capable of cruelty. Contemporaries feared "Mr. Attorney General"; he earned widespread hatred for his bitter, relentless invective as prosecutor. At Sir Walter Ralegh's trial Coke behaved shamefully. Was this, one asked, the way our freedoms came to pass—in reverse, as it were? Strange, that social progress can be achieved through an instrument so far from perfect! My workbook argued the point. "Coke was brutal beyond any excuse. Must I love him, must I even *like* him?" "No!" I wrote. "But I must be engaged with him, married to him, at one with him yet independent, rearing back to look at him."

Thinking back, it seems naïve; one forgets the deep involvement that comes with a five- or six-year book. As a definition of marriage proper, what the workbook said would not do. But as a definition of biographical marriage it is valid enough. Perhaps what the biographer needs is not love so much as identification with the hero. Whether or not one likes one's subject, it would be fatal to choose a hero with whom one could not identify. "Relate" is the current psychiatric phrase. A biographer can relate to the most diverse and seemingly unsympathetic characters. Something in the subject's life has touched the biographer's own experience, coming close to his own ambition or desire.

Biographers approach their books at certain stressful periods in their lives. (The lives of artists are bound to be stressful; without stress they would feel themselves lapsing unconscious.) Tchaikovsky went through his days in a state of neurotic anxiety that at times bordered on madness. "Fear and I were born twins," said Thomas Hobbes, the English philosopher, in one of the more surprising confessions of history. Perhaps

16

COPYRIGHT © 1968 BY CATHERINE DRINKER BOWEN

fear, like neurotic anxiety, is to some natures a necessary stimulus. I think no one could write the story of these lives who had not experienced neurotic fear, just as one could not write of Benjamin Disraeli if he had not felt ambition, or of Balzac if he did not himself know the *furor scribendi*. "The need to express oneself in writing," said André Maurois, "springs from a maladjustment to life, or from an inner conflict, which the adolescent (or the grown man) cannot resolve in action."

Maurois goes on to confess that he wrote his first biography, *Ariel: The Life of Shelley,*

because it was an expression of one of my conflicts. Shelley had come from a family from which he wanted to escape, and so did I. The problem of Shelley was also my problem. My personality was also expressed in *Disraeli.* He was Jewish. I was Jewish myself. He was for me an example of how to get on with a Christian society. Proust, Châteaubriand and Balzac I did because I admired them as writers. The choices were guided by my inner feelings, whether I can get on with this man . . . I couldn't accept the idea of spending three years of my life with someone I didn't like.

On the other hand the biographer is himself puzzled at how completely he can identify with diverse and seemingly unsympathetic characters. The surprise comes later, when he reads his published work. While he is writing he is too absorbed to be thinking about such things as identification. When the biographer has chosen his subject and sits down to read, what he is actually doing for the first three or four months is making the acquaintance of his hero. Everything comes as grist to this mill: time, place, climate; the hero's friends, his enemies, his appetites physical and spiritual. Any least word about the hero's appearance, how he looked and dressed, is cherished as a lover cherishes the most fugitive news of his beloved.

Yet one can be deceived, at first reading and first study. It may indeed be years before biographer and hero come to terms; it is extraordinary how the material can lead one astray. Theodor Reik, in his book *Listening with the Third Ear,* has told how Lytton Strachey changed his mind about Queen Victoria while he was writing her biography:

Studying the early life of the young Queen, [Strachey] did not like her very much. He saw her as a spoiled, overly self-assured and level-headed girl. He treated her at first with a certain ironical remoteness and with little sympathy. The more he studied her life and the more he began to under-

stand her personality and the environment that helped form it the more sympathetic he became. At the end, when he speaks of the Queen in her last years, you feel genuine human warmth, appreciation, and admiration for an impressive personality. He started with little affection for his subject, and ended practically in love with the old lady.

With Sir Francis Bacon I had somewhat the same experience. I began his biography influenced by immediately previous years of reading for the life of Sir Edward Coke, who was Bacon's bitter rival both in the law courts and privately. Alexander Pope had called Bacon the wisest, brightest, meanest of mankind, and I was inclined to agree. But when I studied Bacon's works and his career more deeply I recognized my bias and saw that my hero's fall from high estate was no matter of smallness or meanness but tragedy in the grand manner, to be approached not with condemnation but with awe.

Even the biographical scene—the time and the place—can enlarge a writer's horizon. One has sat in the long Parliament with Cromwell, or at the Constitutional Convention with Madison and Washington. One has walked the London streets in a plague year and has seen doors in the houses of the sick black-lettered: *"Lord have mercy on us."*

Is all this to have no influence, leave no scar? Can the author put it from him merely by writing *finis* to a book? Even dreams leave their residue; a day, a week can be colored by a fleeting picture seen in sleep. As to the effect a biographer's hero can have upon him, there is no way of overemphasizing it. To spend three years or five with a truly great man, reading what he said and wrote, observing him as he errs, stumbles, falls and rises again; to watch his talent grow if he is an artist, his wisdom develop if he is a statesman—this cannot but seize upon a writer, one might almost say transform him. When the book is done the author returns to the outer world, but actually he will not be the same again. The ferment of genius, Holmes said, is quickly imparted, and when a man is great he makes others believe in greatness. By that token one's life is altered. One has climbed a hill, looked out and over, and the valley of one's own condition will be forever greener.

Mrs. Bowen's new book, The Craft and the Calling, *from which this article is excerpted, will be published soon by Atlantic-Little, Brown.*

WOODEN DELIGHTS

An obscure Pennsylvania carpenter
named John Scholl left the world a legacy
of charming toys and beautiful fantasies

Every so often the world of American folk art museums and collectors discovers a new star to add to its firmament—a primitive painter, a rustic sculptor. This happened in 1967, when a Manhattan gallery held an exhibition of thirty-seven astonishing wood carvings by a carpenter named John Scholl. Born in Württemberg in 1827, Scholl emigrated to Pennsylvania in 1853 and lived there until his death in 1916. But despite his unquestioned talent as a folk artist, his work was known only locally until his recent discovery.

No other state has proved such a rich mine of folk art as Pennsylvania. The credit for this must go to the thousands of immigrants from the southern part of Germany along the Rhine called the Palatinate, as well as from neighboring Baden, Württemberg, Alsace, Lorraine, and Switzerland, who settled there in the seventeenth and eighteenth centuries. These freedom-loving, devout, and able farmers—Mennonite, Amish, Dunkard, Lutheran, and Reformed —became the dominant strain in the eastern Pennsylvania counties of Northampton, Lehigh, Berks, Dauphin, Lancaster, Lebanon, and York. By the Revolution they numbered one hundred and sixty thousand. It was this stock that produced the so-called Pennsylvania Dutch.

The Germans of Pennsylvania were a people who delighted in the decoration of the utensils of everyday life; and their regularly recurring designs—motifs like the tulip, the heart, the bird, and the wheel—are famous everywhere.

The major source of inspiration for this decoration

was religious, and since the Pennsylvania Germans were Protestants, the feelings that would have been expressed in the furnishings of their churches had they been Catholics found an outlet in their homes. A matter of serious debate among specialists in Pennsylvania German art is whether these people fully understood the meaning of the symbols they used. Did they know, for instance, that in German religious art the tulip was often used instead of the traditional lily to symbolize purity and chastity, or that from ancient times the spoked wheel represented the sun and the cross? It would be foolish to say that at all times and in all places every Pennsylvania German artist knew these things, but when the symbols were painted on hymnals and baptismal certificates or were carved on tombstones, there can be little doubt that they were intended as something more than mere whimsical decoration.

In the 1850's—after the failure of the democratic revolutions of 1848 in the principalities and kingdoms of Germany—a new wave of Germans came to America. Among these immigrants were John Scholl and his wife, Augusta. Attracted by the large number of Germans already in Pennsylvania, they settled first in Shenandoah, in the eastern part of the state, but soon moved northwest to heavily forested Potter County, on the New York border. There, in a colony of Germans called Germania, Scholl plied his trade as a carpenter. He built his own house and barn, the houses of many of his neighbors, the church, the general store, and the brewery. There he and his wife raised nine children and lived a quiet life ordered by their devout Lutheran faith.

Local tradition insists that Scholl began at the age of eighty to carve the creations that have now made

Left: Flowering Circle With Doves, *a colorful Scholl creation designed for hanging. Above: A photograph of the artist in 1913 at the age of eight-six, three years before his death.*

CONTINUED ON PAGE 23

19

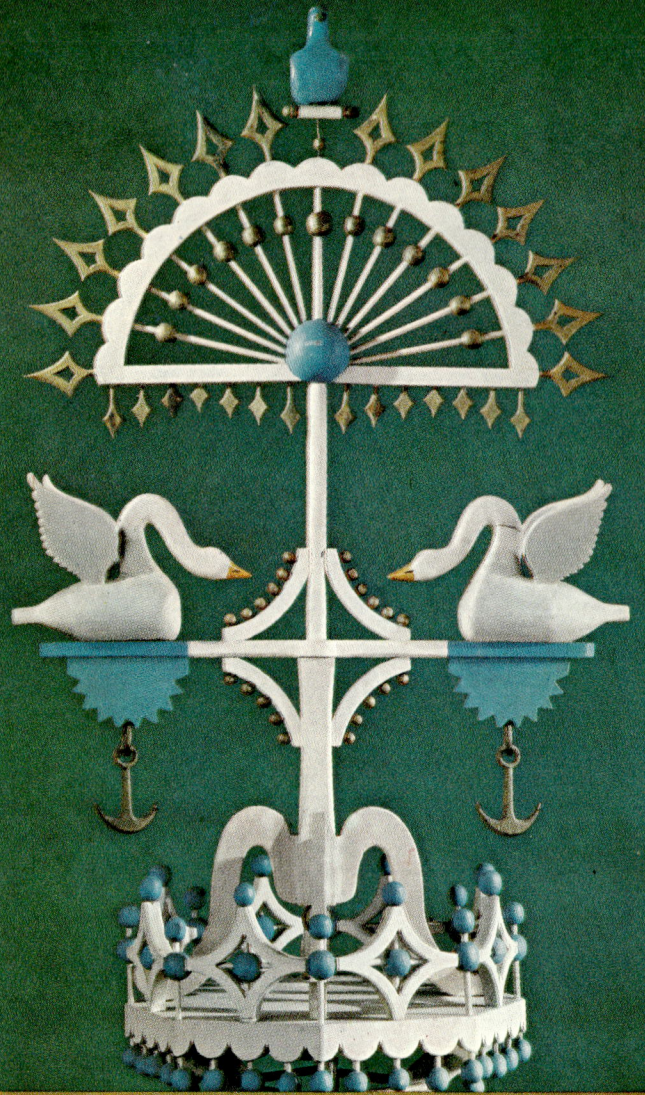

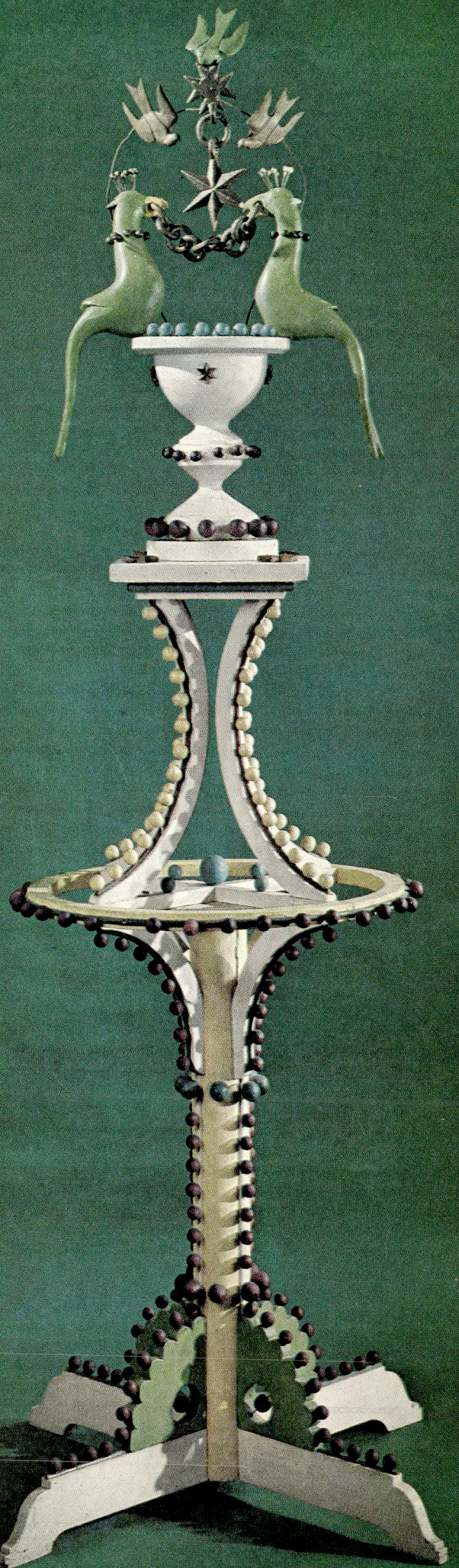

John Scholl's works exhibit a rich variety of imagery. In those on the opposite page—Music (far left), Crested Swans, and Flowering Circle—he has made use of some of the most popular Pennsylvania German symbols: the star, the swan, and the blossoming flower. Song of Victory (above) effectively combines a number of symbols: David's lyre; the thirteen stars of the original states; and the crossed arms of the military services—the infantry, artillery, cavalry, and navy. Fountain With Peacocks (right) uses the bird that is the ancient symbol of immortality, as well as the dove of the Holy Spirit and a fountain, long an image of self-renewal, to express the artist's faith in the eternal life.

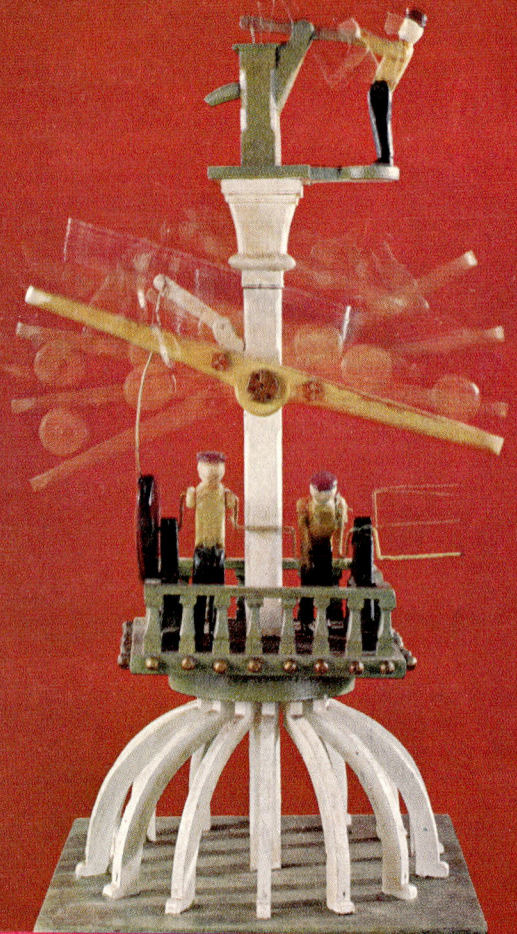

him famous. But even though he lived to be eighty-nine, there would not have been sufficient time for him to have used his jackknife and razor blade, his saws and rasps, to fashion the forty-five objects—some of them seven feet tall—that he has left us. It is more likely that he began creating his fantasies at an earlier age, probably around the turn of the century.

Though Scholl came to America too late to qualify as Pennsylvania Dutch, and settled more than a hundred miles from the Pennsylvania Dutch heartland, it is obvious that the inspiration of his designs springs from that source. If Scholl's creations are reminiscent of anything, it is of the Pennsylvania Dutch trivets, with their combinations of hearts, circles, and stars.

But of Scholl must be asked the same question that is asked of other Pennsylvania German artists: Did he always use the Pennsylvania Dutch symbols with a full awareness of their ancient meanings? In pieces such as *Flowering Circle With Doves* it is most likely that he employed the symbols primarily because he thought them beautiful. Yet there can be little question that in a work such as *Fountain With Peacocks* the appearance of two important symbols of eternal life is more than mere coincidence. Here Scholl has carved not two birds having a drink of water, but a reaffirmation of the Christian belief in immortality.

What sets Scholl's work apart from all other Pennsylvania German folk art is its architectural quality. It has the air of having been made by one who has built houses. Scholl piled symbol upon symbol and then tied the whole thing together in a way that reminds one of the fretwork on the porches of Victorian cottages and the scrollwork that decorated their sharply pointed gables. This effect is heightened by the fact that Scholl painted his creations in shades favored by the Victorians—gold and white, soft blues, greens, and reds, and mustard yellow. As a final architectural touch, he often constructed special stands for his carvings, stands rich with beads and volutes.

In addition to his fantasies, Scholl made toys that work—ferris wheels and carousels that revolve and carry carved birds and people. He also made action toys with little men who, when activated by an ingenious system of wheels, pulleys, and cranks, pump and grind and march. In their mechanical ingenuity Scholl's toys hark back to the work of the cuckoo-clock makers of the Black Forest in his native Württemberg.

Scholl never sold any of his creations and never gave any away, but kept them in the parlor of his house. After his death in 1916 his carvings remained in the house for a generation, cared for by his children. For another generation they were stored in a barn; but in the 1960's some of the Scholl grandchildren began to think that his work might be of interest to others. As a result, the Stony Point Folk Art Gallery of Stony Point, New York, acquired the carvings and arranged for an exhibition of Scholl's creations at the Willard Gallery in Manhattan. As soon as they were seen they became a sensation and were quickly bought by museums and collectors.

Looking at the photograph of John Scholl that accompanies these pictures of his work, one cannot help wondering what he would think of the attention that his fantasies and toys are receiving. The answer is not too difficult. Since he carved to bring pleasure to himself and his family, he could only be pleased that his creations have brought joy to a far wider circle than he would ever have dreamed possible. —*David G. Lowe*

BELOW AND PAGE 19: MUSEUM OF EARLY AMERICAN FOLK ART

Opposite page: Four of the ingenious action toys that John Scholl carved for his own and his family's amusement. At top are a revolving Soldiers on Parade *and a working* Pump and See-Saw; *at bottom, a whirling* Crossed Arms With Acrobats *and a cleverly articulated* Farmers With Pump, Churn, and Grindstone. *The carved figures of Scholl's toys closely resemble the Pennsylvania German whirligig weather vanes designed in the form of a man with rotating arms and a revolving body. Right, the parlor of Scholl's Potter County home, filled with his creations.*

PAGE 20: ALL, STONY POINT FOLK ART GALLERY. PAGE 21: LEFT, NEW YORK STATE HISTORICAL ASSOCIATION; RIGHT, ADELE EARNEST. PAGE 22: TOP—LEFT, FRED SCHOLL; RIGHT, ABBY ALDRICH ROCKEFELLER FOLK ART COLLECTION, WILLIAMSBURG; BOTTOM—LEFT, STONY POINT FOLK ART GALLERY; RIGHT, NATIONAL PARK SERVICE.

THE JAY PAPERS II:

The Forging of the Nation

Edited and Annotated by RICHARD B. MORRIS

States they were, united they were not; while their Secretary for Foreign Affairs sought to pull them together, Europe waited for them to fall apart

In 1786, two years after he became Secretary for Foreign Affairs, John Jay posed for this portrait by Joseph Wright.

Would the Articles of Confederation prove a viable instrument of government? Could the thirteen newly independent states forge an effective union? Would America enjoy a lasting peace? These were some of the questions that concerned responsible statesmen in the years following the Treaty of Paris of 1783. By reason of his central role in the administration of the nation's foreign affairs, John Jay played a crucial, if not decisive, role in shaping the Confederation's destiny. Perhaps no better illumination is cast on the shape and course of events in those years than is provided by the Jay Papers. Now housed in Columbia University's Special Collections, Jay's correspondence plots the nation's fever chart. When a new Constitution had been adopted and a durable union forged, the fever broke.

In the first installment of selections from the Jay Papers, in the February, 1968, AMERICAN HERITAGE, *we shared Jay's frustrating experiences in Spain, where he attempted to secure recognition and aid from the autocratic court of Charles III for the rebellious thirteen states. We then journeyed with Jay to Paris, where his tenacity and acumen were key factors in the negotiations with the British to end the American Revolution.*

The arduous and protracted sessions in Paris left Jay run-down physically and mentally, and the reports he was receiving of intrigue and dissension in America did nothing to lift his spirits. As much as a year before, at the height of the preliminary peace negotiations, Jay had written his close friend, the New York lawyer-patriot Egbert Benson: "Our power, respectability, and happiness will forever depend on our Union." But after the treaty had been signed it became apparent that the "United States," as the new nation styled itself, was far from united. Under the Articles of Confederation, ratified in 1781, it was merely a congeries of governments which did not always see eye to eye and had difficulty in acting together. And Jay's remark to Benson about respectability had point: the great powers of Europe, not only Britain but France and Spain as well, had very little respect for the new nation, weak and insignificant as it was. They were, in fact, rather hoping that it would fail. For one thing, the success of America's revolt against its monarchical motherland might arouse similar expectations among their own subjects; for another, there would be some attractive pieces to be picked up should the house so divided against itself come tumbling down.

Of all these things John Jay was conscious as he affixed his signature to the definitive treaty of peace with England on September 3, 1783. When he took ship for America the following May with his wife and family, planning to return to private life and the practice of law, he had no way of knowing that many of his country's problems were soon to be dumped into his

BY GEORGE HOLLAND, 1797; STOKES COLLECTION, NEW YORK PUBLIC LIBRARY

Jay began his work as Secretary in Federal Hall, New York City—the columned building in this water color—then the seat of the national government. He had only one deputy and two clerks, one of whom covered for the others at lunch time.

lap. Reaching New York on July 24, 1784, he was greeted by the news that Congress had appointed him Secretary for Foreign Affairs. A letter from Charles Thomson, secretary of the Congress, apprised Jay of the gloomy prospects for the Confederation.

Philadelphia, September 8, 1784

Dear Sir,

 . . . I wish exceedingly to see and converse with you not only on the subject of your acceptance but on the general State of our Affairs. There is at present no person whose business or whose duty it is to attend to matters of National Concern. The Committee of the states have in my opinion very unwarrantably separated, and though the Chairman has written to the several states to send on a delegate to form a Committee at Philadelphia, I have little hopes of their meeting. The Superintendant of Finance is busy in winding up his Affairs so as to quit his Office; as to the department of foreign affairs our Ministers abroad are left wholly to themselves without the least information of what is passing here. And the several States seem to be acting as if there was nothing beyond their respective bounds which claimed their attention or deserved their notice. Our public credit is again verging to a precipice and the seeds of jealousy and internal commotions seem to be springing up while at the same time I am far from thinking we are secure from the insidious designs of our late enemy [Britain], or the deep rooted jealousy of our Southern neighbour [Spain]. Yet gloomy as the prospect appears it only wants a little common sense, and common attention in the states to brighten the scene, to ensure public tranquility and private happiness and to render our situation enviable; and on your acceptance I greatly rely for these purposes.

 . . . Be pleased to make my most respectful compliments to Mrs. Jay and accept the assurance of the unfeigned affection of

Dear Sir, Your friend and Servant
CHA. THOMSON

25

Jay found New York a ruined city. The lower section of town had twice been gutted by fire, and the parts which the flames had spared had scarcely recovered from the wounds of military occupation and the wanton stripping by departing Tories. His initial impression of affairs was cautiously optimistic, but within three months Jay noted signs of impending dangers. To Benjamin Vaughan, who had been the British intermediary in the peacemaking, he wrote, "The Policy of Britain respecting this Country is so repugnant to common Sense that I am sometimes tempted to think it must be so.... It is certain that we are trading at a wild Rate, and it is no less true that your People are giving most absurd Credits to many who neither have or ought to have any at Home." (It is revealing of Jay's anti-imperialist stance that in the same letter to Vaughan he condemned Great Britain's policy toward India: "Do justice and all is easy; cease to treat those unhappy Nations as slaves, and be content to trade with them as with other independent Kingdoms.... Your Tribute indeed would be at an End, but it ought not to have had a Beginning, and I wish it may ever prove a Curse to those who impose and exact it in any Country." Save for John Quincy Adams, so high an American official did not venture to criticize the British position in India again until the Presidency of Franklin D. Roosevelt.)

Meanwhile, Jay was buckling down to his work as Secretary for Foreign Affairs, for which he was paid the munificent salary of four thousand dollars a year. He expressed displeasure at the prospect of having to travel to Trenton, New Jersey, where Congress was sitting, but he was told that Congress would soon settle in New York. He also demanded the privilege of appointing his own clerks. This was granted, and on September 21, 1784, he entered on the duties of his office.

Jay's conception of that office was to prove of the utmost importance in the formation of the executive department. While his friend and predecessor, Robert R. Livingston, had been Secretary, correspondence from foreign nations had been directed to the president of Congress and then referred to Livingston. Jay wanted his office to be separate and distinct from Congress, and insisted that he, not Congress, conduct the foreign affairs of the Confederation. He lost no time in making his position clear, and on February 11, 1785, Congress decided that "all communications to as well as from the United States in Congress assembled on the subject of foreign affairs, be made through the Secretary for the department of foreign affairs, and that all letters, memorials or other papers on the subject of foreign affairs, for the United States in Congress assembled, be addressed to him."

In addition, it became customary for the heads of

AMERICA AND CHINA:

Having sacrificed trade with the British West Indies by seceding from the empire, imaginative New England businessmen looked to the Orient to fill the trade gap. To that end a Bostonian named Samuel Shaw was dispatched for Canton in February, 1784, as supercargo on the Empress of China. She arrived there on August 30, and is seen above at far left in a harbor scene painted on a fan given her captain by the Chinese. On Shaw's return he sent a report to Jay.

... The Day of our arrival at Canton, August 30th, and the two following Days, we were visited by the Chinese Merchants, and the Chiefs and Gentlemen of the several European Establishments, and treated by them in all respects as a free and independent Nation. ... The Chinese themselves were very indulgent towards us, though our being the first American ship that had ever visited China. ... They styled us the New People, and when by the map we conveyed to them an Idea of the extent of our Country, with its present and increasing population, they were highly pleased at the prospect of so considerable a market for the productions of theirs. ...

The Police at Canton is at all times extremely strict, and the Europeans residing there are circumscribed within very narrow limits. ... On the 25 November an English ship, in saluting some Company that had dined on board, killed a Chinese, and wounded two others, in the mandarine's Boat along side. It is a maxim of the Chinese Law that Blood must answer for Blood, in pursuance of which they demanded the unfortunate Gunner. To give up this Poor man was

THE OPENING GUN

to consign him to certain Death. Humanity pleaded powerfully against the measure. . . . [On November 27] the supercargo of the [British] ship was seized . . . and committed to Prison. Such an outrage on personal Liberty spread a general alarm, and the Europeans unanimously agreed to send for their Boats with armed men from the shipping . . . and ours among the number. . . . To what extremities matters might have been carried, had not a negociation taken place, no one can say. . . . A deputation, in which I was included for America, met the *Fuen*, who is the head Magistrate of Canton . . . [who] demanded that the Gunner should be given up within three days. . . . The English were obliged to submit—the Gunner was given up—[the supercargo] was released—and the English, after being forced to ask pardon of the Magistracy of Canton, in presence of the other Nations, had their Commerce restored. . . . The Gunner remained with the Chinese—his fate undetermined. . . .

We left Canton the 27 December. . . . To every Lover of his country, as well as to those more immediately concerned in Commerce, it must be a pleasing reflection that a communication is thus happily opened between us and the Eastern Extreme of the Globe. . . .

The opportunities opened up by this voyage were soon spectacularly exploited by Salem vessels. Aside from its economic impact, the dispatch of this ship may be viewed in retrospect as the innocent beginning of our national interest in Asia, with all it implies for our parlous present and uncertain future there. —R. B. M.

the thirteen states to use Jay as intermediary in their correspondence with Congress. Somehow the notion got around that the Secretary for Foreign Affairs also had some responsibility for supervising the postal system. Congress, by a secret act of September 7, 1785, authorized Jay at his discretion to open letters in the post office. In view of the treatment accorded his own letters by foreign nations when he served abroad, it is understandable that Jay would have hesitated to exercise this singular power, and there is no evidence that he ever did.

Jay also showed caution in another area. He wisely sought no power of appointment (except that of his own staff), and even declined to recommend candidates to Congress. He evaded all sorts of pressures, even those of family and friends. When in 1787 John Adams' son-in-law, Colonel William Stephens Smith, sought Jay's intercession to succeed his father-in-law as minister to England, Jay politely declined. It was not unusual for foreign ministers in other countries to recommend candidates for the foreign service, but, Jay pointed out, "the case is different here." In 1788 a committee of Congress issued a revealing study of Jay's administration of his office which reported:

. . . That two Rooms are occupied by this Department, one of which the Secretary reserves for himself and the Reception of such Persons as may have Business with him, and the other for his Deputy and Clerks.

That the Records and Papers belonging to the Department are kept in a proper Manner, and so arranged as that Recourse may be had to any of them without Delay or Difficulty.

That they find his Method of doing Business is as follows: the daily Transactions are entered in a minute Book as they occur, and from thence are neatly copied into a *Journal* at Seasons of Leisure. This Journal contains a Note of the Dates, Receipt and contents of all Letters received and written by him, with References to the Books in which they are recorded, of all Matters referred to him, and the Time when, and of his Reports thereupon; and in general of all the Transactions in the Department. It is very minute and at present occupies 2 Folio Vol.

His official Letters to the Ministers and Servants of Congress and others abroad, are recorded in a Book entitled *Book of foreign Letters,* and such Parts as required Secrecy are in Cyphers.

His official Correspondence with foreign Ministers here, and with the Officers of Congress and others in the United States, including the Letters received and written by him, are recorded at large in a Book entitled *American Letter book.* . . .

The business of the Office is done by his Deputy and

two Clerks, and whatever Time can be spared from the ordinary and daily Business, is employed in recording the Letters received from the american Ministers abroad. . . .

The Office is constantly open from 9 in the Morning to 6 O'Clock in the Evening; and either his Deputy or one of the Clerks remains in the Office while the others are absent at Dinner.

By inspection . . . your Committee find . . . upon the whole . . . neatness, method and perspicuity throughout the Department.

From this distance it seems extraordinary that Jay could have conducted the foreign relations of the United States government for a half-dozen years in a two-room office. Nevertheless, the record of his scrupulously efficient little department compares favorably with that of its more recent successors housed in the palatial grandeur of "Foggy Bottom" and manned by an army big enough to overawe a Burgoyne or a Cornwallis. Modest though his quarters and incredibly minute though his staff were, Jay was to make of the office the most important administrative post in the land.

First and foremost among the new Secretary's problems were America's relations with the erstwhile mother country. The major piece of unfinished business arising out of the peace settlement was the writing of a trade treaty. The United States had already made such a treaty with France, and would soon do the same with Holland, Sweden, Prussia, and Morocco, but all these countries, even France, were peripheral as far as America's external commerce was concerned. Unless the new United States was to fashion entirely new patterns of trade relations, its prosperity depended heavily on securing reciprocal trade concessions from England, including the right to resume the once lucrative trade with the British West Indies. Lord Shelburne, who had made the preliminary peace treaty with America, was dedicated to reciprocity and ultimately to free trade, but once he was out of office, protectionism was in the saddle in England. In fact, even prior to signing the final treaty the British, in July of 1783, inaugurated a restrictive trade policy against the United States. Jay pronounced it "impolitic and ill timed" and proposed to Thomson in a letter from London that "if Britain should adopt and persist in a monopolizing system, let us retaliate fully and firmly. This nation, like many others, is influenced more by its feelings than reasonings." Sound advice, but once back in the United States and charged with the responsibility for implementing it, Jay soon perceived that the impotent Congress of the Confederation could not unite on such a measure.

A number of other issues complicated the restoration of peaceful relations with England. When the British armies left American soil, they carried with them some 3,000 American slaves; these had never been returned to their owners, nor had the owners received any compensation. There was also disagreement over the boundary line between the United States and Canada in the Northeast. A more serious cause of discontent in this country was the British refusal to give up a whole string of strategic northern and western forts stretching from Lake Champlain all the way west to the vital Straits of Mackinac between Lake Michigan and Lake Huron; these posts controlled America's whole Canadian frontier.

On all these points Secretary Jay pressed for continued negotiations by our emissary to the Court of St. James's, the redoubtable John Adams. As the first minister from the former British colonies, Adams was in a ticklish spot, meeting face to face with his former sovereign, the man whom American patriots had denounced as a tyrant and struggled against so long and bitterly. In a letter to Jay, Adams recounted his presentation to George III.

Bath Hotel, Westminster, June 2, 1785

Dear Sir,

. . . At one, on Wednesday, the first of June, the master of ceremonies called at my house and went with me to the Secretary of State's Office, in Cleveland Row, where the Marquis of Carmarthen received me and . . . invited me to go with him in his coach to Court. When we arrived in the Anti-Chamber, the *Oeil de Boeuf,* of St. James's, the master of the ceremonies met me and attended me, while the Secretary of State went to take the commands of the King. While I stood in this place, where it seems all Ministers stand upon such occasions, always attended by the master of ceremonies, the room very full of Ministers of State, Bishops, and all other sorts of courtiers, as well as the next room, which is the King's bed-chamber, you may well suppose, I was the focus of all eyes . . . until the Marquis of Carmarthen returned and desired me to go with him to his Majesty. I went with his Lordship through the levee room into the King's closet. The door was shut and I was left with his Majesty and the Secretary of State alone, I made the three reverences, one at the door, another about halfway, and the third before the presence, according to the usage established at this and all the northern Courts of Europe, and then addressed myself to his Majesty in the following words:

"Sir,

"The United States of America have appointed me their Minister Plenipotentiary to your Majesty, and have directed me to deliver to your Majesty this letter, which contains the evidence of it. It is in obedience to

CONTINUED ON PAGE 89

THE GREAT SEA BATTLE

DONT GIVE UP THE SHIP

Battle can never be civilized, but in a century of total war and almost total barbarism it is refreshing to look back upon chivalrous combat. If it is gallantry and honor, even quixotism, you thirst for in a barren time, they are at their highest in the duel between His Britannic Majesty's frigate *Shannon* and the United States frigate *Chesapeake*, which met off Boston in the calm, early evening of June 1, 1813. Here is an authoritative and totally absorbing description of that famous encounter, together with an account of the principals, Captain P. B. V. Broke and Captain James Lawrence.

By PETER PADFIELD

The Challenger

Broke Hall stands four square and battlemented, close by the river Orwell below the little village of Nacton in Suffolk. It is an unpretending house. The main gates are plain. The drive leads straight, shadowed and scented by limes either side, a long way before the plain oak front door. To the right the sun flashes off broad reaches of the river; ahead the ground rises and folds around the square house, the old flagstones, and the lawns. Oak trees and evergreens complete its shelter from sea winds. Birds sing among them.

From the gentle high ground beneath these trees the view of the river and the far bank breathes England; there is nothing harsh, nothing swift, no feverish rapids, no sparkling pools, only the broad, easy stream leading in lazy curves to the sea. The far bank about a mile away rises alternately wooded and swelling with green and rich brown fields, pointed up with white houses, more trees, graceful village churches, nothing to jar nature.

The only strange notes in all this peace are provided by the gulls; they pipe as shrilly and excitedly as ever a swarm of boatswain's mates, mingling their sea noises with the land birds. For this is a meeting place—rural Suffolk with maritime England. A hundred sail and more—Britannia's shield—have been anchored between those green banks within cannon shot of the house; their canvas-clouded masts have thrilled generations of slow farmers and laborers and villagers of Nacton, and their great guns in salute have startled the gentlemen's deer in those fields and caused pheasants to rise and drum away like Frenchmen.

Leading from Broke Hall down to the river is another avenue of lime trees. It ends at a sand beach scattered with shingle which runs along the shore, narrowly dividing the grass banks and knotted roots of Suffolk from the mud flats at low tide. Sea wrack in the mazy indentations. Salt smell of estuaries. Here is a silence and peace that is not of the twentieth century.

Here we can drift back through the years without intrusion, through generations of Brokes, through this century and the last until we come upon a boy wandering this same sand, his eyes filled with this expanse of water, his mind with great thoughts of the ships that pass upon it. He is dreaming of the day he can get to sea himself—of the high, giddy adventure and romance of life under those raking spars, the far ports, the Indies, the skirmishes with M. Crapaud, the epaulets of an officer of the king, those *tall* ships! It was not unusual for East Coast boys to be seized in that way.

The boy was Philip Bowes Vere Broke (pronounced *Brook*), elder son of Philip Bowes Broke, Esquire, a solid, landed gentleman with literary tastes—not wealthy, but able to maintain his seat and his station comfortably from the few farms in Essex and Suffolk which went with the Broke estate. He had ambitions for a liberal education for his sons—Winchester, his old school, perhaps, or Eton. But Philip was under the spell of the ships. Young Philip had red hair from his mother, who was a parson's daughter, and from her also a firm religious grounding which admitted of no uncertainties; he was representative, perhaps, of the last generation of educated Englishmen who could go through life without doubt. From his mother and father and the extensive library at Broke Hall he had a taste for books and the Latin poets in their own tongue. He would carry with him through life this love of literature, these classical ideas, this absolute

Opposite page: Philip Bowes Vere Broke, in the full-dress uniform of a captain in the Royal Navy, stands on the deck of the frigate H.M.S. Shannon, his hand resting on one of the "great guns" of which he was so proud. The painting, after the English artist Samuel Lane, was done in the years immediately following Broke's encounter with the Chesapeake. The charming miniature at right is of Sarah Louisa Middleton, Broke's "gentle Loo." The daughter of a Suffolk neighbor, she bore him eleven children; two, Philip and George, followed their father into the Navy.

faith in one God, all mixed in with the quiet beauty of Suffolk, the wild flowers along the edges of the fields and narrow, windy, tree-hung lanes, the slow herds— the sea wind, keen from across the Orwell. He would also carry the stability and sense of station of a Broke descended from countless landed Brokes tracing back to Saxon times. Young Philip would feel the privilege of his position and the responsibilities that this privilege carried, one of which was to set an example in defense of his country—even with his life.

We have moved on from the boy on the sand. He had not comprehended all this yet, and was concerned only with persuading his father that there was really but one career for him, His Majesty's Navy. His father, disappointed, made a compromise: young Philip might attend the naval academy at Portsmouth; this, although a most unfashionable way of entering the sea service and frowned upon by stalwarts of the old school as "a sink of vice and abomination," was probably a kinder introduction for a lad than the fearful squalor of the gunroom in a man-of-war—certainly more likely to encourage study.

So from the age of twelve until he was fifteen, Philip studied the theory and high art of seamanship under canvas and obtained some glimpses into the new principles of gunnery, which had been propounded recently by an Englishman named Benjamin Robins, and which brought the light of science to this hitherto mysterious art. The flight of a ball does *not* conform to a parabola, because the ball is continuously retarded by the air it pushes; and most surprising, the spin imparted to a ball by contact with the side of the bore as it leaves the muzzle will cause it to curve toward that side during its flight.

The naval college instructors were not convinced of the practicality of this science, knowing well that the art of *naval* gunnery consisted in laying the ship so close to the enemy that the shot could not miss, however it left the barrel and whatever it did thereafter. More important was the composition of the gunpowder and its preservation in the damp magazines below the water line. Young Philip learned that the explosive force of the powder derives from its endeavors to expand when transformed into a gaseous substance by the application of a lighted match or—the very latest innovation in the naval service—a spark struck from a flintlock.

Philip's mind was fired by the details of his future profession. The ships he saw riding the Orwell, formerly just brave, graceful symbols of adventure over wider horizons than the Broke estate, took on added interest now that he could see the bones and vital organs beneath their fair curves and canvas. His was an essentially practical mind; his lessons in the craft of seamanship and gunnery had given it something to bite on. Now we can see him down by the river fitting out a fleet of wooden model ships and staging a general action, experimenting with gunpowder to fire their cannon, or, on another occasion, constructing a raft and setting out upon the tide to visit a ship at anchor. This fascination with the mechanics of seamanship and gunnery, this bent for experiment awakened at the naval college, would last him throughout his life.

The years passed quickly while he was learning; then, in 1792, at the age of fifteen, he was appointed midshipman in the *Bulldog* sloop-of-war, and nothing was seen of him at the Hall. But his letters arrived frequently. They were long with descriptions of the strange, brutal, yet intensely stimulating new life he had been plunged into. He was a little lonely when he found the time, for there were not too many lads of similar interests and education in His Majesty's ships. But his eagerness to acquire knowledge and master every smallest detail of the profession soon made him a favorite, and his captain, George Hope, later a good friend at the Admiralty, took him under his wing; when Hope was appointed to another vessel, he took young Philip with him.

But before that—war. The French had beheaded their king, and a number of good naval officers besides, and were attempting to spread their hateful revolutionary doctrine through Europe and the world. Young Philip was not only a seaman now but a crusader, convinced with all the fervor of a romantic youth—and heir to a landed estate—that the war with France was a "sacred cause." At the same time, his letters home came alive with more tales of adventure than he had ever dreamed of by the quiet Orwell, stories of the chase and cutting-out parties in small boats, of boarding merchantmen and being placed in command of prizes, of hunting down sharp privateers, or sailing in close to the enemy's batteries as the eyes of the fleet. As a fighting sailor he was fortunate; almost with his first deep draughts of sea air he was breathing in the trade of war, which no peacetime exercises could have simulated. He was learning naturally and barely consciously the disciplines and aggressive attitudes that went to make the men of the British Navy the most formidable sea-fighters in all Europe.

After three years of small-ship time as midshipman,

Philip Broke grew up in this house, Broke Hall, within sight and sound of the sea. This aerial view is of the garden side; a row of lime trees borders the main drive (to the right in the photograph). The present structure was built about 1526 by Sir Richard Broke, Chief Baron of the Exchequer under Henry VIII, and remained in the family until recent times. It is now owned by a gentleman farmer, Hodsoll Hurlock.

Philip Broke received a commission as third lieutenant of the *Southampton*; he remained absent from the Hall except in letters. He was cruising in the Mediterranean with Nelson's squadron. At the battle off Cape St. Vincent his frigate was employed towing the Spaniards off when they could stand the pounding no longer. But the French had not yet been driven into their harbors, and there was excitement aplenty in which the frigates took a more active part almost every week.

At last, after more than five years' continuous absence, Philip returned to Nacton for his twenty-first birthday, received to a hero's welcome—and rightly so, for he was now a seasoned fighting officer. The great portraits in the Hall looked down on him with approval—and some expectation, perhaps.

After some months breathing the quiet of Suffolk and feeling his pulses slowing to the old, familiar beat of the country, Philip—always a small-ship man and proud of it—was appointed to the *Amelia* frigate, Captain the Honorable C. Herbert. Herbert was a man of some literary taste and talent, and Philip found the atmosphere congenial. He served two years here, experiencing another general fleet engagement and many other excitements before obtaining his promotion to commander.

Now, while his father, who was a staunch Tory party worker, schemed with his political friends to ensure his son's promotion to post rank, young Broke experienced his first independent commands—some inconsequential fire brigs and convoy sloops—before his father's "interest" gained him the coveted step to post captain in February, 1801. Now his career was assured; at twenty-four, he had his foot unshakably on the promotion ladder and could look forward, with or without ships to command, to a steady ascent by seniority up the captain's list, and stage by stage through the rear admirals and the vice-admirals to the very top of his profession—if he could survive that long.

He returned to Broke Hall on half pay, a well-built young man over six feet tall. His weathered face wore a pleasant expression; his speech was assured, and he carried himself with a confidence born of ten years of very active service and the knowledge of his own capabilities this had brought. There was no vanity, though. The anecdotes of the chase and capture, of storms and foreign ports, with which he entertained his avid family were modestly understated. His red hair hung naturally and showed no powder; his dress was unassuming. In company he went out of his way to be pleasant and cheerful.

And now he was often down by the river with his young friend Sarah Louisa, second daughter of Sir

Photographed for AMERICAN HERITAGE *by Anthony Howarth*

ALL PHOTOGRAPHS OF BROKE HALL APPEAR BY COURTESY OF THE OWNER, HODSOLL HURLOCK

Broke Hall has both a rural and a maritime tradition. It overlooks the Orwell's estuary— seen above at low tide—and the pull of the sea on its families has been strong. Wind-driven coastal barges (right) still ply the river's current. One of Philip Broke's ancestors, Captain Packington Broke, was slain while in command of the frigate Fforesight at the Battle of Sole Bay in 1665; Philip and his sons added luster to the family's naval record. But as the scene at left suggests, the Brokes were landowners, too, drawing much of their income from the estate and its farms in Suffolk and neighboring Essex. For twenty-six years after his exploits aboard the Shannon, Broke lived the life of a gentleman farmer. His pocket diaries, which he continued to keep as he had done while at sea, tell of riding and shooting with his sons, of attending parish meetings, of buying sheep and lambs, of gardening and planting trees. After the Broke era, the Hall continued for many years in the possession of their relatives, a family named Saumarez.

William Middleton, Baronet, of Shrubland Park, not far from Ipswich; she was a fair-haired girl with a delicate complexion and very blue eyes—a shy creature in company, but it was obvious that she was very much in love with the naval hero, and he with her. They married in November, 1802.

They were ideally happy together, but as the months on half pay lengthened into years, Philip became increasingly nostalgic about those fine, free days at sea and increasingly impatient of idleness. He wrote to Lord Melville at the Admiralty to remind him of his presence and his eagerness to take advantage of any post command that might fall vacant. While he waited for a reply, he satisfied his restless mind by forming and training a body of local peasantry to arms against the day when old "Boney" might attempt an invasion of the last free country in Europe.

At last, in the spring of 1805, after Broke had been four years on half pay, Lord Melville found him a frigate, not a new or imposing one to be sure, and grossly undermanned like so many of His Majesty's ships in those hard times. It was certain also that no volunteers would come flying to join at the sound of her new captain's name, as they would for Lord Cochrane or one of the other glamorous frigate commanders.

Broke, sir? Who is he?

But for Philip, the *Druid*, a worn sieve of a frigate rated 32 guns, was a ship beyond all ships—his first post command. He was nearly twenty-nine years old, in the prime of manhood, and his brilliant prospects were all before him. Elated by the thought, but suddenly very sad at having to leave his delightful "Looloo" and the two children she had borne him, Philip entered the coach for London, his cases packed with a new captain's uniform, table service, and various flints and locks and sights for the great guns, with which he had been experimenting at home.

And again, for an even longer period, almost nothing was seen of him by the Orwell—only Louisa coming down to the beach with their children in the summer to read his letters:

My dear, beloved Looloo . . . My Sunday devotions bear me home to my Loo: I wish I could pray by her side. Alas! I shall see *no primroses* this May to remind me of my gentle Loo. When shall I sit and read to her again in the shade whilst she ties up the violets? Poor Nacton. 'Tis far away; I must not think of it till I am on my return.

But I must close up this and attend to my wooden mistress. *She* is a *great tyrant!* Give my love to the dear little cherubs around you and Heaven protect you all!

*I*n September, 1806, Captain Broke was posted to a brand-new frigate, the *Shannon*, fresh from the builder's yard. During the next few years, most of which the *Shannon* spent on the French blockade, it became apparent to Broke that many British captains were beginning to grow complacent because of the ease with which they had handled the French Navy. He never permitted this attitude to develop in his ship; indeed, he seemed to regard French impotence as a spur to show what could be done with scientific gunnery, of which he had always been an enthusiast.

He was one of a small band of officers who recognized that the improvements in the manufacture and equipment of the great guns which came about during the previous century had made accurate fire a possibility, at least for close action. The tools were there, and Broke's first action on taking command of the *Shannon* was to fit his guns with sights, then to set about training his officers, and through them the men, in their use.

He considered as a fault in gunnery any shot that went above or below the men on the enemy's gun decks. Dismasting or unrigging practice he regarded with contempt unless effected by the special dismantling service guns which he ordered on the enemy's wheel or yards. Each shot, each charge of grape or canister from his main batteries, he considered wasted unless coolly aimed to kill men.

During the next five years, as the *Shannon* ranged up and down the French coast, he had little opportunity to put his theories into practice in combat. But Broke kept his gun crews practicing nearly every day at sea until the use of sights became as much a habit as any other part of the loading and firing procedure and was unlikely to fail in the test of action. As a fighting unit his frigate was among the best ships in His Majesty's fleet.

In 1811, as war between Britain and the United States drew nearer, the *Shannon* was ordered to Halifax, headquarters for the North American station. In June of 1812 war finally came, and during the next six months, in a series of single-ship actions, the tiny United States fleet put the Royal Navy to shame: the *Constitution* bested the *Guerrière*; the *Wasp* defeated the *Frolic*; the *United States* subdued the *Macedonian*; and the *Constitution*, scoring a second victory, destroyed the British frigate *Java* off the coast of Brazil. In February, 1813, Broke had a letter from his former skipper, Sir George Hope, at the Admiralty: "Why don't you get a look at these Yankees," the Admiral wrote, "and not allow them to bully us in this way." In less than four months, Captain Broke would have his chance for revenge.

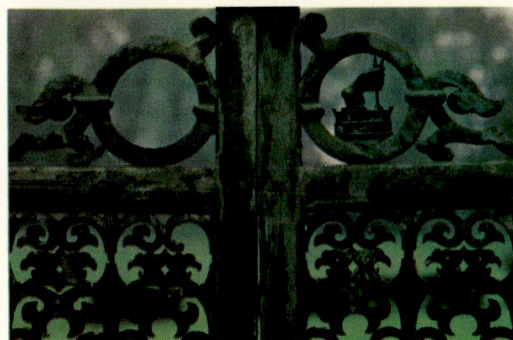

Today the rural aspect prevails at Broke Hall, but memories of the Shannon persist. At top is one of the rooms in the house, remodelled by Philip Broke to simulate his cabin aboard ship; one of his sea diaries and a ceremonial sword (see Cover) lie on a table. Elsewhere on the estate is a gate made from timbers of the Shannon; her figurehead (left) adorns a greenhouse at Shrubland, the home of Lady Broke's family.

The Challenged

In 1813 Captain James Lawrence of the United States Navy was just thirty-one, and like Broke he burned with ambition for glory in action. Like Broke also, he consistently trained his people for that action at the great guns, and was a strict disciplinarian without ever crossing the border to needless brutality or sadism; indeed, he commanded the same respect from some of his midshipmen that Broke did from his Shannons. But whereas Broke was calm and good-humored almost to the point of phlegm, Lawrence was impulsive and passionate.

His ancestors were of English stock, but his immediate forebears were American citizens of some prominence in Burlington, New Jersey, where he was born in October, 1781. Like Broke, he early showed a desire to go to sea, despite his parents' endeavors to put him to the law, and eventually he had his way, attended a three months' course in theoretical navigation, and entered the United States Navy as a midshipman in 1798.

Commissioned a full lieutenant in 1802, he distinguished himself in the war against the Barbary pirates by taking a small boat into the heavily armed harbor of Tripoli and helping to burn the captured American frigate *Philadelphia*. In 1808, the year of his marriage to Julia Montaudevert, he was appointed first lieutenant of the *Constitution*, and after only seven months, still a lieutenant, got his first sizable command, the 12-gun brig-of-war *Vixen*. He briefly commanded the sloop *Wasp* and the brig *Argus*, and in October of 1811, promoted to master commandant—roughly the equivalent of a present-day commander—he took over the *Hornet*, 18 guns. It was on her quarter-deck that he was to make his reputation.

On the afternoon of February 14, 1812, the *Hornet*, on a southward cruise looking for British prizes, sighted off Guiana near the mouth of the Demerara River the smartly turned out but indifferently commanded British brig-of-war *Peacock*. After one inconclusive exchange of broadsides, Lawrence came down on the *Peacock* from to windward, placed himself close alongside her starboard quarter, and proceeded to cut her to pieces with the superior weight of carronade served by his expert gunners. With water flooding in through shot holes, she hoisted her ensign downward.

It was an infinitely sad day for the Royal Navy. And as one British officer subsequently described the contest, "if the *Peacock* had been moored for the purpose of experiment she could not have sunk sooner." Lawrence remarked to an acquaintance that his clerk had reported the time of the action as eleven minutes, "but I thought fifteen minutes was short enough so I made it that in my report." This, if truly recollected, is a remarkable coincidence—as will appear.

Lawrence immediately became the latest in the growing line of U.S. naval heroes. He had suddenly become "Captain Jim," the toast of the eastern seaboard, whose *Hornet* had stung the *Peacock* to death in less time than any previous engagement in the war. After a year of shore duty, Captain Lawrence was posted in May, 1813, to the *Chesapeake*, a fast and exceedingly handsome frigate then at Boston preparing to go out and test the British blockade. Part of the blockade was the frigate H.M.S. *Shannon*, Captain Philip Broke.

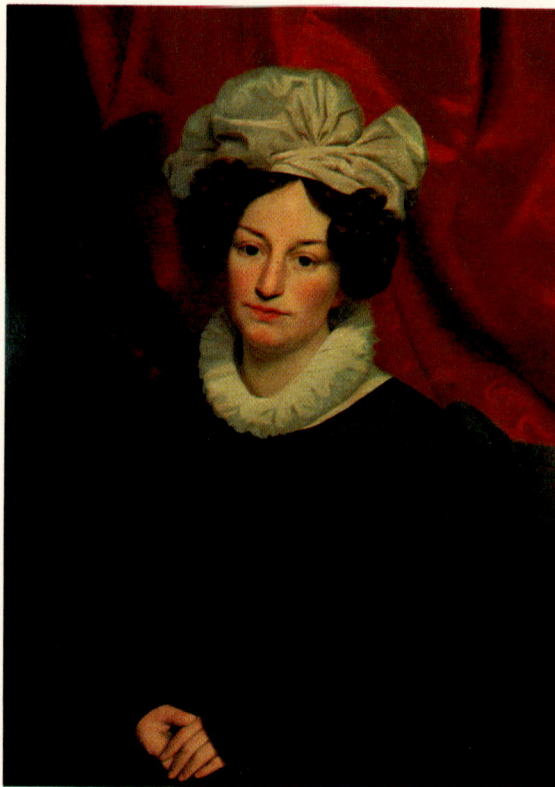

James Lawrence, seen at right in a portrait by Gilbert Stuart, was remembered by a contemporary as "tall, a little under six feet, with a handsome, manly face and dark hair with side whiskers combed up. . . .His proportions were good and his movements graceful, and he carried himself as one born to command." He was also a bit of a dandy, and before an action attired himself in full uniform. Julia, his wife of five years (left, in an anonymous portrait), was the daughter of a French sea captain. At the time of the battle, they had an infant daughter, and Julia was expecting a second child. "I believe our darling is a year old today," Lawrence wrote to his wife a month before he went out to meet Broke and the Shannon; "kiss her affectionately for me." He was never to see either of them again.

Shortly before his victory over the *Peacock*, Lawrence had sent a challenge to H.M. sloop-of-war *Bonne Citoyenne*, lying at anchor in the harbor of San Salvador. The British captain, carrying a valuable cargo of specie, had refused to fight, and the incident had received wide publicity on both sides of the Atlantic. Now, on Monday, May 31, 1813, Captain Broke, cruising off Boston, decided to pay Lawrence off in his own coin: he had sent in verbal challenges via fishermen; now he started drafting a careful letter challenging him to single combat. He took infinite pains. The impression it would make on Lawrence might mean the difference between action or a dull end to his career. "Sir, As the Chesapeake appears now ready for sea, I request that you will do me the favour to meet the *Shannon* with her, ship to ship, to try the fortune of our respective flags. To an officer of your character, it requires some apology to proceed to further particulars. Be assured, sir, that it is not from any doubt I can entertain of your wishing to close with my proposal, but merely to provide an answer to any objection which might be made, and very reasonably, upon the chance of our receiving unfair support. . . . I assure you that what I write, I pledge my honor to perform to the utmost of my power. The *Shannon* mounts twenty-four guns upon her broadside and one light boat gun— eighteen pounders upon her maindeck, and thirty two-pound carronades on her quarterdeck and forecastle, and is manned with a complement of 300 men and boys (a large proportion of the latter), besides thirty seamen, boys and passengers who were taken out of recaptured vessels lately. . . . I will send all other ships beyond the power of interfering with us, and meet you wherever it is most agreeable to you, within the limits of the undermentioned rendezvous, viz. from six to ten leagues East of Cape Cod lighthouse; from eight to ten leagues East of Cape Anne's Light; on Cashe's ledge, in latitude 43 North; at any bearing and distance you please to fix, off the South breakers of Nantucket, or the shoal on St. George's Bank. If you will favor me with any plan of signals or telegraph, I will warn you (if sailing under this promise) should any of my friends be too nigh, or anywhere in sight, until I can detach them

The Challenge

out of my way; or I would sail with you under a flag of truce, to any place you think safest from our cruisers, hauling it down when fair to begin hostilities.

"You must, sir, be aware that my proposals are highly advantageous to you, as you cannot proceed to sea singly in the *Chesapeake* without imminent risk of being crushed by the superior force of the numerous British squadrons which are now abroad, where all your efforts, in case of a *rencontre*, would, however gallant, be perfectly hopeless. I entreat you, sir, not to imagine that I am urged by mere personal vanity to the wish of meeting the *Chesapeake*, or that I depend only upon your personal ambition for your acceding to this invitation; we both have nobler motives.

"You will feel it as a compliment if I say that the result of our meeting may be the most grateful service I can render to my country; and, I doubt not, that you, equally confident of success, will feel that it is only by repeated triumphs, in *even combats*, that your little navy can now hope to console your country for the loss of that trade it can no longer protect. Favour me with a speedy reply.

"We are short of provisions and water, and cannot stay long here.

"N.B. For the general service of watching your coast it is requisite for me to keep another ship in company to support me with her guns and boats, when employed near the land, and particularly to aid each other if either ship, in chase, should get on shore. You must be aware that I cannot, consistent with my duty, waive so great an advantage for this general service by detaching my consort without an assurance on your part of meeting me directly, and that you will neither seek nor admit aid from any other of your armed vessels if I despatch mine expressly for the sake of meeting you.

"Should any special order restrain you from thus answering a formal challenge, you may yet oblige me by keeping my proposal a secret, and appointing any place you like to meet us (within 300 miles of Boston) in a given number of days after you sail; as unless you agree to an interview, I may be busied on some other service, and perhaps be at a distance from Boston when you get to sea. Choose your terms, but let us meet."

The guard of Broke's sword is engraved to show that it was presented to him by the grateful guilds of the City of London.

40

The morning of June 1 broke splendidly. The damp fogs and rain of the last few days had given way to blue sky with puffy clouds over the land. The sun rose brilliantly and shone and sparked off the gently heaving ocean, its surface creased with a cool, invigorating breeze from northward. Broke tapped his barometer and noted it was still rising. Promise of a fair summer's day. But more than that if he had judged Lawrence aright—much more.

He went on deck and acknowledged the salute of his first lieutenant. James Watt, too, had been lifted by the sun. The big man's face was animated and there was a glint in his eye which entirely matched Broke's mood. No need to express it; on such a morning words were superfluous.

Today?

The *Shannon* slid easily through the now friendly blue water southward toward Boston. Cape Ann receded gradually on the quarter*; stretching around as far as the eye could see to starboard lay the green and peaceful countryside of New England with its tall beeches and pines clustering thickly down to the dry, pinkish rock by the shore. Smoke curled lazily from the chimneys of timber frame houses, small fishing boats were putting out from the coastal towns—snuggling roofs and narrow, twisting streets like the West Country of England—and beyond lay all the English names, Bradford, Georgetown, Broke's own Ipswich, Haverhill (the same distance away as the Suffolk Haverhill from the Suffolk Ipswich), Andover, Gloucester, Weymouth, Braintree, Abington, Bridgewater, Kingston, Plymouth, Wareham, Sandwich—and Boston itself. Strange to be fighting these half-countrymen of theirs. . . .

Presently, beyond the spur of Nahant and the cluster of fishing craft after cod and halibut, perch or haddock just south of Pea Island, the far view of the city presented itself clear

* The asterisks that appear throughout this article indicate terms that are defined in the Glossary on page 51.

The Battle

in the morning light. The clustering masts and spars of scores of blockaded vessels marked the outline of wharves stretching down to Boston Neck and Dorchester, and behind them the houses and public buildings rose to Beacon Hill, bright sun glinting off paintwork and windows and white stone, monuments to a wealthy mercantile community.

Then, as the *Shannon* slipped nearer and got an open view into President's Roads between the trees on Deer Island and Long Island, they saw her— a sleek frigate showing gun ports along her side and a fresh bright band of yellow paint below them extending right up in the bows to her fiddlehead,* her rigging above set taut, her royals [see *sail**] crossed and her furled white sails stopped with rope yarns* ready to drop on the instant.

There she lay!

Broke's heart pounded. Up until that moment there had always been the chance that she might somehow have slipped out unnoticed and unreported. But there she was—the *Chesapeake*—and ready for sea. He had not realized quite how much he depended on her—his passport to glory, above all his *release* in action for all the warlike tension built up over seven years of gunnery planning and improvements and drill—like a spring wound tight his company demanded release. And so did he. He shuddered at the violence of his feelings.

He stood the *Shannon* closer in toward the Boston lighthouse, close-hauled to the light breeze which was backing ever more westerly, until within about two miles he luffed* up and fired a gun. Could the *Chesapeake* resist this challenge?

Here was a British frigate entirely alone, her weathered sides streaked down from the gun ports and chains with the signs of long cruising, flaunt-

ing a faded blue ensign at the very mouth of a United States Navy base, firing a single, teasing gun. What American commander could submit to this in the present mood of the Navy and the country?

Of course Lawrence had no option. His fiery spirit demanded that he accept this plain challenge; the confidence inspired by his recent easy victory over the *Peacock* and all the American frigate successes to date left no room for doubts, his own ambition left no time for hesitation. That is—if the *Shannon* was truly alone. So long as this was not just a trick to draw him out on this fine westerly breeze and into the arms of one or two of the *Shannon*'s consorts ready to appear in the offing.

Lawrence's attention had first been called to the strange sail between eight and nine o'clock that morning. Lieutenant George Budd, the officer of the deck, had sent a midshipman down to report, as he supposed, a frigate. Lawrence had gone on deck and then ascended the main shrouds for a better view, soon coming to the conclusion that she was a large frigate. Returning to the deck he hailed a passing pilot boat and directed her to reconnoiter outside the harbor and report back to him if the strange sail was alone, meanwhile ordering all hands to prepare the ship for sailing and to heave short on the anchor cable. Afterward he went below to his cabin and wrote a short letter to the Secretary of the Navy to acquaint him with his decision:

Since I had the honour of addressing you last, I have been detained for want of men. I am now getting under way to carry into execution the instructions you have honoured me with. An English frigate is now in plain sight from my deck; I have sent a pilot boat out to reconnoitre & should she be alone I am in hopes to give a good account of her before night. My crew appear to be in fine spirits, & I trust will do their duty.

Lieutenant Page [the *Chesapeake*'s first lieutenant] is so ill as to be unable to go to sea in the ship. . . . Commodore Bainbridge has ordered midshipmen Cox and

Ballard to act until your pleasure is known. They are both fine young men, and I am confident from their long service, will do everything that can be expected from any commissioned lieutenant.

Then he wrote a short note to his brother-in-law about prize money due for captures during the last cruise, ending:

. . . An English frigate is close in with the lighthouse, & we are now clearing ship for action. Should I be so unfortunate as to be taken off, I leave my wife and children to your care, and feel confident you will behave to them the same as if they were your own. Remember me affectionately to your good mother, Mary and Cox and believe me,

Sincerely yours,
J. LAWRENCE

P.S. 10 A.M. the frigate is in plain sight from our deck and we are now getting under way.

As the *Shannon* fired her gun, Lawrence ordered one of his own to reply, and had the fore-topsail loosed so that it hung shivering in the breeze. One of the sailors hoisted a white flag bearing the words "Free Trade and Sailor's Rights" to the foreroyal masthead. Then they waited for the pilot boat to return.

Certainly Lawrence could have rationalized his decision: the British blockade was tightening every day; now that the British government realized that the war was more than a simple misunderstanding, and the Admiralty was awakened to the need for more ships of force to contain the U.S. Navy and the scores of privateers preying on trade, it was only a matter of time before it would be impossible to break their blockade in fair weather. That might mean waiting for the winter gales before he could get out. His orders, which left him great freedom to exercise his own judgment, were to proceed to the mouth of the St. Lawrence River and attack the troop convoys and supplies going to the relief of the British Army in Canada; they contained the unarguable assertion that "it is impossible to conceive a

naval service of a higher order in a national point of view than the destruction of the enemy's vessels with supplies for his army in Canada and his fleets on this station." But if he had to await the winter gales he might be too late. The supplies and reinforcements would have arrived. And what was the alternative? Simply to go out now while the wind and the opportunity favored, bring in this insolent British frigate while she lay unsupported, quickly make good whatever damage was sustained in the process, and then sail safely in obedience to his orders before the British realized the blockade was broken and dispatched a squadron or a ship of the line* to contain him. Perhaps this was his reasoning; but undoubtedly the decision to fight also came from deeper sources than reason.

Many and varied have been the criticisms levelled at Lawrence for going out with an allegedly untrained crew and raw officers and fighting before he had worked his men up into a team. It is true that Page, his new first lieutenant, was ill in the hospital, and the other lieutenants had been moved up one. It is also true that these officers were young and one had not drilled before the day of action with the men he commanded. But again Lawrence had to face the alternative: what chance would he have if he waited until he was outnumbered or outgunned? Besides, he had faith in his lieutenants; the first, Augustus Ludlow, had been nine years at sea, having entered as a midshipman at twelve years old; he was exceptionally able and together with Budd, the second, had been with the *Chesapeake* during her last cruise and obviously knew her well. The two juniors, Cox and Ballard, had both sailed with him in his previous commands and had been promoted from midshipmen on his recommendation. He had no reason to doubt their capabilities; quite the reverse. Age was no bar; Lawrence himself had been about Cox's age when he had his first taste of hand-to-hand

fighting in the Mediterranean, and only a year older when he was first lieutenant at Decatur's brilliant *Philadelphia* exploit. As for experience in action, that could come only in action, and no amount of working up could provide more of it than they had had while sailing on the *Hornet*.

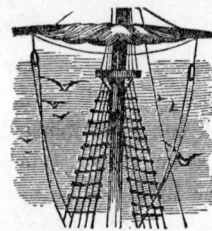

HE other criticisms are perhaps even less valid. The men were not raw; of the 388 officers, men, and marines on the *Chesapeake's* pay list on June 1, 279, or nearly three quarters, had served during the ship's previous cruise. There were no landsmen among them; the lowest rating apart from boys (thirteen in all) was ordinary seaman. They were exceptionally well trained at the great guns, as Lawrence had found during his drills in harbor. Although they were, it is true, dissatisfied about not having the money due for six prizes captured during the ship's last cruise, it is impossible to believe that they were drunk, as some writers have stated, or that they included a large number of foreigners, as other critics would have it. Lawrence had observed them for nearly a fortnight; he knew them to be first-rate American sailors and gunners, many of whom had learned their trade in the British service—a few of whom were in fact British deserters. There was also a detachment of volunteers from the dockyard, possibly from the *Constitution*, which was still under repair; these came aboard at the last moment and their hammocks and gear lay in the boats and across the booms when the frigate sailed. These men too, however, were seasoned sailors and fighters who had already been the victors in two frigate actions, and they were possessed of a splendid morale.

Finally, the two ships were very well matched. The *Chesapeake* was launched in June, 1799, and got away to sea the same year. She was thus seven years older than the *Shannon*, but in all other respects she was as equal an opponent as could be found anywhere. Instead of being 145 feet on the keel as originally planned, she was 127 feet 5 inches, and her length between perpendiculars (English measurement) was 151 feet; the Shannon was 150 feet 1½ inches. The *Chesapeake* had a molded beam of 40 feet 4 inches, the *Shannon* 39 feet 3 inches. The *Chesapeake* carried fourteen long 18-pounder cannon each side of her main deck; so did the *Shannon*. The *Chesapeake* had ten carronades,* 32-pounders, either side of her spar deck, with one long 18-pounder which could be shifted to whichever broadside was required; the *Shannon* on her present cruise fought eight carronades, 32-pounders, each side of the upper deck (six on the quarter-deck and two on the forecastle), and in addition she had two long 9-pounders; these were mounted at the after end of the forecastle and the forward end of the quarter-deck on special swivel brackets raised high above the deck to have a clear fire overall and with facility of elevation to 33°, especially for use either against the enemy's tops* or to dismantle the wheel. Broke had also fitted a launch carronade 12-pounder in the starboard entry port, and a brass 6-pounder to port. Thus both ships had a broadside of fourteen long guns on the main deck and eleven carronades and others on the upper deck, although the *Chesapeake* had a small advantage in weight of shot from the upper deck.

Lawrence knew his men; he had every reason for confidence. The only thing he did not know was the exceptional quality of the opposition. And how should he have guessed that this *Shannon*, which had been flaunting herself before Boston and sending in verbal challenges for weeks, was not simply another lamb for the slaughter? How was he to know that she marked instead the final flowering and high point of the ancient art of broadside fire from carriage-mounted cannon, and that a more destructive vessel of her force had probably never existed in the history of naval warfare?

Lawrence had no idea. He had weighed what he did know in scales heavily weighted by his temperament, and had come to the inevitable conclusion. As he saw the *Shannon* teasing him on this bright morning with the wind fair in the west, he saw only his brilliant opportunity.

Expecting that the pilot boat's report would be favorable, he had the quarter boats lowered and the women from the berth deck sent over the side with their scanty baggage; they expected to be back aboard that evening and cried no farewells—only shouts of encouragement. As they landed by the fort they waved and cheered the British frigate and yelled taunts, looking forward to a closer view when their brave, boastful menfolk brought her in.

The citizens of Boston were equally sanguine. The day's work was forgotten as they rushed to the waterfront or the roofs of nearby buildings to view this latest British ship offering herself as a prize to their naval heroes. Fishermen filled their boats with sight-seers to follow the *Chesapeake* into action; the coffeehouses were abuzz with preparations for a great celebration supper to which it was proposed to invite the surviving officers of the *Shannon* together with Lawrence and his triumphant men. And at the navy yard a wharf was cleared to accommodate the *Shannon's* riven remains when she was brought in. Never was optimism about the result of apparently equal combat so unequivocal.

Even if he had wished, could Lawrence have refused to go out?

The *Shannon* meanwhile tacked and a call to quarters was sounded. The men went through the ritual of the great gun drill without firing. Broke, who had written his letter of challenge closely following his draft, sealed it, then wrote a postscript on the outside, "We have thirteen American persons on board which I shall give you for as many British sailors if you will send them out; otherwise, being privateersmen, they must be detained." The day before, the *Shannon* had captured and burned an American fishing vessel and taken her captain, Eben Slocum, prisoner. Now Broke had Slocum unchained and brought up, and told him that he was a free man if he would agree to deliver the letter. Slocum agreed, and was shortly put into a fishing schooner that the *Shannon's* jolly boat* ran aboard.

As the schooner left her side and pointed inshore for Marblehead, Broke climbed the main shrouds with his long glass and settled himself in the top. He did not expect to have to wait for Slocum to reach the shore. Under the circumstances this morning, the letter should scarcely be necessary. He knew his man. The wind and the weather were fair for sailing; the chance of breaking the blockade in a single action in full view of the people of Boston would be too much for the

Kedge-Anchor, BY WILLIAM N. BRADY, 1872

Sailors' mess on a warship around 1813

spirited captain of the *Chesapeake*. In any case, it was obvious from the papers that the Americans were becoming quite too brash, and they would not expect Lawrence to refuse the challenge presented by the *Shannon* alone.

He trained his glass over the masts and yards of the frigate standing up so boldly, searching for another sign of movement. Below him the great cannon went rumbling and thudding against their port sills, then back again —then out. The only other sounds were made by the water plashing gently against the bow, and the occasional hoarse orders from the officers of the quarters. The sun was warm against his neck and the breeze full in his face.

But after that first response from the *Chesapeake,* nothing further seemed to happen. She just lay there with the topsail flapping unsheeted. In the other direction Slocum's small boat was making slow progress against the offshore breeze; he could not reach Salem for some time yet—but surely, surely

A gun crew services a big naval cannon.

Lawrence would never need a *paper* challenge. . . .

At 11:30 Broke shut his telescope and climbed down to the officer of the watch on the quarter-deck, who happened to be Provo Wallis, the second lieutenant. "Beat the retreat if you please," he said with the disappointment obvious in his voice. "But, Wallis, I don't mean this for a general quarters. She will surely be out today or tomorrow."

The *Shannon* beat back and forth across the harbor entrance under easy sail to the light and variable breeze, making little way, towing her jolly boat astern from a short painter. The small boat had been left down in the water after capturing the fishing schooner so that she would not obstruct the fire of the stern chase guns. She yawed across the smooth green shadows in the frigate's wake.

At midday Wallis ordered meridian.* The marine sentinel on the quarter-deck upturned his half-hour sandglass, and from the belfry forward came the four double peals followed immediately by the pipes shrilling for

dinner. The men, animated by the pleasant weather and their close view right into the heart of enemy territory, excited by the prospect of a wild break in routine when the American frigate came out, clattered down to their mess tables.

On the quarter-deck Lieutenant Charles Falkiner relieved Wallis for the afternoon watch. They both stood gazing over toward the *Chesapeake*'s spars and hanging topsail over the bright land. The barometer was high and rising. The wind had blown the clouds off and the sky was a clear, blue bowl of summer.

"She has not moved yet?" Falkiner asked.

"The Captain is sure she will come out."

Presently the marine at the sandglass called out the half hour and the bell was struck once. The pipes shrilled for grog and the rough pitch of the men's voices from below swelled and grew more frenzied as the watered rum loosened their tongues. The noise struck up through the gratings over the hatchway—roaring laughter, snatches of song, stage-Irish obscenities to rile the new Paddys who were too stupid to understand anyway, all mixed with coarse boasts of what they were going to do to the Yankees when they dared come out. They knew they could. If anyone could turn the trick it was their flaming redheaded captain. A tartar at the great guns; but they knew they could handle them now and shoot straight across the surface whatever the roll on her—none of your dismasting games—into the hull and give it to the men and never mind about the rigging, the Captain said. They knew that if he could get her alongside yardarm to yardarm, they could flush the boasting Yankees from their pride. If anyone could do it, the Shannons could.

The babble of sound floated up to Broke, who had taken his position with a telescope in the maintop again. But why wouldn't she move? Every minute gone by was a minute of this

fine day wasted—and would it eventually be just another day to add to his six and a half undistinguished years?

He could see that Slocum's boat had still not reached shore.

As he looked back toward the *Chesapeake* his blood stopped momentarily, and then pumped hard. There was a cry from the lookout, "She comes! Sir, the frigate has made sail!"

What a picture she made! She had sheeted home* all together and was walking* out over her short cable helped by the ebbing tide. He watched her through his glass for a moment to make sure there could be no mistake, then hurried down on deck.

The voices from below had ceased as the word spread like a thunderclap among the men. They were all on deck lining the bulwarks and hammock nettings and even in the lower shrouds, straining to get a better sight. And they were quiet. Now that the moment was upon them their high spirits gave way to a sort of awe. The Yankee frigate was coming for them.

Broke felt their eyes on him, and knew that Watt close by was waiting for a word. He stepped back to the main shrouds and levelled his telescope again. There could be no doubt. She was walking down steadily toward the lighthouse with the tide and the wind behind her—she was surrounded by a clutch of small craft like ducklings in her wake, and among them some fairsized cutters and a large schooner, probably armed, and all of them crowded with Americans coming out to see the sport. What a spectacle they made with their gay sails and myriad colors against the land! He could imagine his opponent, Lawrence, on the frigate's quarterdeck, a large, handsome, willful fellow by all accounts—and confident, too. He would expect to give those people of his a show.

Broke fought down his mounting excitement and turned to Watt. "I hope to have the pleasure of shaking hands with Captain Lawrence today." Watt smiled.

They wasted little time discussing

the immediate situation because it was obvious to both that the *Shannon* was far too close to Boston and that if by mischance they were dismasted or otherwise crippled they would be in danger from boarding parties from the shore. The helm was put up to wear* ship, the jib set, and when they were around on a southeasterly course the topgallants and the forecourse were dropped and sheeted home. The *Chesapeake* meanwhile set all her studding sails* alow and aloft and walked out after them, a splendid, tapering mass of white sunlit and shadowed canvas against the green land.

All the officers were up on the quarter-deck now, and those marines and waisters* on deck were talking with hushed excitement. Broke called them to silence. Then he went below to his great cabin for the last time before it was dismantled for action. He fell to his knees and committed to God's care his beloved Louisa and his dear children and the *Shannon* and all her people, and he prayed earnestly that he might not fail any of them when the moment of trial came. And if it were God's will—let it be the *Shannon* to raise the proud old union flag again.

IS servant was stowing his gear ready for carrying below, and the carpenters were banging away at the timber partitions that formed his suite of rooms. They soon had them apart and carried them down to the holds with his few pieces of furniture and his books; now the gun deck presented an unbroken sweep of planking down each side inboard of the cannon: from the manger* forward where the goats were tethered, down past the main hatch coaming, which was surrounded by 18-pounder balls like strings of black beads in their shot racks, past the foot of the mainmast [see *mast**] with its cluster of stanchions, up again to the great windows at the stern through which the sun was striking in diagonals. Dappled reflections off the water rippled along the beams overhead.

The chase to seaward continued slowly down the fitful afternoon breeze. Broke had the carpenters erect a table on the quarter-deck and a canvas screen just forward to shield it from the men's gaze, and invited his commissioned officers to dine with him. They gathered around the white cloth gleaming with his silver service and glassware, claret in decanters making a splash of color between their shadows —Watt and Wallis, Falkiner and the two marine officers, Johns and Law, each backed by his own servant, each a little constrained by the occasion and by an effort at unconcern. And whenever they stood up to glance over the starboard-quarter hammocks, there, like fate itself, was the towering spread of the *Chesapeake*'s canvas, always just a fraction closer, the sun molding white highlights on the starboard side of her studding sails, and the ripple at her bow. A picture for an artist against the clear blue of the sky! The small craft accompanying her were straggling now; only the schooner seemed able to stay the pace in the light breeze.

When they had finished eating and the servants had cleared the plates, but while the port remained, Broke rose to his feet and looked at his officers in turn. "Well, gentlemen, no doubt we shall shortly be in action," he started, as if announcing nothing more serious than a gun drill. "It will be a satisfaction to me if we all take wine with each other—and shake hands all round before we go to our quarters." This was an old custom which had fallen into disuse. The chairs scraped back; the officers stood with him and raised their glasses across the table, then bowed, straightened up, and drank deeply to their friendship.

Below decks all was ready for the action. In the steamy, dark cockpit below the steerage the surgeon and his mate had laid out their armament of saws, knives, probes, drills, and forceps, which glistened dully in the candlelight from the heavy lanterns hung around the cockpit. The deck below was spread with old, scrubbed canvas; half-tubs gleaming with water stood ready to receive amputated limbs, others were placed near the sponges and bandages and tourniquets, still another half-tub was filled with warm water to take the coldness from the instruments before they entered flesh.

Forward the old gunner, having seen to the damp brushwood screens all around the hatchways up which his cartridges would be passed, and more damp screens before the entrance to the magazines themselves, was busy filling flannel cartridges with powder, helped by a little band of his mates, stacking them carefully inside the copper-lined door.

Above on the main deck, alternate cannon had been loaded with one ball in addition to the one they always had in them at sea; the others had one round of shot, one of grape. By the side between each gun port was a half-tub of salt water in case of fire, and by each breech, but placed out of range of possible leaping, stood another half-tub of water with lighted slow matches stuck in the rim in case the lock failed. A third bucket contained fresh water for refreshing the crew. Nettings of wads were placed handy between the guns, and the rammers, sponges, and worms* laid in parallel on the deck, handles inboard as if at drill; the ends of all the tackles were neatly flaked,* the flints carefully placed and adjusted in the locks, the tampions* removed from the mouths that poked outboard; all that was needed now before firing was the correct adjustment to the quoins* for horizontal aim. The deck had been wet and sprinkled with sand, hoses were uncoiled like snakes over the hatch gratings, the pumps were rigged.

Similar preparations were visible on the forecastle and quarter-deck for the carronade batteries, and the small arms had been laid inboard of them for the boarders. Above, the yards had been slung with chains and further secured against falling by stoppers to their halyards so that if cut below the stoppers by shot they would still hold. Buckets of water had been prepared on hoists so that the sails could be wet down just before the action.

Meanwhile Lawrence, fearing once more that he might be following the *Shannon* into a trap, rounded to and lay pointing northwesterly toward Salem, and fired a gun. Broke had the *Shannon* brought to in the same direction and hove all aback, and fired a gun in reply. He discussed with the officers whether they were far enough from the harbor, but decided that as there was still plenty of daylight it would be advisable to try to draw the *Chesapeake* still farther out. So when Lawrence, apparently satisfied with Broke's action, put his helm up and filled again, standing toward him, Broke did the same.

By this time, about 4:00, the *Shannon* had run some fifteen miles from Boston, which was out of sight astern. Broke, his table and canvas screen cleared from the quarter-deck, shortly decided that the time was suitable for allowing the *Chesapeake* to close, and he ordered the topgallants to be taken in and the staysails* lowered. The hands were piped to grog. The kids were brought up from the manger and thrown overboard. Broke watched them struggling as they drifted astern.

The *Chesapeake* was barely four miles away and was steadily closing the gap of blue water. Her cloud of canvas was broken gaily by the red and blue splashes of three ensigns from the main and mizzen, and still at the fore-royal was the white flag with "Free Trade and Sailor's Rights" emblazoned across it. This was what they were fighting for—not the economists' definition but simply the freedom to trade with whatever country they wished, without the fear of impressment.

By 4:50 the *Chesapeake* was some two miles astern and Lawrence ordered his studding sails to be taken in, the royals furled, and the royal yards sent down on deck. Broke noted this, but kept his own royal yards across, as he expected that the light breeze might die away with the evening. At 5:10 he asked Watt to have the drum beat to quarters; the men assembled and stood quiet and grim in double rows between the cannon, looking almost as they had at the morning's drill—but with a tension about them which had been lacking then. The quiet was intense.

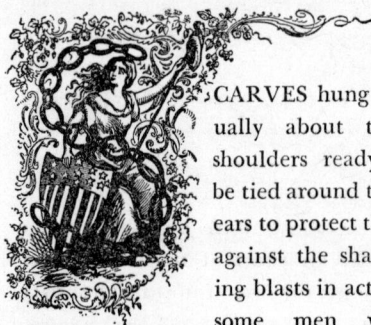

SCARVES hung casually about their shoulders ready to be tied around their ears to protect them against the shattering blasts in action; some men were bare-chested with another scarf holding their white or blue duck trousers around their waists, others had striped shirts tucked in or hanging outside like smocks. Everything was clean in case a ball plowed the cloth into their flesh.

The officers had donned worn old uniforms and their fighting swords for the fray, and Broke had adorned himself with a top hat as better protection for his head than the uniform cocked hat. When the men were all assembled, Broke went to the break of the quarter-deck. The men of the upper-deck quarters and the marines, brilliant in their scarlet and white-crossed tunics, drew up on either side along the gangways; the men of the main deck looked upward from below the boats and spars across the open hatchway.

"Shannons," he started when they were still. "Shannons, the time has come to show the superiority you have acquired in managing your guns and in marksmanship. You know the Americans have lately triumphed on several occasions over the British flag. But this will not daunt you—we all know the truth—'twas disparity of force that enabled them to do so." He paused.

"But they have gone further—they have said and published in their newspapers that the English have forgotten how to fight." He looked around at them. "Shannons, you will let them know today that there are Englishmen in this frigate who still know how to fight. You have drilled long and earnestly. You have acquired such skill with the great guns that I believe no frigate afloat can stand beside you. *Now* is the time to put that drill to the test of action. Throw no shot away. Aim every one. Keep cool. Work steadily. Fire into her quarters—main deck to main deck, quarter-deck to quarter-deck. Don't try to dismast her. Kill the men and the ship is yours."

The sailors growled their appreciation. Broke held up a hand.

"And if it comes to close quarters, don't hit them about the head for they have steel caps on. Give it them through the body."

The low growl broke out again. Broke raised his voice. "You know the day—'tis the Glorious First of June.† And I have great hopes of adding another shining laurel to it, for I have no doubts that we will triumph. Remember your comrades—from the *Guerrière,* from the *Macedonian* and from the *Java*—you have the blood of *hundreds* to avenge today. The eyes of all Europe are upon you."

There was complete silence as Broke mentioned the three British frigates that had been lost, and now several of these sturdy sailormen around him wept openly with emotion.

One of them, named Jacob West, who had been in the *Guerrière* when she was taken and had subsequently been repatriated and drafted to the *Shannon,* raised his voice, "Sir, I hope you will give us revenge for the *Guerrière* today."

† The Glorious First of June was the last day of a British-French sea battle fought in 1794, at a point over 400 miles from the French coast. The British, trying to intercept a convoy of corn that the French had bought in America and were transporting home, won a brilliant victory, although they failed to capture the convoy.

"You shall have it, my man," Broke replied. "Now go quietly to your quarters. And don't cheer!"

The men dispersed back to their guns, the waisters and idlers* to their stations for manning the braces, and the marines along either gangway, muskets held loosely. Broke stationed two of the *Shannon*'s quartermasters at the weather* spokes of the wheel, and a man named James Reader, alias Adam Read (a recaptured sailor), at the lee wheel, making certain that a chance shot would not leave the steering unattended. Then he walked forward to his 9-pounder swivel crews and instructed them to concentrate on the American wheel. "She must not get away!"

The *Chesapeake* was well within range now, but Lawrence was careful to keep just clear of the *Shannon*'s wake so that no guns would bear on her. She had shortened to fighting canvas and was coming on at between three and four knots under full topsails, foretopmast staysail, and jib. Lawrence's men were waiting quietly at their quarters. Their earlier grumbling about the prize money owing them had been quieted when Lawrence sent them down to the purser by twos and threes to collect checks. Now, calling them together, he addressed them from the quarter-deck as Broke had addressed his people. After stirring their imagination and confidence by reciting the unbroken list of American frigate successes, he ended with a telling reference to his own latest victory. "*Peacock* her, my lads," he had finished. "*Peacock* her!" The Americans stood to their guns, certain that they would do just that. And it was very plain that "Captain Jim" intended to go in to close quarters immediately, for he had instructed his lieutenants to add canister and bar shot to the one round, one grape, already in the guns.

Broke now shortened to single reefed topsails and jib and lay the *Shannon* to with the wind just forward of the starboard beam. The jib was allowed to shiver, and, the main yard being braced square, the maintopsail was shivering so that she had bare steerage way under the fore and mizzen topsails alone. The spanker* was held simply by the throat brail,* ready to drop in an instant should they need leverage at the stern to turn her up into the wind quickly, and the cr'jack* braces were manned. She lay like a wary fighter waiting to respond to whatever her opponent attempted.

The quiet minutes drew out agonizingly. The *Chesapeake*'s masts stood taller as she walked down toward the *Shannon*'s taffrail* at a fine angle from the starboard quarter. Every detail was bright and clear. Her three ensigns and the motto flew gaily to leeward. The sun picked out the barrels of the marines' rifles along the spar deck, and more rifles in the tops, which were crowded with faces peering toward the *Shannon*. The rigging was taut and through its maze of lines and furled canvas there was a clear view to the quarter-deck and the wheel and Captain Lawrence standing high on a gunslide, tall and unmistakable in cocked hat, heavy gold epaulets, snowy shirt above his best blue coat laced with gold and buttoned across his chest; he had dressed himself carefully for the occasion, his haid braided in a queue and tied with black ribbon. His first lieutenant, sailing master, and midshipmen aides stood nearby.

Broke in his tall hat, with Watt close beside him, stood right aft at the *Shannon*'s taffrail watching the American vessel closely and trying to fathom which side she would attack. There were three courses open to her. First and most unlikely, she could luff up suddenly and bring her port broadside to bear before the *Shannon* could answer with her full broadside—but she was coming too slowly to do this without risk of hanging in irons,* especially if a chance shot carried away some vital rigging. Her most likely course would be to put her wheel up and come under the *Shannon*'s stern to rake. Alternatively she could come fairly alongside with her port bow ranging up the *Shannon*'s starboard quarter.

Broke's best plan, according to accepted doctrine, was to wear while she made her approach, and to try to half rake with the port broadside as she conformed to his movement. Broke dismissed this plan; he knew the value of keeping his ship steady for the gunners to take good aim, and he had little faith in a raking fire from a ship under way and swinging. Besides, this would throw the ships into action at comparatively long range, and the last

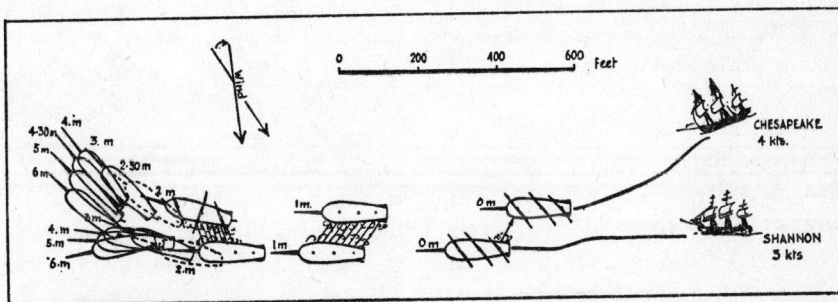

The battle between the Chesapeake *and the* Shannon *lasted only eleven minutes— but, as Mr. Padfield puts it, "in those eleven minutes . . . more men were killed or wounded per minute than in all of Nelson's and Villeneuve's great battleships combined at the battle of Trafalgar." The author's minute-by-minute drawing of the fight shows how it happened: the* Chesapeake, *overtaking her adversary at 5:50 P.M. at a speed of four knots, received a devastating series of shots from the* Shannon's *fourteen starboard 18-pounders as she drew alongside. With a large part of her crew already dead or disabled, the* Chesapeake *luffed; then, about six minutes after the start of the action, she drifted back into a collision with the British frigate, enabling Captain Broke and an adequate number of his crew to board.*

47

thing he wanted was a maneuvering match which might leave him dismasted so close to his enemy's base and at this late hour. He wanted to draw Lawrence alongside, yardarm to yardarm, where the ferocity of the close action would tell in favor of the ship with superior drill and discipline; this must be the *Shannon*.

"Close quarters was always Captain Broke's teaching—his wish—his hope and his principle," one of the *Shannon*'s midshipmen recalled later. "It is then that every element in a sea fight even to the noise, the smoke and confusion has its greatest effect to weaken the energies and overpower the martial faculties of the enemy."

So he left his wheel steady and his jib and mainsail shivering, offering his barely moving frigate to Lawrence from whichever side he chose to take her, challenging him similarly to dispense with opening maneuvers—but watching closely nevertheless, ready to meet whatever movement he chose.

"Sir, may'nt we have three ensigns" —it was one of the carronade hands nearby, his voice tight with suppressed excitement—"like she has sir?"

Broke turned and glanced briefly up at the *Shannon*'s single, faded blue ensign fluttering from the gaff.*

"No. One is sufficient." He added, "We have ever been an unpretending ship." But he called out to the Scot who was captain of the mizzentop, "Make fast a stop at each side of the flag!"

When he turned to observe the American frigate again it appeared that she had put her helm up. Watt said, "She's bearing up* to rake!" Broke called out for the jib to be sheeted in and the wheel starboarded. Walking forward with his speaking trumpet, he called down to the gun deck through the open skylight which normally served his cabin, telling the men to lie down on deck. "Stand by for raking fire from aft!"

Whether Lawrence intended to rake but thought better of it when he saw the *Shannon* coming around to answer

Aloft to furl sail on a square-rigger

him, or whether it was just a temporary adjustment in his line of approach, he almost immediately resumed his former course. Broke, watching carefully, did likewise. Now he knew he had his man. Lawrence had accepted the challenge; he was going to run alongside! To make their speeds more nearly equal, therefore, he ordered the maintopsail braced sharp up so that it would fill like the fore and mizzen, and then, walking to his skylight again, he called out to his main-deck gunners to fire when they bore on the *Chesapeake*'s second main-deck port from forward. Wallis at the after quarters and Falkiner, forward, had the quoins of the starboard battery set to give horizontal fire to windward under the present easy press of the topsails.

Broke, meanwhile, walked forward to the starboard gangway and stood at the entrance port, where he had a clear view around the vessel over the waist hammocks and would be able to see his first guns taking effect. His every action had been under the keenest surveillance from the silent, waiting men of the upper deck quarters. Now one of these, named Rowlands, who had been in the *Guerrière* when taken and was craning over the canvas screen around the maintop to get a better view, was so delighted with Broke's calm and self-possession and the precision of his orders that he ejaculated, "Ah! That's the man for me!" And picking up his musket from where he had laid it, he concentrated on the American frigate, now nearly upon them.

Lawrence was bringing her up in fine style. Aware of all eyes from the small spectator craft which had caught up to within a mile or two while the

frigates shortened sail, conscious of their admiration and support, he carried his ship up and almost aboard the *Shannon*'s quarter. This was how the *Hornet* had made her approach to the kill—"*Peacock* her, my lads!"—but he was coming in closer even than that, buoyed up by thoughts of another quick and shattering victory. His marines were waiting in orderly ranks. He aimed to give them every opportunity with their rifles.

"He had no talk, but he inspired all about him with ardor," one of his colleagues, Stephen Decatur, recalled. "He always saw the best thing to be done, and he knew the best way to execute it, and he had no more dodge in him than the mainmast."

Lawrence held on as close as good seamanship allowed without danger of accidental collision; his bowsprit reached out almost to the *Shannon*'s taffrail. He noted the peeling paint, the streaks of rust down her sides, the patched sails, the faded union flag at the foreroyal, the old blue ensign at the gaff, the jolly boat swaying slowly in the smooth of her wake—another tired craft, too long on the station?

He called out, "Luff her!"

The quartermaster lent his weight to the spokes. The *Chesapeake*'s bow swung up into the wind paralleling the *Shannon*'s course with only forty yards separating them laterally. The American company roared out three exultant cheers across the small gap of water.

The Shannons gave no reply; it was one of Broke's peculiarities to insist on silence in action as well as in drill so that orders could be heard clearly. They waited quietly, screwing up their courage in the awful moment before the holocaust broke, holding tight lips, tight nerves, expecting a fierce contest but determined not to submit. Scarves drawn tightly about their ears, they watched the gun captains bending over the sights all down the starboard battery, all the guns laid precisely horizontal for the slight list—"Throw no shot away. Aim every one. Keep cool.

Work steadily. Fire into her quarters—main deck to main deck, quarter-deck to quarter-deck. Don't try to dismast her. Kill the men and the ship is yours. The eyes of all Europe are upon you. . . ."

The ripple of water from the bow of the American vessel could be heard distinctly through the ports as they waited. Bill Mindham, captain of the aftermost main-deck gun, suddenly saw her martingales* down to the dolphin striker* showing very close against the bright afternoon, passing slowly forward across his sights. Next he saw the dark stem, with leaves picked out in gold chasing, up to the proud black scroll of the fiddlehead, then the broad yellow band leading down from it around the curve of the bow, down to the level of the gun port sills as she came on—he could see each plank and fastening clearly, even each scratch in the fresh paint. As the first bridle port* moved across the barrel of his piece the dispart* stood fairly in its center. He felt a tight ball of excitement in his throat; they had her! The *Shannon* was quite steady under the easy canvas, the guns were exactly lined for height—this was ten times easier than practice at a mark.

He could see the second port with the muzzle of its gun poking through —now! He jerked the lanyard, the lock snapped, splutter of powder, sparks upward, and the great breech came leaping toward him like thunder, smoke clouding back through the port and blinding all view. As the trucks thumped to the deck and the tackle men heaved frantically taut, he heard the aftermost carronade go off just above his head, and then a fraction of a second later there was a roar from his left hand as the thirteenth main-deck gun came on target. There was a choking smell in his nostrils, fighting blood rushing to his head.

Broke, standing above in the open gangway port, watched the shadow of the *Chesapeake* cross his beloved *Shannon*'s weathered quarter and saw his first two main-deck shots splintering home right on target. He was aware of the crackling of small arms from the American marines and the scream of a ball through the air. Then his own twelfth main-deck gun went off and almost simultaneously the second carronade from the stern. He left the entrance port and walked back to the quarter-deck, satisfied that his broadside was horizontal and all guns would be effective; as he went he noticed the *Chesapeake*'s jib suddenly lose its wind and shiver slack—the sheet had already been cut.

Forward in the American frigate the slaughter was dreadful. Most of the gun's crew standing by the right of the foremost gun, which was the point of the *Shannon*'s aim, were dead or injured. Some had been laid flat against the timbers of the manger, pieces of others were blown straight across to the opposite port. The lieutenant of the first division, Budd, together with other survivors, pulled the bodies clear so that the gun could be fired, dispatched the wounded down to the cockpit, the dead into the sea.

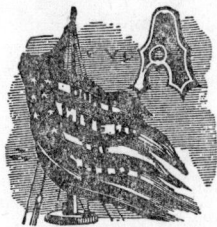

S the *Chesapeake* ranged up with almost a knot superior speed, the destruction spread aft. The two balls or ball and grape from each British gun, travelling comparatively slowly before their charges of old and often damp and clogging powder, smashed through the side timbers, spreading jagged splinters and mowing down the guns' crews. Above them the British carronades, loaded with one round and one grape each, were spreading equal destruction along the *Chesapeake*'s upper deck and gangway, and the 9-pounders detailed by Broke for dismantling the wheel had already dispatched the original quartermaster. Another had taken his place. Captain Lawrence himself had a musket ball in his leg from a marksman in the top; one knee of his snowy white breeches was spreading with red.

He realized that he had too much speed, a situation aggravated by the fact that his canvas was now blanketing the *Shannon*'s and further increasing the difference in their rates of sailing. He ordered the wheel put down for a pilot's luff, a temporary yaw into the wind to shiver the sails and take the way off. This maneuver was helped by the loss of wind from his jib, and the *Chesapeake* turned away, veering her stern half toward the *Shannon*. All of the American ship's guns were in bearing by now, and the comparatively unhurt midships and after crews had begun firing with an energy equalling the *Shannon*'s own; but as they were manning lee guns and were without the meticulous arrangements for horizontal fire that the British ship could boast, too many shots hit below the main deck and banged against the copper exposed above the water line. A number took effect among the guns' crews, however, bringing death and splinters, the sudden shock of wounds —smashed bone and muscle, limbs flying, and blood pulsing through clean cloth, spreading, tacky underfoot.

The immaculate silence which had been observed as at drill disintegrated into a grunting, cursing, even cheering confusion of sound as the crews reloaded feverishly and the tackle men hauled the great pieces out with a run.

In brief intervals when the piled-up smoke blew clear, the marksmen in the *Shannon*'s tops had vivid glimpses down to the *Chesapeake*'s upper deck; the planking was scarcely visible—"the hammocks, splinters and wreck of all kinds driven across the deck formed a complete cloud." The American marine officer, Lieutenant James Broom, and the sailing master, William White, were taken off, as were also two midshipmen and a number of marines; Lawrence, having limped down from his gun slide, leaned on the binnacle for support. Two of his helmsmen had been killed and a third was at the wheel. The easy *Peacock* had turned into a hawk with red claws.

Down below in his gun deck the fourth lieutenant, Ballard, fell mortally wounded, and forward in the first division, whose guns were now out of bearing, Lieutenant Budd realized with a shock of horror that out of some one hundred and fifty men who had started the action on the gun deck only about fifty were still on their feet, able to work their pieces.

S the *Chesapeake* continued to turn up into the wind most of her shot struck forward in the *Shannon*. Thomas Selby, able seaman on the forecastle, had his head smashed from his body. Neil Gilchrist was cut in two by a 32-pounder ball. Thomas Barry, a young lad, was taken off by a star shot across his middle. A 32-pounder carronade ball struck a case of shot for the *Shannon*'s 12-pounder, which was stowed in the main chains, and drove it through the timbers to scatter like lead hail across the gun deck. The Shannons moved their wounded from the dangerous space near the leaping cannon and into the arms of the sick-bay party, pitched the lifeless through the ports, and found themselves caught up in a primeval lust for killing which swept the quarters like a red cloud, turning them berserk. They cheered and yelled obscenities, dripping sweat as they worked with superhuman frenzy, mindlessly handling the tackles and sponges and rammers whose feel and motion they knew as well as their own leathery palms.

The *Shannon* reeled and shook to the discharge of her own guns and the occasional staggering shock of the enemy's blows as the *Chesapeake*'s well-drilled crews, decimated as some were, still poured in a ragged volley from the midships and after guns.

On the American quarter-deck the third helmsman fell, and the wheel itself was smashed and the tiller ropes cut by Broke's dismantling guns. The *Chesapeake,* out of control and with the helm still slightly a-lee, continued to luff into the wind, helped around by her spanker, whose brails had been shot away so that the canvas blew out and flattened against the mizzen rigging. The fore-topsail halyard had also been cut by a shot, and the yard having no chain slings* or preventers* —a sign of careless overconfidence perhaps—had fallen on the lifts* and shivered the canvas; her head turned farther from the *Shannon*.

Broke, seeing this, and thinking that she was trying to disengage under cover of the smoke and deafening confusion, ordered the wheel down to chase her, then walked forward to direct the two 9-pounders to aim for the *Chesapeake*'s head yards, not realizing that these had already been disabled. As he passed by the main shrouds, lifting one leg high over an obstacle on deck, a 32-pounder ball from the *Chesapeake* knocked a monkeytail* from the 9-pounder swivel, and flew on, according to witnesses, between his legs. The captain of the gun, Driscoll, fell to the deck with both knee caps fractured by the flying metal. He was carried to the mainmast, where he sat weeping with mortification at being out of the fight. The loader of the same gun received a grape shot just below his stomach, an agonizing wound. He loaded the gun nevertheless, then fell to the deck in torment, beseeching anyone nearby to put a hand into the wound and remove the shot. "I shall do well enough if you will only do that." He died later.

By now all the *Shannon*'s aftermost guns were out of bearing, since the *Chesapeake,* despite her luff, had surged on past them. The carronade crews from the quarter-deck had consequently left their pieces at a word from Broke, picked up muskets, and swarmed forward onto the booms and the boats, from where they started firing over the heads of their own marines, drawn up along the gangway, into the blue mass of the opposing marines.

Their fire winged diagonally across the American decks as the *Chesapeake*'s totally unbalanced canvas accelerated her turn into the wind. Her yards were caught aback. The canvas slapped loosely against the masts and she lost way, then started drifting astern, back toward her eager adversary. Broke's second lieutenant of marines, John Law, saw her approaching through the smoke clouding up from the forward guns and, hoping to get some orders for his division, which was still drawn up out of the fight on the disengaged gangway, observed to Broke that she was preparing to board.

"No, sir," Broke replied. "She is crippled and cannot help herself." Nevertheless he ordered Law to move his men onto the forecastle. Then, directing his forward carronades to fire among the massed American marines, he ordered the helm up and the mizzen topsail to be shivered, in an attempt to throw the *Shannon* away from the approaching stern of the other. The American ship was helpless in irons and he wanted to pour in more shot before there was any question of boarding. Unfortunately, the *Shannon*'s jibstay was parted by a shot at this moment, and she fell off very slowly.

On the wreck-strewn quarter-deck of the *Chesapeake* Lawrence realized that his ship was falling foul of the Britisher and ordered the boarders up. Lieutenant Ludlow yelled down through the hatchway; Midshipman William E. McKinney, a bare fourteen years old, scampered down the main ladders and went forward to tell Lieutenant Budd of the first division; then he worked his way aft, piping out instructions to Lieutenant Cox of the second division, and calling out to the third division, whose aftermost guns were still in bearing and were firing. Meanwhile, another of Lawrence's aides, Curtis, was trying to find the bugler, William Brown. This man, who had no duty in action save to

Glossary

abaft. Behind.

bear up. To steer closer to the wind.

bridle port. A bow port through which hawsers are passed in mooring.

carronade. A type of short iron cannon of large caliber.

cr'jack. Short for *crossjack*. The lower yard on the mizzenmast (see *mast*). *Cr'jack braces* is applied to all braces on the mizzen.

dispart. A metal sight set upon the muzzle ring of a piece of ordnance which enables the gunner, in calculating the proper elevation of his weapon, to correct for the difference in the diameters of the barrel at the breech and the muzzle.

dolphin striker. A spar extending downward from the bottom of the bowsprit cap.

fiddlehead. A wooden ornament similar in shape to the head of a violin, used in place of a figurehead to decorate the bow of a ship.

flake. To coil or arrange a rope so that it will run out smoothly.

flying jib boom. A light extension to the jib boom.

gaff. A spar which projects behind a mast to extend the head of a fore-and-aft sail not set on a stay.

idler. A sailor who has constant day duty and therefore is not assigned any night watches.

in irons. A position in which a vessel is rendered incapable of maneuvering, occurring when a ship is turning at a slow speed and the sails are not catching wind from either direction.

jolly boat. A ship's small boat, used for errands or rough work.

lift. A rope or chain from the mast to the end of a boom, or at each end of a yard, to support or lift it.

loblolly boy. A surgeon's attendant or steward.

lubber's hole. A hole in a top (see *top*) through which a man may crawl when going aloft.

luff. To steer or sail nearer to the wind.

manger. A small space across the deck immediately behind the hawseholes. The after end has a strong coaming to prevent the ingress of the sea when the hawseholes are open.

martingale. A rope or chain for staying the end of the jib boom to the dolphin striker.

mast. Frigates have three masts: the foremast, farthest forward; the mainmast; and the mizzenmast.

meridian. A navigator's observation of the sun or stars, taken when the reference point is directly overhead; thus, if the navigator is shooting the sun, he does so at noon.

monkeytail. A short iron lever for aiming a swivel gun.

preventer. A line designed as an extra support for a mast in case of damage to the headstay, the line that keeps the mast from falling backward.

quarter. The after part of a vessel's side. An approaching vessel is said to be on the quarter when it is coming up from astern at an angle of 45°.

quoin. A wedge-shaped device for blocking up a gun to aim it.

rope yarn. Fibers twisted to form a strand of rope.

sail. The principal sails on each of a frigate's three masts are (from deck to top of mast) the course, the topsail, the topgallant (*t'gallant*), and the royal.

sheet home. To haul sails out to the yardarms, as in setting sail.

ship of the line. A war vessel larger than a frigate, with three gun decks and sixty or more guns. Also called *line-of-battle ship*.

sling. An extra support for a yard to prevent it from falling in case of accident or battle damage.

spanker. A fore-and-aft sail set behind the mizzen. It has a mast and generally a boom.

spritsail. A square sail spread on a yard under the bowsprit.

staysail. Any fore-and-aft sail fastened on a stay.

studding sail. A sail set outboard of square sails in good weather and when the wind is fair.

taffrail. The rail around the deck at a ship's stern; the upper part of a ship's stern.

tampion. A stopper placed over or in the mouth of a gun or cannon when it is not in use.

throat brail. A rope that is attached to the outer lower corner of a sail and passes through a block at the jaws of the gaff to furl the sail.

top. A platform at a lower masthead that spreads out the topmast shrouds and acts as a platform for setting or taking in sail and, in battle, as a perch for sharpshooters.

waister. A green hand or an old sailor whose duties are confined to the waist of the ship.

walk. To sail. Used with *down, out, over*.

wear. To turn about by swinging the bow to leeward, or away from the wind; to veer; the opposite of *to come about*.

weather. Toward the wind; the opposite of *lee*.

worm. A small corkscrewlike wire, either on a long handle or attached to the end of a gun sponge, used to withdraw fragments of unconsumed cartridge from the barrel of a cannon.

stand by with his bugle at the break of the quarter-deck, a passive spectator of the wreck and carnage, had not unnaturally tried to find shelter from the musketry sweeping the deck. He was crouching under the disengaged side of the longboat, which was stowed in its chocks just three feet forward of his duty position. When Curtis at last found him, he yelled at him to blow —blow for the boarders—but the

A frigate's gun deck cleared for action

wretched man was so terrified or stupefied by the noise and frantic confusion that he just crouched there, trembling. Curtis left and ran down the main hatchway to call the boarders by word of mouth.

The confusion was, if anything, worse below. The *Shannon*'s main-deck fire was half raking from the port quarter as the *Chesapeake* hung in the wind, drifting down toward the muzzles. Lawrence's stern windows had been beaten in and the fir beams and timbers had been shivered into clouds of splinters that brought death and terror to the men of the after quarters, who had been virtually untouched at the commencement of the action. The men of the first division, up forward, who had taken the first brutal, methodical assault of the *Shannon*'s guns and whose own pieces had been out of bearing for some minutes, had no work to take their minds off the crashes and screams from aft; they were either lying on the deck to try to escape the fire or were crowding over to the disengaged starboard side, where they

took refuge by the galley. A few men from the comparatively unhurt second division in the waist followed their lieutenant, Cox, as he rushed with drawn sword for the main hatchway, crying, "Boarders away!" but most retired to starboard and mingled with the beaten men of the first division.

There was also a steady stream of wounded being taken below to the cockpit. Lieutenant Ludlow, hit by a musket ball, was among them, leaving Lawrence the only officer on the upper deck—apart from some midshipmen forward. Already Lieutenant Ballard of the third division, which was now taking the hardest pounding, had been carried below by his midshipman.

Lieutenant Cox meanwhile gained the quarter-deck only to find that his captain had been hit with a second musket ball—this time it was a desperate wound just above the groin—and, in pain, was clinging to the binnacle to keep himself upright. Cox, who had been with Lawrence all his sea life and who had the same respect and affection for him as Broke's men had for him, sheathed his sword and, ordering the men to "rush on," hurried to hold up his captain. Lawrence asked him to show him the way to the cockpit, and Cox, helped by two sailors, took the Captain painfully to the ladder and down. As they reached the gun deck Lawrence recognized his young aide McKinney, and called out to him to hurry up the boarders.

On the *Chesapeake*'s forecastle the boatswain, Adams, had been mortally wounded; midshipman John D. Fisher had rushed aft on hearing the call for boarders. But he saw no signs of an organized body of men there, simply a few leaderless individuals held in an enfilading fire from the whole length of the *Shannon,* and a few carronade men valiantly working their pieces through the roar and the smoke. He thought a mistake must have been made and once more went forward. Here he found that an order had been passed to board the fore tack and haul aft the head sheets to shoot the ship

clear. The wounded Adams growled, "They are shot away!"

But it was too late anyway. The *Chesapeake* had been increasing her pace astern, and now her wrecked port quarter gallery crunched against the *Shannon*'s timbers. The fluke of the *Shannon*'s working anchor, which had been stowed on a gangway to be out of the way, tore in and held. At the same time the Americans' spanker boom swung over the *Shannon*'s marines, who were lined up two or three deep and still firing as fast as they could load. Broke's boatswain, Stevens, hurried to lash the boom inboard to keep the ships together.

Broke meanwhile was leading a charmed life. Having narrowly escaped the ball that put Driscoll out of the fight, and having been untouched by all the American marines' bullets aimed for his tall hat, he was standing beside his clerk, John Dunn, his purser, George Aldham, and the marine sergeant, Molyneux. A shot from one of the *Chesapeake*'s after carronades struck the bow of the launch just forward of him and knocked a cloud of splinters away to leeward, temporarily halting the marines of the second division, who were moving along the port gangway in orderly fashion to take up station on the forecastle. Almost immediately afterward another of the American carronades erupted only feet away, knocking in the hammocks just beside him and smashing both Dunn and Aldham to the deck with pockets of grape across their lower stomachs and hips. They lived for scarcely an hour.

Broke was not conscious of his escapes as, standing on a forecastle carronade slide, he peered over to try to ascertain the situation on the *Chesapeake*'s decks. He himself had no intention of boarding, but he suddenly realized that there was no one to oppose him. The American marines had long been in an intolerable position. They were massed on the gangways under the concentrated, half-raking fire of grape from the *Shannon*'s forward carronades. Also, they were exposed to fire from the *Shannon*'s first division of marines, from the gun crews of the after quarters in the boats above them, and from the expert and chosen marksmen in the tops; now those American marines that remained, their officers dead, were falling back on the forecastle. The gun crews of the *Chesapeake*'s after carronades were also fleeing forward in the smoke caused by a grenade which had exploded the arms chest by the Americans' mizzen and spread flame briefly up the luff of the spanker.

Now the quarter-deck lay just four feet from him—practically deserted!

As he saw all this through the thinning smoke, a sailor just forward came to the same conclusion and leaped up on to the forecastle hammock cloth, shouting, "Captain Broke, now is a fine time to board her, for damn the man that's alive on her quarter-deck!" He crossed over to the *Chesapeake*'s bulwarks, but a shot from an American marine dropped him.

Broke realized that the opportunity to board was fleeting: the ships were touching at a small point only, and the *Chesapeake*'s head was being blown around before the wind. Her yards were still braced sharp up and as soon as her sails filled she would tear herself away from the lashings Stevens was putting on the spanker boom. There was not a moment to be lost; he must get as many men over as possible in the brief time they had. He was the nearest.

Dropping his speaking trumpet, he drew his sword and cried, "Follow me who can!" He climbed to the working anchor, thence over the hammocks just abaft* the forecastle bulwarks, and down onto the protruding muzzle of the *Chesapeake*'s deserted aftermost carronade, using it as a step up to the hammocks atop her bulwarks. Then he dropped down on to the enemy quarter-deck.

Sergeant Molyneux followed close behind, with William Stack, his coxswain, and Bill Mindham; several others were swarming over the bulwarks with cutlasses, and more were creeping and running along the spanker boom from out of the boats where they had been firing muskets. An Irish sailor named James Bulger leaped over without any weapons at all, then realized his mistake and grabbed the first thing he saw on the enemy's deck—a boarding pike. Wielding it, he went roaring after the others who were following the shiny black hat of their captain. Lieutenant Charles Falkiner, who had come up from the gun deck as the ships crashed together, saw his opportunity and jumped across. So did Lieutenant Watt, after seizing the white ensign which he always laid ready at hand across the capstan before going into action.

Broke, running forward on the deserted, blood- and wreck-strewn quarter-deck, saw a lone figure by the mizzen standing his ground and pointing a pistol at him. He brought his sword up in a swinging, backhand cut and laid the man's pistol arm open against the mast, then ran on toward the port gangway, toward the inert forms of marines and others who were lying wounded and had thrown their arms from them.

OME way ahead of him a small party of Americans gathered on the forecastle and prepared to face the attack. Below in the stench, blood, and dim, wavering light, mutilated men groaned and uttered involuntary sharp cries as they were carried to the entrance of the cockpit to await medical attention. The surgeon, John Dix, hurried to Captain Lawrence as he was supported in great pain down to the stanchions at the foot of the ladder. Lawrence called for his aides. "Tell the men to fire faster! Don't give up the ship!" They carried him straight to the operating table. "Doctor," he said, "go on deck and tell the commanding officer to fight the ship till she sinks." He countermanded the order immediately and told the surgeon's assistant to send the loblolly boy* instead.

Lieutenant Cox, having left him at the ladder, returned to the main deck fired by his spirit, and seeing that the after guns still bore against the *Shannon*'s side, helped Midshipman Russell, alone at the thirteenth gun, to depress and fire it. Then they both went to the fourteenth gun and fired that. There was no one else; the men had either been driven from their quarters by the terrible pounding and splinters or had gone up at the cry of boarders.

Lieutenant Ludlow, although he was wounded and receiving attention in the cockpit as the ships fell together, led a number of the Americans in a rally up the main hatchway and succeeded in pushing a party of Shannons back as far as the binnacle before another wave of the cursing, yelling Englishmen came storming over the hammocks with pikes and cutlasses and forced them to retreat again. Foremost in the British charge was John Collier. He saw an American marine pointing a rifle as he rushed him, heard the explosion, and felt the blast as the ball flew by his ear. There was a cry behind as the next man took the shot in the throat and fell. Collier came on. The marine threw down his useless rifle and turned and ran. Collier followed him down the starboard gangway toward the forecastle, where Broke's small party of boarders, having pressed through a disorderly volley of small-arms fire, was meeting spirited cutlass and bayonet resistance from some American marines. A number of former British sailors who had previously deserted to the American service were fighting with the defenders. These men knew they would be promptly hanged if they were captured. Lieutenant Budd had rallied another small party from the gun deck up the fore hatchway, and the fighting was hot.

Then the second wave of English led by Collier came rushing into them.

53

The marine whom Collier was chasing jumped through one of the bow ports and climbed down to enter his ship again by the main-deck bridle port; others followed him. Lieutenant Budd received a saber cut across the arm and fell back down the hatchway he had emerged from.

Aft of them Lieutenant Ludlow had also received a cutlass wound, a severe one across the head, and he fell; the remnants of his party were fleeing before the blood-maddened Englishmen and the Irish, wild with excitement. James Bulger's American boarding pike was red at the tip; he charged into the forecastle fray cursing, "And then did I not spit them, beJasus!"

Lacking officers, lacking support from below, and driven back by the irresistible fury of the boarders, the American resistance fell apart. Some men bolted out of the carronade ports down over the side like the marine, others leaped for the fore hatchway and tumbled down.

N the gun deck below, Lieutenant Cox became aware of the commotion up forward as they clattered and fell off the ladder, while others from the gun deck, having removed the gratings from the hatchway to the berth deck below, jostled each other to get down. The panic was contagious. He ran toward them, drawing his sword.

"You damned cowardly sons of bitches! What are you jumping below for?"

A midshipman, Higginbotham, who was nearby, asked Cox if he should try to stop them by cutting a few down.

Cox looked at the stampede; they were too tightly crowded and too terrorized. "No, sir," he said sadly. "It is of no use."

By this time the American frigate's topsails had filled and torn her away

from the lashings that Stevens had been securing when he was struck in the arm by grape from the American's mizzentop swivel. Now, leaving some of her port quarter gallery on the fluke of the *Shannon*'s work anchor, the *Chesapeake* walked away forward. As her port side crunched against the British forecastle, the after end of her foreyard, which was still braced up sharp, came in contact with the forward end of the *Shannon*'s foreyard, which was also braced up sharp, and the midshipman from the *Shannon*'s foretop, John Smith, seeing the split-second opportunity presented, ran out along the yard and over onto the *Chesapeake*'s. By this time most of the American foretopmen, seeing their forecastle virtually overrun, were fleeing down the shrouds; the sight of Smith storming toward them along their own yard, with a French cavalry saber he had acquired from a captured privateer, was enough to panic the rest, and they scampered over the weather side. The last to escape was a large midshipman wearing enormous fisherman's boots; he jumped for a backstay which had been cut by shot and was dangling over the forecastle, and slid down it. Smith jumped on the same backstay and followed him down so closely that they fell on deck together, with the American underneath. Broke was nearby and he put out an arm to restrain Smith as the terrified American tumbled away.

Meanwhile Midshipman Cosnahan, stationed in the *Shannon*'s maintop, had found his aim impaired by the lower corner of the topsail, and had scrambled down and seated himself astride the main yard. From here he had a splendid view of the American mizzentop, whose seven occupants were keeping up a spirited fire on the British boarders below them. Cosnahan started picking them off one by one, passing his empty musket up through the lubber's hole* into the top after each shot and receiving another loaded one. He dispatched three Americans in this way; three others fled, but one

man, hidden from him by the timber of the lower mast and topmast together, remained firing down on the English boarders. He could not be removed until a Shannon came running up the shrouds and grappled him with bare hands. After a short struggle, the Britisher, who was a large, muscular fellow, shouted, "Stand from under!" and the American sailed from the top and crashed into the starboard quarter boat.

Now, as the *Chesapeake* forged across the *Shannon*'s bows, carrying away the British jib stay, jib, flying jib boom,* spritsail* yard, and rigging, she ceased to touch the side at any point, and the marines and others preparing to follow the first boarders found a widening gap of sea preventing them. In all, sixty men, perhaps less, had gained the enemy's deck in the minute or so available. But they were enough. The American organization had been completely shattered by the grape and musketry sweeping the deck prior to the boarding, and the gun crews of the main deck had been demoralized by the raking fire to which most of them had been unable to reply; they had consequently lacked the cool discipline necessary to resist the ferocious British charge. And when both the surviving officers were hit, all cohesion was lost. The Americans became simply individuals trying to save their lives. As the American frigate sailed herself away from the *Shannon* her upper deck was virtually a British possession.

Broke saw the victory as clear cut. He tried to tear his frenzied men from slaughtering the few outnumbered Americans and British deserters who still fought for their lives on the forecastle, but as he was concentrating on this, three other Chesapeakes, probably those chased down from the foretop by Smith, rushed on him from behind with weapons picked up from the deck. Collier, fortunately nearby, yelled a warning, and Broke turned in time to knock aside the first thrust from a boarding pike, and put his sword through the man. Before he could recover, however, the second assailant swung a clubbed musket which knocked off his hat and crashed down on his shoulder, and the third dealt him a ferocious saber cut from half behind on his left, parting his skull down to the brain cavity. Broke, stunned, fell to the deck with blood welling from the wound and down the side of his face and neck. The American was about to finish him off on the deck when a British marine, John Hill, ran the man through with a bayonet. The other two Americans were making off as the British rallied to their captain's aid. Collier yelled, "One of them fellows has cut the Captain's head!" and William Stack, Broke's coxswain, chased the nearest over the booms and dispatched him from behind as he was going below. The other was hacked to death by Collier and other enraged Shannons.

Broke, faint and weak, tried to pull himself into a sitting position. The whole side of his face, muffler, shirt, and uniform was red with his own blood, and on the deck where he had fallen, blood was mixed with the contents of a burst cask of quicklime. Midshipman Smith hurried to help him, as did Bill Mindham.

Meanwhile another tragedy had overtaken the British on the quarter-deck. Watt, who had boarded with his white ensign, had temporarily been halted by a shot through the foot as he dropped onto the American deck. By the time he recovered himself and went to the mizzen halyards to haul down the American flag and raise his ensign over it, he found that some other Shannon had beaten him to it, and a small blue ensign was already waving above the Stars and Stripes. Determined to raise his larger flag, however, he ordered both to be hauled down and was about to bend on the white ensign when a charge of grape from the *Shannon*'s seventh main-deck gun carried off the top of his head and killed or wounded five others among his party. This gun had been engaging the *Chesapeake* through Lawrence's

stern windows while the ships had been locked together, and it seems likely that it was elevated and fired into Watt's group as the ships separated because the gunners saw the blue ensign descending and assumed the men hauling it down must be Americans. Or it may simply have been a case of excitement, the lock tripped before the quoin was properly home.

The British recovered quickly from the shock and hauled up the blue ensign again over the Stars and Stripes. Lieutenant Wallis in the *Shannon*'s main deck ordered the cease fire, and went up to the quarter-deck to try to ascertain the position. Forward on the *Chesapeake*, Bill Mindham, binding Broke's head with the neckerchief he had been wearing about his own head, drew his captain's attention to the symbol of victory.

"Look there, sir. There goes the old ensign up over the Yankee colors!"

Then, with Smith's help, he lifted Broke to his feet and supported him slowly along the gangway to the quarter-deck. He eased the Captain down on a carronade slide with his back against the bulwarks.

Meanwhile the boarders had rushed down the main hatchway, chasing a few Americans before them. These had fled on down the steerage ladders while the British rushed ahead to where the last of the forecastle party were squeezing down the fore hatchway to the berth deck. Some of these faced them and there was a ragged volley of rifle fire, but the British were frenzied with the excitement of victory, and once again the fury of their onslaught drove the unorganized, leaderless Americans back. Both Lieutenants Budd and Ludlow had, by then, been taken to the cockpit; after the first few shots there was little resistance.

Captain Lawrence, lying below, heard the rush down the ladders and asked what was happening. On being told that this was the enemy boarding he cried in an agony of the spirit, "Then blow her up! Blow the ship up!"

Two decks above, Broke sat dizzily on the carronade slide, suddenly cold in the shade of the bulwarks and faint from loss of blood. He was still hazily aware, through the confusion of shouting and pounding feet, the press of movement, light and color, and the deep, throbbing pain splitting his skull, that they had won—*won!* The old blue ensign flew proudly over the Yankee flag—he was sitting on the Yankee quarter-deck. He remembered coming aboard—over the hammocks, dropping down on the planks —deserted—only that one strange fellow aiming his pistol at him—it seemed but a moment ago. . . .

Midshipman Smith had left him. After cutting the halyards to the main peak so that the last American flag fluttered down from aloft, he had gone below in the wake of the tumultuous

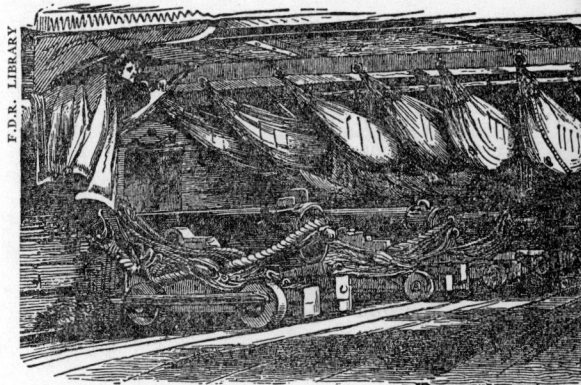

Hammocks were slung over the guns

boarders. The main deck that greeted his eyes was a terrible scene of ravage. The rays of the low evening sun were striking diagonally from the port quarter, through the great, shattered windows which had received most of the fire, glinting along the muzzles of the deserted guns, all awry on their split carriages and missing trucks, ropes and side tackles astraggle—sunlight lighting jagged holes in the side timbers where solid shot had entered, brightening the splinters of raw wood. Below, the scuppers were dark with blood; patches of blood stained the deck and even the beams overhead, and fragments of flesh, scalp skin with pigtails, unrecognizable pieces of gore, slivers of flesh, were plastered loosely about the timbers. On the starboard side forward, the fingers of a dismembered hand were sticking above a port as if their owner had pushed them through from outboard. Pieces of limbs still covered with blood-soaked clothing were scattered among the wreckage and loose ropes on deck as if kicked out of the way, and among them were the still forms of those who had been killed in the rush of boarders, and others lying, moving faintly.

Amid this ghastly scene, highlighted by the bright sun and contrasting shadow, the Shannons moved like tigers, indifferent or unaware of the carnage, exulting in their success. There wasn't a Chesapeake to be seen on his feet. All the Americans had fled or been driven below; the British were securing the gratings over them. Smith, glad of the opportunity to get back into the fresh air, was about to mount the ladder and convey the stirring news to Broke—while he still lived— when one of the Shannon's main-deck guns went off (by accident, it was later learned) and the ball mowed straight across the deck and through the port side timbers, fortunately without wounding anyone. Smith ran to a gun port and shouted, "Cease fire! This ship is secured!"

As if to disprove it, there was a rifle shot from the berth deck below, and a British marine, William Young, who was standing guard over the main hatchway, fell, mortally wounded. Fury welled up in the Shannons, and they began firing their muskets among the penned Americans below them.

This fresh outbreak of shots and screams shattered the calm of the upper deck. Broke, now barely conscious from loss of blood, and wavering, ashen-faced, on his carronade slide, asked what was happening. On being told, he directed that the Americans be driven into the hold. It was his last order in the battle; he fainted.

Lieutenant Falkiner, who had been resting on the booms between the gangways to recover his breath after the heady rush and excitement of the fighting, had jumped to his feet at the noise and rushed below. Seeing his men out of control and firing down at the helpless prisoners, he lined his pistol at the head of the nearest and shouted that he would blow out the brains of the next man to fire a shot. In the quiet that followed this announcement, he called to the Americans to send up the man who had killed William Young.

"The Chesapeake is taken," he added. "We have three hundred men aboard. If there is another act of hostility, you will be called up on deck one by one—and shot."

The contest was over. From the time of the first Shannon gun until the last, mistaken shot across the maindeck, it had lasted eleven minutes by Lieutenant Wallis' watch. Wallis had handed it to the gunner, Richard Meehan, as they went to quarters, and the gunner had timed the shots in the security of his magazine below decks.

Both ships had swung around before the wind now and were heading easterly within easy hail of each other, the Chesapeake drifting out of control, the Shannon, under the command of Lieutenant Wallis, coming up under her lee. The Shannon's jolly boat was hove alongside, a party of marines and sailors embarked, and they pulled across the short space of water and

---

Mr. Padfield, who lives not far from Broke Hall, spent many years in the British merchant service. In 1957 he crossed the Atlantic with Alan Villiers in the Mayflower II. Among his books on the sea are The Titanic and the Californian and An Agony of Collisions. Our text, with certain adaptations, is taken from his new book, Broke and the Shannon, published in England by Hodder and Stoughton.

For technical advice in the presentation of the article the editors wish to thank E. B. Potter of the faculty of the U.S. Naval Academy and Joseph C. Bruzek, curator of the Academy's museum.

---

scrambled up the side of the defeated Chesapeake, shouting greetings and congratulations. As they reached the deck they fell silent. Broke was lying propped against the bulkhead with a quiet group around him. His face was white beneath its weathering; Mindham's neckerchief, dark with blood over the left side, covered his forehead, and beneath it his red hair was matted. Patches of white lime looked like a crude powdering over it.

"He breathes yet," someone said.

They lifted him gently and, slinging ropes under him, eased him down into the jolly boat, then pulled back to the Shannon and carefully lifted him aboard. His cot was rigged up in the space which had been his cabin, and a canvas screen hurriedly erected around it as a temporary shelter before the partitions were restored. The Shannon's surgeon left his wounded in charge of the assistant surgeon, and came up to attend him. Wallis hovered anxiously nearby. They removed Broke's stained coat and muffler, his formerly white shirt, and Mindham's stiff neckerchief. The doctor washed the blood off his face and neck and, parting the tangle of matted hair, gradually revealed a deep cleavage extending for some four inches over his left ear toward the corner of his mouth. Between the depressed sides of the wound at the top of his head they could see the outer membrane of his brain pulsing gently.

Wallis was appalled at the severity of the gash; it seemed impossible that Broke could survive. And the doctor gave him no hope. Strong as he was, the Captain had but a slim chance indeed.

While undressing him they found a delicate chain with a blue satin satchel, now sticky with blood, hanging around his neck. Inside was a lock of blonde hair. When they had put clean bandages around his head and settled him back in his cot, Wallis took the keepsake down to his cabin and stowed it carefully. He would deliver it to Louisa after Broke died.

BY ROBERT DODD, 1813; NEW-YORK HISTORICAL SOCIETY; OVERLEAF: LITHOGRAPH BY L. HAGHE AFTER PAINTING BY J. C. SCHETKY, 1830; NEW-YORK HISTORICAL SOCIETY

The commencement of the battle is shown in the aquatint above. Captain Lawrence did not live to file a report, but many years later Provo Wallis, who had been the Shannon's *second lieutenant, retained a vivid memory of the events. "When we were within about two or three miles of the [Boston] lighthouse," he wrote, "we hove-to, hoisted our ensign, and fired a gun. The challenge was immediately accepted by the* Chesapeake, *who let fall her foretopsail and also fired a gun, hoisting at the same time a large white flag at the fore, which, upon close acquaintance, we found inscribed, 'Free trade and sailor's rights,' the idea for which they declared war against us. . . . We continued hove-to until she was nearly within gun-shot . . . At ten minutes to six, being then within pistol-shot, she gallantly rounded-to, and ranged up close on our starboard (weather) quarter, and the battle began."* **Overleaf**: *This scene shows the* Chesapeake *coming up and passing the* Shannon *to starboard. The big guns are in action and the tops are crowded with sharpshooters. "The cannonading continued for only eleven minutes,"* Wallis *remembered, "when the* Chesapeake, *who had got before our beam, was taken aback, and . . . dropped into us just abaft our fore-channels."*

On the opposite page and below are two views of *Broke leading his men in boarding the* Chesapeake *after the two ships had drifted together. His apparel is quite different in the two pictures; apparently the one below, in which he is wearing a tall top hat, is the more authentic. Wallis' account continued: "Broke, who saw the confusion on board of* [the Chesapeake], *ran forward, calling out, 'Follow me who can!' and jumped on board, supported by all who were within hearing. A minute had hardly elapsed before the ships had separated, and a general cry was then raised, 'Cease firing,' and by the time I had got upon the quarterdeck from the aftermost part of our maindeck the ships had got so far asunder that it was* impossible *to throw any more men on board of her; but it was unnecessary, as they hailed, 'We have possession.' I must here observe that no orders were given to prepare to board; but the happy moment was seized as already described." Broke himself had his skull laid open by a saber and his first lieutenant was killed; command devolved upon Lieutenant Wallis, who secured the prisoners.*

UNFINISHED WATERCOLOR, *Melee on Board the Chesapeake*, ARTIST UNKNOWN; COURTESY HON. J. V. B. SAUMAREZ

George Budd, Wallis' opposite number in the Chesapeake, *described the scene aboard the American frigate in a letter to the Secretary of the Navy: "In about twelve minutes after the commencement of the action we fell on board of the enemy, and . . . . I found that the enemy had succeeded in boarding us, and had gained possession of our quarterdeck. I . . . then made an attempt to regain the quarter-deck, but was wounded and thrown down on the gundeck. . . . . On my being carried down to the cock-pit I there found Captain Lawrence and Lieut. [Augustus] Ludlow, both mortally wounded; the former had been carried below previously to the ship's being boarded, the latter was wounded in attempting to repel the boarders." Lawrence—shown in a romantic engraving above—had been wounded in the lower body by musket fire during the exchange of broadsides; he died three days later. Next day (right) the victorious* Shannon *and the* Chesapeake—*the British ensign flying above her own colors—arrived in Halifax to a tumultuous welcome. On the voyage northward, First Lieutenant Ludlow, briefly rallying from his wounds, heard that one of his fellow Chesapeakes was complaining that it had been an unfair fight. "Let me hear no more of it," he retorted. "We were fairly beaten."*

On June 2, the day after the battle, a light breeze from the southwest sprang up, and the *Shannon*, with the captured *Chesapeake*, filled to it and set course northward for Halifax. During the next few days Lawrence, stricken in mind by the remembrance of his ship being boarded and taken, and suffering acute pain from peritonitis resulting from the musket ball embedded in his vitals, sank into a delirious coma. He tossed and waved his arms, crying out again and again the ever-remembered words: "Don't give up the ship!" He died on June 4 off the Sambro Light at the entrance to Halifax.

A few days later, as Broke still lay motionless between sheets at the home of a friend in Halifax, the body of his gallant rival was lowered over the side of the *Chesapeake* in a mahogany coffin draped with the colors he had defended with such spirit, his sword placed on top. A twelve-oared barge received the coffin, then pulled for shore with slow strokes to a discharge of minute guns; the barge was followed by a convoy of gigs and pinnaces containing naval and garrison officers. Arrived at King's Wharf, the party disembarked and re-formed in solemn procession on shore behind a funeral firing party, each man with a black band on his left arm. Following the coffin came the surviving American officers and midshipmen from the *Chesapeake*, then British garrison officers, post captains of the Royal Navy, staff officers, and finally the dignitaries and citizens of Halifax. "Six of the oldest [Royal] Navy Captains carried the pall, which was one of the colours of the *Chesapeake*," wrote an eyewitness. "This, they said, was considered a particular mark of respect by naval men, as it was a token that he had defended his colours bravely, and that at this time they should not be parted from him. The procession was very long, and everything was conducted in the most solemn manner. . . . There was not the least mark of exultation that I saw, even amongst the commonest people."

A few days after the burial service, First Lieutenant Ludlow was interred near his captain; later both coffins were removed to the United States.

Meanwhile the critically wounded Broke had begun to make a slow recovery, and before long he was able to dictate a report of the battle. It is an interesting coincidence that although the *Shannon*'s logbook recorded the time of the action as ten minutes, and Lieutenant Wallis' watch had recorded it as eleven minutes, exactly as Lawrence's clerk had recorded the time of his *Peacock* action, Broke, like Lawrence, thought fifteen minutes quite short enough and made it so in his official dispatch. As he later confided to a midshipman, "I stated fifteen minutes that there might not be any disputes. I thought I could give them the difference."

Captain Broke returned to England in November to scenes of wild excitement and the news that he had been raised to the rank of a baronet of the United Kingdom. The long-awaited reunion with his family was almost too much for him to bear with composure. Louisa was crying with happiness, and the children—so much bigger than he remembered—bounded and bubbled around them.

In 1815, after peace had been made with the Americans, he settled finally at Broke Hall and took up the duties of country gentleman and fond husband and father, to which he had been so looking forward. He never went to sea again. For the next twenty-six years he and Louisa lived simply at Nacton, visited occasionally by old Shannons, Sir Philip reliving his days of glory through the distinguished naval careers of two of his sons. He died peacefully in his sleep at six in the evening of January 2, 1841. The following day his coffin was borne to the tomb of his ancestors in the little parish church close by. Two years later his beloved Louisa followed him there.

And now, if you make the journey to Nacton on the river Orwell just below Ipswich you will still see the church where they lie; and in the Broke Chapel there is a white marble plaque inscribed: "To the memory of SIR PHILIP BOWES VERE BROKE, Baronet & K.C.B., Rear Admiral of the Red, who died on the 2nd of Jany 1841 in the 65th year of his age. . . . In his profession which was his choice from infancy he was ardent and persevering. After a long period of service at sea his professional skill was signally exhibited on the 1st June, 1813. . . . Also of SARAH LOUISA his wife."

The remains of Captain Broke and his wife rest in a chapel of the little parish church (left) at Nacton. Those of James and Julia Lawrence—and of the Chesapeake's *first lieutenant, Augustus Ludlow—are in New York City's Trinity Churchyard (right). Lawrence's epitaph ends with: "Neither the fury of battle, the anguish of a mortal wound, nor the horrors of approaching death, could subdue his gallant spirit. His dying words were* 'DON'T GIVE UP THE SHIP.'"

How Harding Saved

When the administration of Warren G. Harding took office in March, 1921, one of the duties it cheerfully assumed was acting as undertaker to the Treaty of Versailles—at least as far as the United States was concerned. Although Woodrow Wilson had been one of the treaty's godfathers, the Senate had not been disposed to ratify it or to have anything to do with its concomitant, the League of Nations.

Still, there was enough pro-League sentiment among a small group of senators and congressmen to engender discussion of whether Harding might be persuaded to work out some sort of compromise. Newspaper cartoonists, having had a field day over the League struggle, now depicted Harding valiantly striving to "find" a treaty which somehow would accomplish the impossible and appeal to all sides. Eventually this led to some wisecracks by the press about where the Versailles Treaty—the document itself—actually was. On the surface all this was treated in jest, but behind the scenes in the State Department a minor crisis developed.

Meticulous to a fault, Secretary of State Charles Evans Hughes suddenly awoke to the fact that he really did not know where the official American copy of the Versailles Treaty was. Obviously his embarrassment, to say nothing of Harding's, would be painful if the press discovered that the administration was ignorant of the treaty's whereabouts. On July 11, 1921, in a letter marked PERSONAL, he wrote to Harding's private secretary, George B. Christian, Jr., as follows:

My dear Mr. Christian:

There are some inquiries, with obviously humorous import, as to where, physically, the Treaty of Versailles is at this time. It appears that Mr. Wilson brought it back personally from Paris; that it was sent to the Senate and returned by the Senate to the White House. The general practice with respect to treaties which have not been ratified is to have them sent back from the White House to the Department of State, to be put in the archives. Apparently the Treaty is not here, and I should like to know whether it is at the White House merely to avoid a confession of ignorance which I should otherwise have to make and which might be a subject of some comment.

Faithfully yours,
CHARLES E. HUGHES

On the same day, July 11, Christian replied:

My dear Mr. Secretary:

I have your personal letter of today inquiring as to the whereabouts of the Treaty of Versailles. I personally know nothing whatever about it, but Mr. Forster [Rudolph Forster, executive secretary of the White House staff] tells me that after its return by the Senate it was sent from the office to President Wilson at the house, and that is the last he *knows* about it. He thinks, however, that President Wilson took the Treaty with him.

Sincerely yours,
GEORGE B. CHRISTIAN, JR.

Warren G. Harding

The new President wanted it . . .

His private secretary couldn't find it . . .

George B. Christian, Jr.

Christian's reply did not allay Hughes's anxiety. The Secretary of State had little desire to approach Wilson about the treaty, in view of the recent tense and vitriolic fight over the question of its ratification. On the other hand, he was piqued by the thought that the ex-President might indeed have taken the document when he left office. Cautiously, he answered Christian on July 12:

My dear Mr. Christian:

I note that Mr. Forster says that after the return of the Treaty of Versailles by the Senate it was sent from the office to President Wilson at the house, and that is the last Mr. Forster knows about it. Has any search been made or do you think that it is necessary to have a search made to determine whether the Treaty is in fact at the White House? I suppose that all papers were removed from the White House proper and that all receptacles were emptied. If this is so, of course it would do no good to search in that quarter. I simply wished to be sure of my ground before bringing the matter to the attention of Mr. Wilson. Of course, he had no right to take the Treaty with him

the Versailles Treaty

By ROBERT K. MURRAY

when he left office, as it was the official copy belonging to this Government and belongs in the archives of the Government, although not ratified.

Faithfully yours,
CHARLES E. HUGHES

Christian immediately ordered a search of the White House files, and before the day was over had this reply in the Secretary's hands:

My dear Mr. Secretary:

I have your letter of July 12th. A careful search has been made at the White House proper for the document to which you refer and I find that no papers of any kind were left there by President Wilson. It is my understanding that those papers not returned to the office were taken by President Wilson with him.

Sincerely yours,
GEORGE B. CHRISTIAN, JR.

The Secretary of State now found himself in a difficult situation. Although the whole matter had been handled

The Secretary of State was embarrassed about it . . .

Charles Evans Hughes

The old President knew where it was all the time.

Woodrow Wilson

with the utmost secrecy, the press had surmised that something was amiss because of the gingerly manner in which the administration was treating humorous quips about the treaty. The Washington *Post*, for example, speculated that the treaty was "lost, strayed, or stolen," and that "no one knows where it is." Harding had scheduled a press conference for July 15. Rumors now

circulated that reporters intended to ask the President quite specifically where the document was. Secretary Hughes decided that he must act.

Carefully observing protocol, and with constrained formality, Hughes sent a message to ex-President Wilson asking what had become of the treaty document. (Wilson had moved to the house on S Street in Washington where he was to die three years later.) By noon on July 15—the news conference was set for 1 P.M.—no reply had been received. The disquieted Secretary of State closeted himself briefly with President Harding, and the two agreed that if the question came up, the President would merely indicate that the document was in safe hands, and that no one need worry about it.

While Harding was left to face the reporters, Hughes returned to the State Department. There he found this letter, delivered personally by Wilson's secretary:

My dear Mr. Secretary:

When the Treaty of Versailles failed of ratification by the Senate the copy of the Treaty accompanying this note was returned to me personally with the official notification from the Senate that votes sufficient for the ratification could not be obtained.

This was at the time I was very ill, and the copy was put in my private fireproof files for safekeeping, and when my effects were transferred from the White House to my present residence this copy of the Treaty was of course transferred with other papers under the conditions of safety with which it had at all times been surrounded.

I beg now that if it is convenient to you, you will permit me to deposit it with the Department of State. I am therefore sending the copy by my secretary along with this letter.

Cordially yours,
WOODROW WILSON

P.S. I know that your judgment will justify me in asking the favor of having a formal receipt sent me for this copy.

The pains Wilson took to assure Hughes that the treaty had been properly cared for, and the hint of distrust in the curt postscript, make an interesting psychological footnote to the League struggle of a year earlier. Secretary Hughes, much relieved, quickly complied with Wilson's request for a receipt and immediately phoned George Christian, hoping to reach Harding before the President started his news conference. Christian told him it was too late: the conference had begun.

Harding, however, evidently managed to answer ques-

CONTINUED ON PAGE 111

George Washington's Monument

What does a nation give a man who has everything? If a man happens to be the country's first citizen, he may be rewarded with honor and fame and the respect of high office; after death, his name can be assigned to the archives of public memory. All of this happened to George Washington, who was certainly first in the hearts—though not, as it turned out, in the pocketbooks—of his countrymen.

The easy, inexpensive gestures, such as memorializing his name on everything in sight, including counties, towns, a state, a mountain, and the Federal City itself, were accomplished readily enough. But building an appropriate monument, the cost of which was reckoned at twenty-five cents for each citizen at the time of Washington's death in 1799, was something else again. It took more than a century from conception to completion, and its progress was marred by turmoil, rancor, niggardliness, religious bigotry, theft, and incompetence. But the ultimate disgrace to the memory of this decisive man of unity was that the project (viewed on these pages through the lens of Francis Hocker about 1875, from a tower of the Smithsonian Institution) was left untouched, in Mark Twain's phrase, like "a factory chimney with the top broken off" for twenty-one years.

Why was it so difficult to erect a memorial to the nation's greatest and, more significantly, least controversial hero? The problem was financial. Naturally, different people had vastly different ideas for the monument. But even when there was agreement, the funds were seldom appropriated—starting with the unani-

mous decision of the Continental Congress in 1783 to put an equestrian statue of General Washington wherever Congress itself would eventually be situated. Washington was flattered, and said so. And he later approved the plan of Pierre L'Enfant, designer of the capital city, to locate the tribute on the projected Capitol Mall at the point where it passed the front of the proposed President's home.

But nothing happened until Washington's death, when Representative John Marshall interrupted the eulogizing to remind his fellow legislators of their sixteen-year-old unfulfilled promise. What Marshall had in mind, however, was not a statue but a tomb, located not on the Mall but beneath the rotunda of the Capitol. Even though the late President had specifically stated in his will that he wished to be buried at Mount Vernon, Martha, "taught by the great example which I have so long had before me never to oppose my private wishes to the public will," reluctantly agreed. But several decades of debate later, when Congress finally acted upon Marshall's resolution, the Washington heirs reneged, and the Capitol mausoleum has since remained empty except to store the black-draped presidential catafalque.

Then in 1833 a concerted effort was begun to implement the dream of the Continental Congress and the vision of L'Enfant. That year a group of citizens, exasperated by the failure of the two houses of Congress to agree on an appropriate memorial, organized themselves into the Washington National Monument Society, choosing John Marshall, by then Chief Justice, as their leader. Perhaps, they reasoned, private citizens could achieve what partisan politicians demonstrably could not.

Initially their optimism seemed justified. The first public subscription, which limited donations to one dollar a person, raised a modest $28,000 in three years. The society was sufficiently encouraged to announce a design competition; it was won by architect Robert Mills, who conceived an elaborate pantheonic and statuary-cluttered pedestal dominated by a six-hundred-foot obelisk. Though this design was widely publicized, the society concentrated from the beginning on only the obelisk itself.

Yet Americans simply would not contribute, despite an unending series of fund-raising gimmicks. Nor was Congress especially interested in even obliquely committing itself to a project estimated to cost in excess of one million dollars. Undeterred, the society continued to pass the hat. In 1839, the hat was held by thousands of deputy marshalls, who were then launching the decennial federal census. "The rich will, it is hoped, be munificent in their donations," a circular letter from the society to the marshalls explained, "while from those in inferior circumstances any sum will be thankfully received." The former dollar limit now served only to

separate the impecunious from those who were promised an elegant lithograph of Mills's winning monument design, autographed by such political luminaries as Zachary Taylor, James K. Polk, Henry Clay, Millard Fillmore, John Quincy Adams, Daniel Webster, and Albert Gallatin. To make sure that the marshalls remembered to mention the monument, the society raised the commission on collections from ten to twenty per cent.

The results were hardly spectacular, but they were encouraging enough to rekindle the society's hopes. A committee of ladies was formed to sponsor fairs and social events; the Masonic fraternity was tapped, as were the nation's sailors by the Secretary of the Navy; and the Secretary of State instructed all U.S. consuls to seek contributions from Americans living abroad. By 1847, the society's coffers contained about $87,000, enough to begin construction. The leaders promptly announced the laying of the cornerstone on Washington's Birthday the following year, and asked Congress for a deed to the property. But Congress did not approve the site (relocated some one hundred yards southeast of L'Enfant's original position, to ensure a better foundation) quickly enough, and the ceremony had to be rescheduled for the Fourth of July.

More than fifteen thousand people, led by President Polk, attended the gala proceedings, which were ornamented by the presence of Martha's grandson, George Washington Parke Custis, prolonged insufferably by a ninety-minute oration by House Speaker Robert C. Winthrop, and climaxed by a pyrotechnic display in the evening. The 24,500-pound marble cornerstone—stuffed with such trivia as a 1783 penny, the thirty-first annual report of the American Colonization Society, and sev-

Robert Mills, whose design (left) won the 1835 competition, envisioned a colonnaded base below a towering obelisk, with underground vaults for the bodies of national heroes. Among the losing entries there was a Syrian-style edifice (right), submitted by architect H. R. Searle. Forty years later attempts were made to redesign the memorial in the fashionable style of English Gothic or Romanesque. A discarded example of the latter (far right) was prepared by Colonel Thomas Casey, the engineer who completed the monument in 1884.

enty-one different contemporary newspapers—was ritually laid in place with the same silver trowel that Washington had used in 1793 to begin construction of the Capitol building.

The most encouraging aspect of the ceremonies, from the society's perspective, was the attendance of so many government officials, whose numbers included an obscure congressman named Abraham Lincoln. Such official sanction, together with general prosperity in the nation, would speed the monument to completion. Or so everyone thought. Fund appeals now went out, not just to individuals and organizations but to banks and even to the various states. When Alabama offered to provide a stone tablet instead of cash, the society seized upon the suggestion and began soliciting commemorative plaques for the interior walls. They came, by invitation, from various sources: states, fire companies, clubs, Indian tribes, and other friendly nations. It was an inviting idea, but one with nearly disastrous consequences.

In just six years, the society had managed to push its grand design 152 feet into the sky, and everything seemed to be proceeding smoothly. Then, early on the morning of March 6, 1854, a group of Know-Nothings, members of the xenophobic and anti-Catholic American party, broke into the premises, stole the slab sent by Pope Pius IX from Rome's Temple of Concord, and presumably hurled it into the Potomac. The society, properly scandalized, fired its delinquent night watchman and offered a $100 reward for the arrest of the thieves. But nobody was ever arrested, and when contributions dwindled to a trickle, work was suspended. In desperation, the society turned again to Congress; this time the lawmakers pledged to appropriate $200,000 on Washington's Birthday in 1855. But the night before, the Know-Noth-

ings struck a second time: what they "stole" this time was the monument and the society itself. A number of American party members had quietly joined the society, making them eligible for election as officers; by surreptitiously inserting newspaper advertisements announcing the society's annual balloting, they were able to seize control at a private (and presumably illegal) predawn meeting. Congress, in disgust, rescinded its promise of construction funds.

During the three years the Know-Nothings were in charge, they managed to collect a mere $285.09 and added only four feet to the monument. Since this was accomplished with inferior marble that had previously been rejected, it had to be removed when the control of the society passed back into respectable hands in 1858. Taking the bad stone down proved rather difficult, since one of the block and tackle hoists was "lost" and the other had collapsed. The society applied for and was quickly granted a congressional charter to eliminate any future rump elections, but public confidence in the project had been shattered.

Now the stub, unfinished, stood untouched until 1879. Cattle and sheep and pigs, mobile provisions for the Union armies, grazed about its base during the Civil War. After Appomattox, despite the anguished efforts of the society, about the only things raised on behalf of the monument were the periodic voices of prominent politicians. Several states, beginning with New York, voted appropriations, but the offers were made on a matching-fund basis. The society was unable to raise the necessary sums.

Finally, on Washington's Birthday, 1873, a select committee of the House recommended a massive injection of federal aid for the purpose of completing the monument in time for the centennial of the Declaration of Independence. The report was never voted upon, yet it was the centennial that indirectly ended the impasse over the monument. Philadelphia had requested a joint session of Congress in that city as part of its celebration; the House agreed, but the Senate refused. The ensuing furor in the press stung the patriotic instincts of many senators, and on July 5, 1876, a joint resolution to complete the structure was introduced and quickly carried without a dissenting vote; the figure finally agreed on was $200,000, in four annual installments.

The society gratefully deeded the thirty-acre monument site back to the United States, and a new completion date was announced: October 19, 1881—the hundredth anniversary of Cornwallis' surrender at Yorktown. Only two questions remained to be resolved: Should the design of the monument be changed to conform with contemporary architectural tastes? Could the present foundation support the projected monument? Inertia on

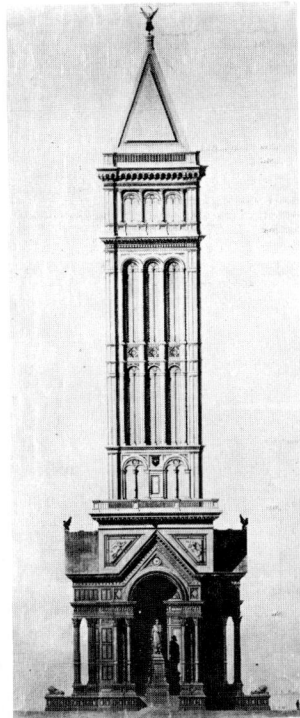

COLLECTION OF PATRICK HAZARD

When the Army Corps of Engineers took command of the monument construction late in 1879, they began by excavating the base (below) to strengthen it with a concrete "skirt." Then an elevator (above) was installed to haul up the stones, thus speeding the structure's completion.

the part of a Senate public-works committee ended the debate on aesthetics, and an ominous report from Lieutenant Colonel Thomas Lincoln Casey of the Army Corps of Engineers made it clear that the base would have to be considerably strengthened with additional concrete footings. Previous engineering surveys had also urged that the height of the monument be lowered. This view prevailed after the U.S. minister to Italy, George P. Marsh, discovered that the classical proportion of obelisks called for a height about ten times the base line. Since the monument's base measured slightly more than fifty-five feet, the engineers redesigned the shaft to reach a height of 555 feet.

President Rutherford B. Hayes laid a second cornerstone in 1880, and the work was now pressed upward in earnest under Casey's direction. Once the foundation had been reinforced, the most serious problem the engineers faced was trying to match the Maryland marble facing on the first one hundred and fifty-two feet. The next thirteen two-foot courses were faced with Massachusetts marble, but the contractor defaulted, and the rest of the stone was quarried in Maryland. Later these New England blocks weathered to a different tone, thereby producing the visible "ring" around the monument. But the Army's main objective was to finish the project as soon as possible. And on December 6, 1884, in a raging gale, six men climbed precariously to a wooden platform high atop the monument carrying the largest piece (100 ounces) of aluminum ever cast. (Before this tip was set in place, it had been displayed in New York and Washington, where visitors frequently asked to be allowed to step over it, so that they might later claim to have stepped over what was then the world's tallest structure and is still the world's highest piece of masonry.) At the moment of capping, a flag was unfurled, a salute was fired, and the assembled workmen and dignitaries hurled their cheers into the wind.

The formal dedication was not held until the next Washington's Birthday. President Chester A. Arthur, the fourteenth Chief Executive to be named ex officio president of the monument society (a practice still followed today), gave a brief talk. He then retired to the comparative comfort of the House of Representatives for a lengthy speech, written but not read by the ailing Robert Winthrop, who had spoken and spoken and spoken almost four decades earlier at the original cornerstone ceremony. Three years later, or one hundred and five years after the Continental Congress first entertained the idea of a memorial to George Washington, the structure was opened to the American public.

The editors wish to thank Professor Patrick D. Hazard of Beaver College, Glenside, Pennsylvania, for his assistance in the preparation of this article.

In S. H. Nealy's sketch of the 1884 ceremony, project superintendent P. H. McLaughlin places the tip on the capstone as rigger James Hogan releases the flag. Watching, from left, are B. R. Green, Captain G. W. Davis, Colonel Casey, and Lewis O'Brien.

"Take the hatred away, and

"The Recorder's Court of the City of Detroit. In the name of the people of the State of Michigan, Robert M. Toms, prosecuting attorney in and for the said County of Wayne who prosecutes for and on behalf of the people of said state in said court comes now here in said court in the September term therefor, A.D. 1925, and gives the said court to understand and be informed that Ossian Sweet, Gladis Sweet, Joe Mack, Henry W. Sweet, Morris Murray, Otis O. Sweet, Charles B. Washington, Leonard C. Morris, William E. Davis, John Latting and Hewitt Watson, late of said City of Detroit, in said county, heretofore, to-wit on the 9th day of September, A.D. 1925, at the said City of Detroit in the county aforesaid, feloniously, willfully and of their malice aforethought, did kill and murder one Leon E. Breiner; contrary to the form of the statute in such case made and provided, and against the peace and dignity of the people of the State of Michigan."

Behind the matter-of-fact language of this complaint lay a city seething with racial unrest. Ossian Sweet, his wife Gladys (whose name the court clerk apparently had trouble spelling), his two brothers, Otis and Henry, and their friends also mentioned in the complaint were Negroes. The dead man, Leon Breiner, was white. He was, it appeared, the innocent victim of a racial pitched battle.

The Sweets had moved into their newly purchased house on the corner of Garland Street and Charlevoix Avenue on Tuesday, September 8, and had been shaken by several telephoned threats of violence. The next evening, they left their two-year-old daughter with relatives and sought help from Ossian's brothers and seven friends who agreed to come home with them. All the men were armed and determined to defend the Sweets and their right to live in the house they had bought. When a crowd gathered along Charlevoix Avenue that evening, the police guarding the house made no attempt to stop unruly members of the throng from bombarding it with rocks and stones. At dusk, Otis Sweet and a friend arrived in a taxi, and barely made it from the curb into the house, pursued by an angry group cursing and flinging rocks. Minutes later, shots rang out from several

windows of the darkened house, and the crowd scattered. The police quickly arrested the Negroes in the house. Only later did the authorities learn that Breiner, smoking his pipe on a friend's porch across the street, had been shot through the back and died not long after he was rushed to a hospital. The Sweets and their friends were charged with murder.

No one in Detroit, white or black, would have given the Negroes much of a chance for acquittal. When arrested they had told evasive, often contradictory stories. The Detroit policemen who had been guarding the house insisted that there had been no overt act of violence, no mob assault to justify the gunfire. Moreover, the three Negro defense lawyers hired by Mrs. Sweet's mother were treated with studied contempt by the Detroit police, who simply refused to let them see their clients. The attorneys secured a writ of habeas corpus, ordering the police to produce the defendants in court on Friday morning, thirty-six hours after their arrest, but when the time came only an assistant prosecutor showed up; he told the judge that local feeling was so intense he dared not risk bringing the accused outside the walls of the city jail. Not until four o'clock that afternoon did the Sweets and their friends get any legal advice. The following morning they were arraigned and formally charged with murder.

Thus far the case had received no national publicity and hence had aroused little interest outside of Detroit. But this changed immediately when the eleven defendants received the rather startling news that Clarence Darrow was going to defend them in court.

At first glance, it was hard to see why the Sweet case attracted "the attorney for the damned," as Darrow was sometimes called. Thwarting and denouncing the death penalty had long been Darrow's forte, but this clause of Michigan's penal code had been abolished. Also, at sixty-eight, Darrow had supposedly retired from criminal law. But a closer look at Darrow's career made his defense of the Sweets readily understandable. After nine years as a small-town lawyer in his native Ohio, he had

UPI

This couple, Ossian and Gladys Sweet,

you have nothing left" <small>By THOMAS J. FLEMING</small>

moved to Chicago in 1888 and soon won fame as a defender of labor before hostile judges and jurors. Tall, rangy, and intense, Darrow built his sympathy for the underdog on a somewhat sketchy philosophy of scientific determinism combined with a profound passion for social justice. He proved equally brilliant at persuading juries to pity and sometimes to acquit accused murderers. His climactic triumph in this field was his 1924 defense of the young Chicago "thrill killers," Nathan Leopold and Richard Loeb, whom he saved from the electric chair. By this time Darrow was selecting his cases for their precedent-setting potentialities. The defense of Leopold and Loeb had been a blow against the death penalty; and he had just spent the summer of 1925 battling William Jennings Bryan and the fundamentalists of Tennessee over the right of a young teacher named Scopes to teach the theory of evolution in the public schools. "I had determined not to get into any more cases that required hard work and brought me into conflict with the crowd," Darrow later wrote. "I had fought for the minority long enough. I wanted to rest. . . ."

But a committee from the National Association for the Advancement of Colored People had called on Darrow in New York, where he was visiting his friend and fellow attorney Arthur Garfield Hays, chairman of the American Civil Liberties Union; the committee convinced Darrow that the Sweet case was as important to Negro freedom as Scopes's had been to academic freedom. The N.A.A.C.P. had been fighting hard on the legal front for more than a decade against white attempts to contain Negroes in ghettos. In 1917 the United States Supreme Court had ruled that municipal ordinances enforcing segregation were unconstitutional, and now the N.A.A.C.P. was deeply involved in contesting the legality of property holders' convenants prohibiting the sale of homes to Negroes. To the N.A.A.C.P. the Sweet case represented another and more dangerous segregationist technique —mob violence.

Behind this N.A.A.C.P. move to engage Darrow was a bitter argument between Walter White, the organiza-tion's assistant secretary, who had rushed to Detroit to investigate the case, and the Negro lawyers already retained. In his report White passed harsh judgments on two of the three, calling Julian Perry "a man of no personality" and Cecil Rowlette "a blustering, noisy, pompous individual with a very inflated opinion of his own ability." Rowlette had angrily protested the idea of hiring outsiders, arguing that a white lawyer would hurt rather than help. Finally he threatened to walk out if a white lawyer was hired. Walter White calmly pointed out that a prominent white lawyer was the Sweets's only hope of gaining "the best white sentiment" of Detroit, which was at present totally alienated because most people felt the killing was unwarranted. In a letter written the following day, September 17, White added an even more ominous note: "There is sentiment even among colored people that the firing began too soon. If they had waited fifteen or twenty minutes until the attack on the house had reached its full fury there would have been little to the case. But we've got to see it through. . . ."

There was ample reason for Arthur Garfield Hays to bring the Civil Liberties Union into the case as well, and on October 12, he and Darrow arrived in Detroit to interview their new clients. By this time the case was on the docket at Recorder's Court. The presiding judge was Frank Murphy—future governor of Michigan and associate justice of the U.S. Supreme Court—a handsome, thirty-five-year-old Irish-American who had been elected two years earlier on a nonpartisan ticket by one of the largest majorities ever cast for a judge in Detroit. Murphy had assigned the case to himself because, he told a friend, "every judge on this bench is afraid to touch [it.] They think it's dynamite. They don't realize that this is the opportunity of a lifetime to demonstrate sincere liberalism and judicial integrity at a time when liberalism is coming into its own." Murphy's first act when the case reached his jurisdiction was to release Gladys Sweet on bail. Even this gesture, Hays said, "aroused the fury of the community."

Hays remembered the first meeting with their clients:

wanted to live in this house.   *The white neighborhood*

We were ushered into a small room, dimly lighted by a dirty window, furnished with a table and a few broken chairs. Our clients were summoned. They seemed cheered by our visit but not hopeful. They had spent sixty summer days in a dingy city jail; and Negroes in Detroit involved in a killing have reason to be pessimistic. On the face of it our case was not strong. It seemed clear that Breiner had been shot by the fusillade from that house.

To make matters worse, the attitude of the eleven defendants was not very helpful, from a lawyer's point of view. They had what Hays called "a very human desire" to support the "original and inept stories" they had given the police when they were first arrested. One man stubbornly maintained that he had been taking a bath when the shots were fired. Another was frankly proud of the whole episode: It had taught the whites a lesson, hadn't it? Most difficult of all was getting anyone to admit that those inside the house had been frightened. "They had become heroes in the eyes of their race," Hays said. "Not all of them cared to admit they had been scared." It took a great deal of argument to convince them that their defense depended almost entirely upon their state of mind at the time of the shooting.

Judge Murphy had granted Darrow two extra weeks to prepare his defense. The lawyer undoubtedly read closely the hundred pages of testimony taken during the pretrial examinations conducted in mid-September under Murphy's supervision. Under angry cross-examination from the three Negro attorneys, police and civilian witnesses had stubbornly insisted that Charlevoix Avenue had been quiet on the night of September 9, and that there had been no provocation whatsoever for the Sweets suddenly to blaze away with guns. Finding witnesses to rebut this proved almost impossible.

The trial began on October 30. The courtroom was divided into two unequal parts, with space in the smaller half for two to three hundred spectators. The larger half was the well of the court, with the judge's bench and witness box against the marble wainscoted rear wall. On the left was the prisoners' bench, where the eleven Negroes sat awaiting judgment. Ossian Sweet, the leader of the group, was a handsome, dark-skinned man with a small black mustache. His slender, twenty-four-year-old wife was so light in color that she had grown up in an all-white neighborhood in Detroit without experiencing an iota of prejudice. She wore her thick dark hair parted in the middle and coiled loosely at the back of her neck.

During the Scopes trial, Darrow had taken advantage

of his small-town-Ohio roots and had out-folksied Bryan, the farmers' hero. The newspapers had carried dozens of pictures of the two tieless, rumpled giants, snapping their galluses at each other in the sweltering Tennessee courtroom. But an entirely different Darrow had appeared to do battle in Detroit. He was impeccably dressed and carefully groomed, and his manner was quiet and self-possessed. Beside him, looking almost diminutive in contrast to Darrow's bulk, the New Yorker Hays was equally dapper in dress and crisp in manner.

Opposing them was District Attorney Robert F. Toms, a big, round-faced, fair-haired man with the affable personality of a successful politician. As proof of his lack of prejudice he could point to his appointment of a Negro assistant district attorney. (His critics claimed that he had also appointed two other assistants who were members of the Ku Klux Klan.) Toms's courtroom assistant was Lester S. Moll, a tall, dark, good-looking young lawyer with a rather aggressive manner.

Some friendly observers thought that Darrow should ask for a change of venue; to them he reiterated his long-standing belief that "a man who practices law in the criminal courts should be able to tell something about a man by looking at his face." Darrow liked what he saw in Judge Murphy's sensitive Irish face; he decided to take his chances with him. This meant that the selection of the jury would require extra discretion, and Darrow spent three weeks finding twelve white men (the only Negro venireman was challenged by the prosecution) who met his standards. Not only did he want the jurymen to have no prior opinion on the Sweet case; it was vital that they be equally without prejudice toward the Negro as a human being. Seated at the attorneys' table, Darrow questioned the prospective jurors in what one reporter called "a very colloquial, not to say intimate tone." Sometimes his questions became a casual but moving disquisition on the Negro's bitter journey through American history. For even during the jury selection, Darrow was beginning what he felt was his primary task in the case—educating the jury to the point where they could feel compassion for the Sweets. Writing about the case later, Darrow summed up this goal in an aphorism, "No one ever *judges* anyone else without finding him guilty, no one ever *understands* another without being in sympathy with him. A person who can understand can comprehend why, and that leaves no field for condemning."

Before the first witness appeared, Darrow and Hays moved that the prosecution provide a bill of particulars, which would compel the state to confine the witnesses' testimony to proof of a specific allegation. Darrow knew

exploded and a man was killed. The Detroit police charged the Negroes with

there was no evidence of who had fired the fatal shot. Rather than let the prosecution dredge up all sorts of material and then fit it into a general theory at the end of the trial, Darrow wanted to narrow the argument. Judge Murphy sustained the motion, and the prosecution was therefore forced to state in baldly simple terms its contention that the Sweets had maliciously and premeditatedly armed themselves and their friends and had acted on a preconceived agreement to kill the first white man who so much as threatened to damage Ossian Sweet's newly purchased house.

To substantiate this contention, the prosecution now proceeded to parade seventy-one witnesses to the stand. Inspector Norton M. Schuknecht, who had been in charge of the police detail outside the Sweet house on September 9, insisted that the neighborhood had been quiet, and he proudly testified that he had instructed his officers that Sweet "could live there if we had to take every man in the police station to see that he did." Schuknecht and the other police officers vowed that there were no more than one hundred to one hundred and fifty persons around the neighborhood at the time

and that "there was no congregating." Civilian witnesses made even lower estimates, the favorite figures being twenty-five to thirty.

Casually, quietly, Darrow probed these statements. He forced the police to admit that they had summoned reserves from the station house, and that traffic had been so heavy that two men had been detailed to handle it, with orders to bar further parking on the street. He obtained the additional admission that five minutes before the shooting two policemen had been rushed to the roof of an apartment house across the street. With the civilian witnesses Darrow took another tack. Slouched in his chair, he would lift his head from the crossword puzzles on which he worked while the prosecutor examined the witness. "What brought you to that corner?" he would drawl. Most witnesses answered, "Curiosity."

"About what?"

"Nothing in particular."

"You knew that colored people had moved into that house?"

"Yes."

"Did that have anything to do with your curiosity?"

"Maybe."

"Many people there?"

"No."

"There were strangers there—people you didn't ordinarily see in the neighborhood?"

"Some."

"How many?"

"Twenty-five or thirty."

Most witnesses grimly clung to this stubborn pattern of evasion. But Darrow's relaxed, low-keyed manner got a few to lower their guard. One youngster said, "There was a great crowd—no, I won't say a great crowd, a large crowd—well, there were a few people there and the officers were keeping them moving."

Darrow sprang to his feet. "Have you talked to anyone about the case?"

"Lieutenant Johnson [a police detective]."

"And when you started to answer the question you forgot to say a *few* people, didn't you?"

"Yes, sir."

Darrow also asked almost every civilian witness, "Did you belong to the Water Works Improvement Association?" Thanks to some good reporting by the Detroit papers, Darrow knew that this association had been formed at a meeting in the Howe School auditorium, directly across the street from the Sweet house, on July 12. The organization's name, derived from the nearby Water Works Park, was innocuous, and so, on the sur-

murder. *To their defense came Clarence Darrow, America's noted*

face, was its announced purpose: to "render constructive social and civic service" in the neighborhood. Darrow inquired further. He asked one Eben Draper when he had joined the association.

"A long time ago."

"When did you first hear the Sweets were moving into the neighborhood?"

"That was a long time ago too."

"Did that have anything to do with your joining that club?"

"Possibly."

"Did it?"

"Yes."

"You joined that club to aid in keeping that a white district?"

"Yes."

"At the meeting in the school was any reference made to keep the district free from colored people?"

"Yes."

"How many people were present at that meeting?"

"Seven hundred."

Again and again Darrow wheedled this admission out of witnesses, until the real nature of the "improvement association" was quite evident. But only by sarcasm or innuendo could he shake the general story that there had been no mob. Wasn't it remarkable that so many people had had so much "curiosity" about the Sweet house on that particular evening?

Beneath the surface of examination and cross-examination, Darrow and Toms were fighting a subtle duel for the jury's allegiance. Knowing Darrow's capacity for righteous indignation and searing invective, Toms did his utmost to treat him with maximum politeness and to avoid the least sign of personal rancor. At one point, encountering his adversary outside the courtroom, Darrow exclaimed, "Goddamn it, Toms, I can't get going. I am supposed to be mad at you, and I can't even pretend that I am." Darrow countered by attempting to inject humor into the case whenever possible. Once when the courtroom burst into laughter over one of his wry remarks, Toms lamented to his assistant, "We'll never get a verdict of guilty unless we keep the case serious."

To bolster his argument, the prosecutor compared the Sweet house to an automobile. Suppose, he said, a car with four persons in it was proceeding down a busy De-troit avenue with the curtains drawn. There was nothing unlawful about that. But "suppose that suddenly volleys are fired from four sides of the car, one shot killing a bystander; suppose that on the car being stopped four weapons are found hidden under the cushions or in the pockets of the car; suppose that when arrested none of the four men said a word about the shots except that the driver stated that there would be no more shooting. If we put the Sweet house on wheels, we have exactly the same situation."

Hays and Darrow were on their feet instantly, arguing ferociously against the comparison. As the debate went on, Darrow played one of his shrewdest tricks. A baby began to cry in the back of the courtroom. "Who brought that child in here?" Judge Murphy asked.

With a beguiling smile, Darrow drawled, "That is the Sweet baby. We had her brought in here as an illustration. Had she been in that house that night, she might well have been arrested and tried and the evidence here would condemn her to the same extent that it does the defendants."

Retreating a little, Toms moved to dismiss the charge against Mrs. Sweet. Darrow and Hays had maneuvered him into a tacit admission of the weakness of the conspiracy theory. Mrs. Sweet refused to accept the dismissal, and Judge Murphy denied the motion.

Now it was the defense's turn. Hays opened by arguing the law in the case. He cited *People v. Augustus Pond*, a landmark case in Michigan decided in 1860, which specified that "a man assaulted in his dwelling is not obliged to retreat, but may use such means as are absolutely necessary to repel the assailant from his house . . . if the assault or breaking is felonious, the homicide becomes, at common law, justifiable. . . ."

Then Darrow took over. His argument was deceptively simple. "Our theory is self-defense and we claim the law to be that one is justified in defending himself when he apprehends that his life is in danger and when that apprehension is based upon reason." But the reasonable man is not a fiction, Darrow pointed out.

He is a man with a background, with a color, with the color with which he has been endowed. The question is not what a white man in a city of whites would do under certain circumstances. The question is what a colored man, a reasonable colored man, with his knowledge of the prejudice against him because of his color . . . with his knowledge that there was a

criminal lawyer. Race prejudice,

society of men (a so-called Improvement Association) formed for the purpose of ejecting him from his home; with his knowledge of what mobs do and have done to colored people when they have the power....

To show why and how Ossian Sweet thought as a colored man, Darrow told the jury the story of his client's unusual life and brilliant career. The son of a Florida minister and the grandson of an Alabama slave, Sweet left home at fourteen to work his way through Wilberforce Academy in Ohio and Howard University Medical School in Washington. After practicing medicine for several years in Detroit and marrying Gladys Mitchell, he went abroad to study gynecology and pediatrics in Vienna and in Paris, where he worked at the Curie Institute under Madame Curie herself. Returning to Detroit, Dr. and Mrs. Sweet, now the parents of a little girl, began looking for a home. They selected the house on the corner of Garland and Charlevoix, which was owned by a white woman named Smith who was married to a very light-skinned Negro.

Now, Darrow reminded the jury, during the summer before Dr. Sweet moved into his house Detroit had been rocked by a series of racial incidents. Another highly respected Negro doctor who bought a house in a nearby white district had been driven into the streets by a rampaging mob. At least six similar incidents had occurred within a few weeks, forcing the mayor to issue a proclamation begging the public to avoid "a lasting stain on the reputation of Detroit as a law-abiding community." At the same time, the city's Negroes were seething over the fact that in the previous twenty-two months fifty-five black men had been killed by the police.

With this for background, Darrow put Ossian Sweet on the stand in his own defense and asked him to describe what had happened on the fateful night.

"When did you first observe anything outside?"

"We were playing cards. It was about eight o'clock when something hit the roof of the house."

"What happened after that?"

"Somebody went to the window and I heard them remark, 'People, the people.'"

"And then?"

"I ran out to the kitchen where my wife was. There were several lights burning. I turned them out and opened the door. I heard someone yell, 'Go and raise hell in front; I am going back.' Frightened, and after getting a gun, I ran upstairs, stones were hitting the house intermittently. I threw myself on the bed and lay there a short while—perhaps fifteen or twenty minutes, when a stone came through a window. Part of the glass hit me."

"What happened next?" Darrow asked.

"Pandemonium—I guess that's the best way to describe it—broke loose. Everyone was running from room to room. There was a general uproar. Somebody yelled, 'There's someone coming.' They said, 'That's your brother.' A car pulled up to the curb. My brother and Mr. Davis got out. The mob yelled, 'Here's niggers, get them! Get them!' As they rushed in, a mob surged forward, fifteen or twenty feet. It looked like a human sea. Stones kept coming faster. I was downstairs. Another window was smashed. Then one shot, then eight or ten from upstairs. Then it was all over."

Slowly, quietly, with deep sympathy in his resonant voice, Darrow now asked the crucial question of the trial. "What was your state of mind at the time of the shooting?"

"When I opened the door and saw the mob," Sweet replied, "I realized I was facing the same mob that had hounded my people through its entire history. In my mind I was pretty confident of what I was up against. I had my back against the wall. I was filled with a peculiar fear, the fear of one who knows the history of my race. I knew what mobs had done to my people before."

Darrow asked Sweet if he could tell the jury what he meant by that last sentence, and the doctor proceeded to recite the grisly tale of recent Ku Klux Klan-inspired race riots in both the North and the South. In East St. Louis, Washington, D.C., and Chicago, Negroes had been shot and beaten by white mobs. In Arkansas, four brothers named Johnson—one a physician like Ossian, another a dentist like Otis—had been dragged from a train and murdered. In Tulsa, Oklahoma, Dr. A. C. Jackson, called by the Mayo brothers the foremost Negro surgeon in the country, had accepted a police guarantee of protection when a mob attacked his home. He had surrendered his weapons; five minutes later he was dead. In Texas, Henry Lowrie surrendered himself under a similar promise of safe conduct. The police let a mob drag him from a train and burn him at the stake. It was these victims and many others—Dr. Sweet declared that almost 3,000 Negroes

Left: Detroit, 1943; above: Detroit, 1967

he prophesied, would inevitably lead to tragedy.

had been lynched in the last generation—that Sweet had been thinking about on the night of September 9 in his house on Charlevoix Avenue.

The prosecuting attorneys strenuously objected to this testimony. But Judge Murphy declared it admissible. Now Darrow brought Negro and white witnesses to the stand to counter the prosecution's argument that Charlevoix Avenue had been peaceful and relatively deserted. Three Negroes named Smith told of driving near the corner at about eight o'clock that evening. Their car had been bombarded by stones, and they had been told to get out of sight before they were lynched. The prosecution questioned them intensely on why they were driving in the neighborhood. One of the Smiths, an elderly man, became visibly annoyed. "I was goin' to dinner," he said, "and when I wants to eat anywhere I goes by any street I pleases." Smith told how the crowd began stoning his car, shouting, "There's niggers now!" "Get 'em!" "They're going to the Sweets."

His nephew, James Smith, testified that there had been between five hundred and one thousand people on Charlevoix Avenue. Another Negro couple who happened to drive down the street around the same time estimated the crowd to be over six hundred. A white reporter from the Detroit *Free Press*, who had also happened upon the scene, told how he had had to elbow his way through the people on the sidewalk and the street.

The time had come for the closing arguments. As Darrow rose, the courtroom was tense. It was, he recalled later, "a pitiful and tragic picture. The whole of the space beyond the railing was packed with Negroes. With strained and anxious faces they made a powerful mute appeal to the white men who seemed to be holding in their keeping the fate of an outraged and downtrodden race."

For the jury Darrow recapitulated the Negro's history, trying to make his white listeners understand how prejudice felt from the black man's point of view. He read a poem by Countee Cullen, an American Negro poet:

> Once riding in old Baltimore,
>   Heart full, head full of glee,
> I saw a Baltimorean
>   Stand gazing there at me.
>
> Now, I was eight and very small,
>   And he was no whit bigger,
> And so I smiled, but he stuck out
>   His tongue and called me "Nigger."
>
> I saw the whole of Baltimore
>   From April till December,
> Of all the things I saw there
>   That's all that I remember.

Finally, Darrow bluntly told the jurymen that he wondered if it was possible for twelve white men to give a fair trial to a Negro, no matter how hard they tried.

The Sweets spent their first night in their first home afraid to go to bed. The next night they spent in jail. Now the State wants them to spend the rest of their lives in the penitentiary. The State claims there was no mob there that night. Gentlemen, the State has put on enough witnesses who said they were there, to make a mob.

There are persons in the North and in the South who say a black man is inferior to the white and should be controlled by the whites. There are also those who recognize his rights and say he should enjoy them. To me this case is a cross-section of human history. It involves the future, and the hope of some of us that the future shall be better than the past.

Judge Murphy's charge to the jury was a clear and unwavering exposition of the law in the case. He carefully explained the different types of homicide and emphasized that it was entirely within the jury's province to "consider what were the circumstances which confronted the accused at the time; their situation, race and color, the actions and attitude of those who were outside the Sweet home." All of these things, he said, had a bearing on "whether or not the sum total of the surrounding circumstances as they appeared to them at the time were such as to induce in a reasonable man the honest belief of danger." He also made it clear that Dr. Sweet's home was "his castle, whether he is white or black, and no man has the right to assail or invade it." As for the definition of a mob, Murphy explained that according to Michigan law "if on the night of September 9th there were gathered in the vicinity of Dr. Sweet's home twelve or more persons with clubs or other dangerous weapons, or thirty unarmed, for the purpose of compelling Dr. Sweet to leave his home . . . you will find that such persons were unlawfully assembled."

Darrow later said that Murphy's charge to the jury "scarcely left a chance for them to do anything but acquit." But the jury remained closeted for forty-six weary hours. The room in which they debated was close to the courtroom, and Hays recalled that occasionally when a door opened he and Darrow could hear angry exchanges such as: "What's the use of arguing with these fellows?" "Two of you had these fellows convicted before you came here." "I'll stay here twenty years, if necessary, and I am younger than any of you." A majority of the jury were inclined to acquit, but they could not convince the holdouts, reported to be four or five, and they finally informed the judge that there was no hope of agreement. Murphy discharged them.

A month later the case was put back on the court calendar for retrial. But Darrow now decided it might be better to try the defendants separately. Under the law he had a right to request this, and he singled out Henry

CONTINUED ON PAGE 104

A Dakota Boyhood

If one were to start making a list of things that unmistakably say "America"—things such as the Statue of Liberty, the Lincoln Memorial, and Mount Vernon—one would come very soon to the old buffalo nickel. This handsome five-cent piece with a buffalo on one side and an Indian on the other was unquestionably one of the most American of all United States coins. Its designer, James Earle Fraser, was born in Winona, Minnesota, in 1876, but when he was four his family moved to Dakota Territory where his father, a civil engineer, was in charge of building a railroad. Fraser became a student at the Art Institute of Chicago at the early age of fifteen, went on to the Ecole des Beaux Arts in Paris, was an assistant to the great Augustus Saint-Gaudens, and eventually became one of America's most famous sculptors. But always his early years on the Dakota prairie exerted a powerful influence over his imagination. This influence is reflected in Fraser's most famous works—the statue of an Indian warrior called *The End of the Trail*, the statue of Theodore Roosevelt as a Rough Rider in front of the American Museum of Natural History in New York City, and, of course, the design for the buffalo nickel. When Fraser died in 1953 he left a huge collection of statues, models, letters, sketches, books, papers, photographs, and manuscripts, which last year was given to Syracuse University by his sister-in-law, Mrs. Oliver H. Sawyer. Among the manuscripts was an unpublished autobiography, and from this document AMERICAN HERITAGE is proud to present for the first time the chapter that covers Fraser's formative years in Dakota Territory. In the original manuscript, which has been edited here, the chapter opens in 1880 with the Fraser family newly arrived in the territory and living in a boxcar near the town of Mitchell in what is now South Dakota. After a few months they move to an unfinished ranch house where they manage to survive a typically ferocious northern Plains winter. After such an experience, the coming of the prairie spring makes a deep impression on the young boy. —*The Editors*

By JAMES EARLE FRASER

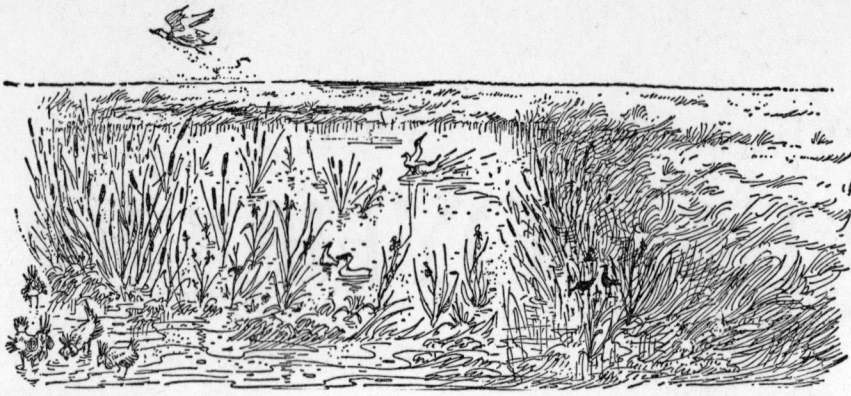

PRAIRIE CHICKENS

Late March found the sun climbing the sky and shedding its warm direct rays on the prairie's hard, crusted snow. In the early spring, latecomers to the plains were surprised at the changed look of the country—the melting snow formed great lakes, which covered much of the landscape. These so-called lake beds were a great convenience for the wildlife, and on windy days or dark nights geese and ducks flying toward the north would settle on them by the thousands to rest and feed. In the calm moonlight they would fly in V formation and their guiding honking could be heard through the night. In heavy weather I have seen great flocks settle down and walk on the open prairie.

There was a vast variety of waterfowl besides geese—black and white swans, brants, teals, mallards, canvasbacks, and numerous other species.

I can't recall seeing a crow, a buzzard, or a robin while I lived in Dakota, but the bobolink with his gay song and bright yellow and white markings was everywhere, as was the meadow lark, the sweetest songster of that region, with possibly the most beautiful song of any bird of the plains. Later, great flocks of blackbirds came when grain had been grown.

Some of the deeper lake beds retained water the year round. These were filled with cattails and flags, and made an ideal spot for the nesting of many kinds of birds, particularly wild ducks, rail, and other waterfowl.

As the shallower lake beds dried and the tender grass shoots and myriads of insects came up from the ground, prairie chickens would gather in thousands to feed. Their chattering produced a strange hum when heard from a distance, much like the sound of a large city. It puzzled us greatly when we first heard it early one spring morning. The curious sound came from the south, beyond a slight ridge where there was a flat strip of moist lake bed about half a mile long and rather wide. My aunt and I followed the sound, which grew louder and louder as we crawled to the top of the rise. There, to our astonishment, on the flat surface of the drying lake bed, we could see prairie chickens racing back and forth in such numbers that it seemed impossible for them to find space to avoid one another in their wild rush. We were amazed to learn that birds were making the strange noise that puzzled us so much—certainly only thousands of them could have produced such a volume of sound.

In spite of the incessant chatter of the hens we could hear the booming of the cocks and see them standing on separate clumps of earth or on a lone rock, each proudly watching his particular flock. The cock seemed like an actor wanting to impress by his vivid presence and strange antics. It was surprising to find that a bird so small could make a booming sound that could be heard for miles. The notes were *boom-ah-boom,* ending with a curious elongation of the same note. During the booming, large orange-colored sacs on either side of his neck would swell and the feathers on the back of his head would rise and stand straight up like horns, giving him a gorgeous and aggressive appearance. And he was ready and eager for a fight.

Any other cock coming near would cause a fierce battle.

These gathering flocks with their chatter and dervishlike dances fascinated me, and I crawled up the ridge to watch whenever I heard them—usually it was during a bright sunrise, but it was more beautiful in a hazy morning mist. After an hour of play and feeding, the prairie chickens would begin to fly; at times a huge flock would rise, making a thunderous sound. They never flew far, but would scatter, land, and run.

The primitive character of the plains distressed my mother, and for the first months in our new ranch house she was intensely lonely. Grandfather was in charge of the ranch, and Father was so busy with railroad affairs that he was unable to see us more than twice a week. The powerful prairie winds whistling around the house corners and under the eaves added to her feeling of loneliness. More and more the wind on the gravel paths in front of the door annoyed her—it was so gusty and violent that it picked the pebbles from the path and blew them against the door unceasingly. Finally Grandfather stopped it by laying down some boards on the path to keep the pebbles in place. Nevertheless, in after years she remembered and spoke often of the gravel peppering the door of our prairie home.

CUTTING SOD

When the spring came, plowing or "breaking" began, and the virgin sod was turned by the plowshare. The sod was so tough that from two to three yoke of oxen were used to pull the plow. The straining oxen, the strong men guiding the plow, the calls of the drivers, and the brilliant sunlight all made a picture of power which I remember vividly. The first breaking was done to build sod barns and to form a ring around the buildings as a prairie firebreak. Later, hay and straw were stacked inside the circle, but more important still, it made possible the cultivation and planting of the very necessary garden. The fertile undersoil, I heard men say, was four feet deep.

As the furrow was cut, it produced a constant cracking sound like a volley of pistol shots, caused by the breaking of incredibly tough roots, or spurs. Some of these spurs were three or four inches long and a half inch through the top, perfectly straight and tapering to a needle point; they were the color of ivory and nearly as hard. The spurs made a fascinating plaything for a small boy, even though they were dangerously sharp.

The new sod was solid and easily cut into two-foot lengths, the size used to build the sod buildings. The walls were constructed by laying two sods lengthwise and the next layer crosswise, so as to make a two-foot-thick bonded wall around the building. The walls were built to a height of about seven or eight feet. The windows were small and near the thatched roof.

A PET ANTELOPE

As for me, my childhood was virtually without the company of other children and their usual playthings. I was not conscious, however, of missing anything, for I caught frogs and toads, and Grandfather aided my interest by adding several kinds of gophers, jack rabbits, and a badger. As I think of it now, these living playthings were much more fun than the usual inanimate toys, and certainly more of an education.

I soon discovered that toads liked attention, became quite tame, and enjoyed having their backs scratched; that jack rabbits fought one another, kicking and biting; and that the badger was vicious—he hated his cor-

ral and finally dug his way out, to everyone's relief. But all of those pets paled in comparison to my greatest prize—a baby antelope.

Old Bob, our top cowboy, rode in one day tenderly holding the little creature in his arms. He was very tiny —I should say about twenty inches tall. His beautiful color was a pattern of tawny brown and creamy white, and his delicate body was exquisite. He seemed so lost and helpless that we all wanted to do something for him. Grandfather built him a movable cage, and after Mother showed me how to feed him out of a bottle he became quite content. Everyone loved the little fellow, and he was the pet of the ranch and the star of my small menagerie.

With the advance of summer my pet antelope grew from a baby into a good-sized boy, but he still followed me around and I had no idea that he might change.

Toward fall, when he was three-quarters grown, a small herd of antelope came by. Before this he had paid no attention to their passing, but he was interested now when he saw these and left the yard like a shot in pursuit. He caught up and joined the herd, much to a small boy's despair. They all disappeared in the distance and that was the last sight I had of my little pet "Lope." Nevertheless, whenever I saw any antelope, I would go out and call "Lope, Lope," but they all flew like the wind. If he was among them he had forgotten his name. Once in the winter when three or four of the little fellows came by close to the house, I thought I recognized him and ran out, but he showed no sign of knowing me. During my years on the prairie, I never saw a buck antelope brought in by a hunter without wondering, Could this be my little "Lope"? I am sure I could never have killed an antelope.

MY INDIAN PONY

Often a few families of Indians were allowed to leave the reservation, and many times we would wake up in the morning and find that they had set up a camp of eight or ten tepees close to our ranch house. On one of these occa-

sions Grandfather thought it might be a good opportunity to get me a pony, so we went to look them over. I found one in the Indians' herd that I liked. He was small and young and I certainly wanted him. My grandfather knew that money wasn't of much value to the Indians, so he had taken along an empty silver watch case attached to a long silver chain. Its covers snapped shut with a click. He showed it to the chief, who was delighted with it, and after a conversation in sign language we made an easy trade. The chief liked opening the case and snapping the covers shut. After searching in a pouch, he found something to put in his new possession. My grandfather said it was probably a sacred charm. The chief strode away waving his hand toward the herd. After much running about, we got my pony and took him home. For the watch case my grandfather thought we might have had a number of ponies! I named the pony "Billy." He was small, even for a bronco, but he was tough and strong. He was a bay color, but his long mane and tail were black. In the winter the hair under his neck and belly grew to be five inches long. I had experiences of all kinds with him, and some of them were not too happy. He was very nice and gentle at times, but, as is the case with most broncos, he was very temperamental.

He wanted to remain in the Indian camp with the other ponies, for which I couldn't blame him, and he wouldn't stay home, so I had to keep him on a picket line. An iron stake with a swivel around its top was driven into the ground and attached to a rope long enough to give him plenty of chance to feed. When he wanted to get away he would go to the end of the rope, lean away from the stake, and walk around in a circle, leaning harder with each step. When the stake was loosened to his satisfaction, he would run as hard as he could straight across the circle, the picket pin would fly into the air, and he would be off. He usually did this when there were Indians near. How he knew, we never discovered, but when we found the camp, there in the herd, with the picket pin and rope dragging, would be my pony. The Indians were amused, and the Indian boys usually helped catch him.

There were many kinds of snakes on the prairie, ranging all the way from rattlers to garter snakes. One kind was exceedingly disagreeable. My grandfather called it a "blow snake." I have no idea what kind it really was, but it was a dark, earthy color, and the one I recall most distinctly had a blunt tail. It turned its head toward us and emitted a foglike vapor which my

grandfather said would make us deathly sick. Then there was the prairie bull snake, which looked very much like a rattlesnake. It would enter the holes in a prairie dog village, possibly to eat the young prairie dogs.

And, by the way, it is true, as has been said, that owls fly out of holes. I have seen them. Maybe they were on the same mission as the bull snake, although they were very small; nor did they confine themselves to prairie dog holes, as I have seen them fly from holes belonging to other animals. They may have wanted a dark place to stay in during the day, or possibly they were looking for leftover food.

WATCHING PRAIRIE DOGS

One of my many pleasures was to watch a prairie dog village, which was an actual village because the mounds were close together and sometimes covered half a mile or more in one direction and a little less in the other. Each mound was about two feet high, and the hole which was at its center was quite deep. It was amusing to see a

large number of prairie dogs sitting on top of these hivelike mounds, to watch their antics and see them fall into their holes when frightened. Probably their snappy bark is the reason for their being called dogs. They were easily scared and would dash for the hole, barking noisily, if anyone came near. They are very difficult to shoot, and a hunter rarely knew whether he had hit

one or not because of their habit of straddling the hole and dropping into it. There was very little grass near the village as the dogs ate up the supply as fast as it grew, and they had to cover quite an expanse of prairie to get enough food.

Then there was fishing, another of my pleasures—such remarkable fishing. The rivers teemed with pike, bullheads, catfish, and perch, although there were other kinds less frequently caught. While fishing in the spring, I often saw the trappers in their canoes come down the Jim River—that's what we called the James, which was the biggest river near Mitchell. The trappers were very picturesque in their buckskins and their beaver caps. They must have had great success, because their canoes were always well filled with pelts.

The mill dam on the Jim River was a wonderful place to fish, so I liked going there. The mill was on the east bank, and the trappers were forced to make their portage around the dam to the west. They would carry their packs and their canoes down the path, re-pack them, and be on their way again. I have modelled a statue of Lewis of the Lewis and Clark expedition from my memory of a trapper I saw at this

place. He was a magnificent figure as he stood against the sky at the top of the dam.

These were legitimate hunters and trappers, but there was the other kind —the pot hunters. They were hated by both the settlers and the cowboys. They hunted on the prairie with double-boxed lumber wagons. Six or eight men walked in front of the wagons with dogs to flush the prairie chickens, which they shot by the hundreds. Within half a day the wagons were filled, the hunters having moved only five or six miles. It was a daily occurrence as they went from one locality to another.

As time passed there were more sod cabins and wood shanties put up here and there to hold claims. The most unsuccessful of these claims were tree claims. Thousands of trees were set out only to have their bark stripped and eaten during the winter by the animals.

It may have been because there were no trees that the grass was so luxuriant. The blue joint grass in particular grew so tall in late summer that it was over my head. When I went to higher ground and looked across the prairie, the view was beautiful. The wind on the grass produced billowing waves that looked like a green-blue sea; that, combined with the wonderful clouds, made an unforgettable picture.

DIAMOND DICK

I liked, always, to investigate the lake beds, and once while riding around the edge of one looking for wild ducks, muskrats, or anything interesting, I was startled by the unusual appearance of a young man who came galloping toward me. He was riding a wonderful-looking horse, but what astonished me was that he actually glittered as he rode. His saddle and bridle were decorated with silver and gold; his black velvet clothing was embroidered with intricate designs in gold; and to top it all, he had an embroidered sombrero on his head covering his shoulder-length hair, and he carried a beautiful rifle. The bright sunlight on his gold trimmings made him more dazzling than any person I had ever seen.

I suppose the glittering young man was also surprised to meet a small boy alone on the prairie. When he came up, he said: "Hulloa—what are you doing out here? Anyway, I am glad to see you. There are some ducks on the water over there and I want to get one. Would you mind holding my horse?" I looked at his gun and said: "It won't be much good if you shoot it with that rifle." He replied: "Oh yes, it will—if I can see it, I'll only knock its head off." After a good deal of maneuvering so as not to get his beautiful high-heeled boots wet, he got near enough to shoot. Many ducks flew. Then he said: "Now, let me hold the ponies, and get me the duck." I kicked off my moccasins and waded in, expecting to see a badly mutilated duck; but on the contrary, I found two shot through the head. He had got two in line and knocked both heads off with one shot. I hadn't seen that trick before and thought it was wonderful. He didn't seem to think that his shooting was extraordinary, but he was pleased. He put the ducks into his saddlebags, said "Thanks," and held out his hand to shake mine. I felt something in my hand as he turned, and I let it drop. "Pick it up," he said, "and now you can say that you shook the hand of Diamond Dick." He jumped on his horse and galloped away before I could return the coin. It turned out to be a ten-dollar gold piece. Diamond Dick was certainly picturesque; he became a famous wild west showman.

Seeing Diamond Dick's gun made me want one like it, but my mother thought that at the age of nine I was too young to have one so dangerous. She didn't know I already had an old musket hidden away. Whenever I did manage to get a discarded gun, it was so old and powerful that when I fired it, it nearly knocked me over. I was very careful of a fairly good one that I got and managed to smuggle it into the house and put it under my mattress, because I wanted it near at hand. But one night, before I could remove the rifle, a visitor was given my room and the gun under the mattress made a very poor, if deep, impression. The guest thought there was something wrong and on investigation found the object. So I lost my rifle.

Uncle Gene had given me very strict instructions on how to handle a gun, and I have always been very thankful to him. He said: "When not in use, a gun should be pointed down to the earth or straight up in the air."

A BULLFIGHT

There were many things to fear on that primitive plain—wolves, snakes, and cyclones—but my greatest fear was of a vicious bull in a herd belonging to a Bohemian family about two miles from where we lived. I had to pass near their place on my way to my Uncle Gene's house. The bull was so ferocious that they had attached a board to his horns. It hung down below his eyes so that he couldn't see directly toward the front. That helped, but he was clever enough to turn his head so that he could see with one eye, or toss his head and flip up the board.

I would skirt the rises whenever I saw a herd of cattle on that range, and I never dared walk in that direction. I always rode my pony. On one or two occasions the bull chased after the pony and me, but we were usually so far away when he spied us that we were able to outdistance him.

The Bohemians' house was really just a cellar. The walls were of stone and extended about two feet above the ground. On these walls there was a gable roof, rather steep, with windows under the eaves.

On one of my visits, as we were going by the house I noticed that there were some cattle in the yard. One of them turned around. It had a board over its face. It was my nemesis the bull. When he saw me he wheeled like a flash and came for me. Without the slightest hesitation I went up the sloping roof of the house like a wreath of mist and stayed there until the bull was out of the way. For some reason he never bothered the Bohemian children. I still believe it would have been only a matter of time until he turned on them. That bull was not to be trusted.

Finally he decided to tear down Uncle Gene's house. It was not very big. He came raging into the yard and began charging against it. Then he

went into my aunt's favorite flower bed bellowing and snorting. We watched him from the windows as my aunt's flowers were being tossed skyward by his crazy pawing. He couldn't see too well with the board over his head, and my uncle stepped out of the door with a gun in his hand, ready to do away with him if necessary, but hoping he wouldn't have to, for the Bohemians were his friends. He picked up a good-sized cobblestone from the flower bed and, taking deliberate aim, threw it with all his strength. It hit squarely in the middle of the board on the bull's head. The shock of the impact sent the bull sprawling on his knees; the board was split in two, and for the first time in several years the bull was able to see clearly. His eyes rolled from side to side showing the whites. He struggled to his feet just in time to receive another cobblestone in the ribs, and instead of attacking as expected, he decided to leave for home. Probably his mind was slightly blurred. My uncle told the Bohemian family of the ferocious efforts to tear down his house. This time the bull had gone too far, and he was killed. After that the prairie seemed a pleasanter and far safer place for me and, I am certain, for everyone else who lived near the Bohemian family.

CYCLONES

The prairie always held me fascinated; it was serene at certain periods and tempestuous at others. In the late summer the threat of a cyclone was always in our minds. Many times when heavy storms came my mother took us into our cyclone cellar, but we never had a cyclone come straight over our ranch, although once a very vicious one cut a path through the countryside just north of us. The open prairie made it seem very near. I remember it as a huge bluish-black cloud in the northwest; beyond it the sky was bright and clear. The center of the great cloud began to whirl and lower from the main body. It kept lowering, lengthening, twisting, and bending this way and that until the black funnel-shaped mass against the clear sky became very distinct. Then it moved swiftly toward the east, the funnel twisting and turning and getting nearer the earth until finally it touched and then clouds of dust rose around it. Shortly afterward it crossed the Jim River. Then the rain came, and it was lost to sight.

MEMORIES of INDIANS

Stories were often told of the danger of Indians, and with such tales very much in mind, I recall how startled I was when while fishing below a lonely cliff I suddenly noticed some moving shadows cast across the water at my feet. I looked up and there on the edge of the cliff stood seven or eight Indian braves silhouetted against the sky, some of them with bodies bare, others dressed in their buckskins. There was no evidence of their families and that frightened me. I was all alone and at least three miles from any house. Instead of coming down to where I

was fishing, they silently disappeared. Where they went I didn't know and I didn't care to find out, but I decided I had fished long enough, got my pony, and rode home at the best possible speed. I looked closely all around me but didn't see them again; probably they were on a hunting trip.

Certain groups of Indians were allowed to come back to the old hunting ground when they became too restless, and, as I have said, they often camped near our ranch. I liked that, for it gave me a chance to play with the Indian boys. They showed me how to make shafts for arrows out of the stalks of cattails. The stalks were so straight and true and, when tipped with a tiny flint arrowhead, evidently made for shooting birds, were very good. They would last a long time; besides, there were so many cattails that when one shaft was used up, another could be made in a few minutes.

One of the sports of the Indian boys which they taught me was the use of those arrows to shoot frogs as they stuck their heads out of the water. It was really quite a mark to try for, but the Indian boys were extraordinarily adept. I learned that Indians used the frogs for their soup pots, which always seemed to be simmering either inside or outside the flap of their tepees. Any passing person was welcome to stop and take a gourd of soup.

All Indians who came to their old hunting ground without leave would be found, and the soldiers would come and urge them to return to the reservation. In most cases it was done very amicably—they seemed satisfied after a few days of hunting.

I had so often heard people say that the poor Indians would be driven into the Pacific Ocean that one day it sparked in my mind the idea for an equestrian statue—*The End of the Trail.* The buffalo nickel was also the product of those early years.

I also have another Indian statue which was inspired by the same period —*The Buffalo Prayer.* In the early

morning just at sunrise I saw a medicine man, or counselor of the tribe, make his prayer. It was for the return of the buffalo. His prayer to the Great Spirit was made after a night in a sweat lodge, having partaken of no food. He went to the creek, bathed himself, put on a few strips of buffalo hide, placed in front of him a buffalo skull, then built a fire of buffalo chips toward the east. A thin column of smoke lifted to the sky and the rising sun shed a glow over the whole scene. The bronze color of the man, his black hair with bits of red wound into his braids, and his religious attitude made an indelible picture in my mind. The Indian boys and I watched from a respectful distance.

A HEROIC MOTHER

For some time after our ranch house was built, we had to carry water from Mitchell, and finally it was decided that we must have a well. It was a long deep dig, but when water was struck, we had great difficulty keeping the well bailed out so that we could wall it.

Stones were scarce on the prairie and it would take a day to pick up one small wagon-box full. Fortunately, this had been foreseen and the prairie had already been searched for stones suitable for walling the well. When it was completed, we had a great supply of water, but it had a strong alkali flavor that I came to like after the first distaste had worn off. I remember distinctly that whenever we went East, I was always surprised at the insipid taste of the water.

This well was the scene of an almost-fatal accident to my three-year-old sister. It was fifty feet deep, held twenty feet of water, and was surrounded by a wellhead of boards with four upright posts supporting the roof, which held a wheel through which a rope ran. One day my sister was standing on the coil of rope beside the wellhead and pull-

ing the rope attached to a bucketful of water which was resting on an inside shelf. The bucket fell and the coil of rope pulled her over the top of the wellhead. My mother, hearing the unusual sound, ran out of the house, and to her horror saw her child slipping over the edge into the well. My sister fell thirty feet, hitting the stones on the way down, severely cutting her head. Unfortunately, there were no men around, so my mother, resisting the efforts of my aunt to prevent her, climbed over and went down the rope, hand over hand, and pulled my sister out of the water. Standing on the stone walling of the well, she took off the child's wet clothes, stopped the flow of blood as best she could, and in some way got off her own skirt to wrap around her. My sister was seriously ill for a long time. Many people came to congratulate my mother for her courage, and a committee from Mitchell presented her with an inscribed silver dish. Where they were able to obtain it puzzled us, for Mitchell, at that time, was a primitive town.

PRAIRIE SCHOOL

When I was about eight, a little schoolhouse was built a mile or so away from our ranch, and when it was finished, settlers from twenty miles around were invited to a dance in celebration of its completion. This was one of those western dances with fiddlers and a man to call the various moves. It was gay and very noisy. There were quite a few children and plenty of good things to eat. The dinner began late at night with an oyster stew. In those days oysters were shipped to Dakota in oblong tin cans. The oysters were excellent and made what seemed to be the favorite soup of most westerners.

This school was the first that I attended. On particularly cold days, when the thermometer was around fifteen or twenty below zero, it was arranged that the children would be picked up by a team of horses with a bobsled and a hayrack full of hay for warmth. I thought it a very satisfactory and delightful vehicle for carrying children in any kind of weather.

In the fall, terrible storms came, and we often thought that the little schoolhouse was on the point of being blown away. It quivered and shook and the lightning glinted and the thunder reverberated through the small building. On one of these occasions, when we children were all very scared, there were simultaneously a terrible flash and a crash. The chimney had been hit by lightning. A great ball of blue-green fire rolled along the top of the iron stovepipe to the stove in the middle of the room and down into the stove with a tremendous crash, leaving us children with our heads on our desks and semiconscious. There were many other storms while I was at school but none quite like that one.

Also, the school must have been built in the runway of timber wolves, because very often we children would be startled and greatly agitated by seeing these great animals trot by, usually going south. We would crowd (I say "crowd"—there were about seven or eight pupils) around the windows, the teacher included, to watch them pass, one or two at a time. I don't recall ever seeing three together. They trotted along, never looking right or left, often within yards of the schoolhouse.

A THIRTY-FIVE-CENT LUNCH

Whenever we took a train journey it was with some difficulty, as there were no sleeping cars in those early days in Dakota. The coaches were heated by small stoves at each end of the car, which the brakeman had to take care of. It seemed like an adequate arrangement then, but now it would certainly be thought primitive.

Often we would ride all night sitting up, sleeping if possible, so that we would arrive in the morning and have the full day in either Sanborn or Chamberlain, and sometimes in Mason City. There were no dining cars, so the trains stopped for half an hour for meals. The station lunchroom served a breakfast, a huge meal—soup or oyster stew followed by steak or fish, vegetables, and two or three kinds of pie—all in thirty minutes. This generous meal cost thirty-five cents.

Occasionally scientists, or relic seekers—which they were, we never knew —came to our ranch. They would ask whether or not we had noticed any mounds. They appeared very anxious and would investigate any place that we could mention. Usually I was persuaded to ride along and show them where such places were. They would dig up any hillock on the prairie's surface and were usually disappointed, although near our ranch they did find a few burial mounds.

The graves sometimes had walls of flat stone, with the floor and ceiling constructed in the same way. One that they found was very old, so they said. It was made like a small stockade with wooden poles about four inches thick lining the walls. The ceiling and floor were made with flat stones such as did not exist in the vicinity. The extraordinary thing about the grave was that the poles in the side walls were petrified; they had become solid stone. The

grain of the wood was clearly visible. I had found many pieces of petrified wood, but this was decidedly more remarkable than anything I had ever seen. On the floor were many articles—numerous flint arrowheads, pots, and other things. These were gathered along with the petrified poles, put into the wagon, and taken away. The Indian chief must have been a great man to have received such a burial and to have his afterlife so well supplied.

A GRANDFATHER ALMOST LOST

Winter on the prairie usually was intense with high winds and heavy snow. The blizzards were so severe, the snow so thick and blinding, that one could see no more than a few feet, nor could he keep his eyes open long.

At those times it was necessary to hold on to long ropes attached to the house when going to the barns and various cribs for feeding the animals. After a great blizzard the buildings, except our two-story house, were entirely snowed under; the drifts covered the thatches. Steps had to be cut into the snow down to the doors. The packed snow was so hard that it was strong enough to carry the weight of a man. When the sun came out and melted the surface of the snow slightly, it would freeze and form a thick crust, solid enough to support a yoke of oxen drawing a load of hay. During the blizzard herds of ponies or cattle would be left to take care of themselves. We always knew where they could be found. They drifted with the wind and snow and we would find them fifteen or twenty miles away in a direct line with the blizzard.

During one blizzard we spent a terrible night waiting for the return of my grandfather, who had gone to Mitchell to get a doctor for my sister. The doctor came out on his pony but my grandfather had walked. It was early in the evening, and the doctor reached our house just as the blizzard arrived over the prairie. (The doctor was forced to stay with us for two days.) When my grandfather failed to reach the ranch, the night was spent watching and putting candles and lamps in all the windows. It seemed impossible for anyone to live through such a night on the prairie. We knew he had started home because the doctor had passed him just before the snow began to fall. Grandfather told us later that he had stumbled through the blizzard from evening until two o'clock in the morning, when he came to the railroad track some miles west of Mitchell. He knew that he must be west of the town so he followed the tracks east and came into the roundhouse an hour later, more dead than alive. Most of the time he had been trailed by prairie wolves, which he could see dimly. He knew they were waiting for him to fall. He kept them off by shooting at them from time to time. He certainly was strong, as many a younger man might have died in such a blizzard.

BIRD SONG

After I learned that we were leaving Dakota—which had been a place of wonderful adventure for me—I became very lonely and sad. I dreaded going away, and from my final days on the prairie I have a vivid memory of a spring morning on Firesteel Creek.

A strong desire to go fishing for the last time in my favorite haunt got me up at daybreak. I went to a beautiful turn in the creek where I could usually catch large black-barred perch. I rode there, as I often did, on my little Billy—the last time I ever rode him. The fresh morning air was soft with a scent of earth and water such as comes only in the early spring. It was completely silent—the silence of a primitive prairie. Suddenly above me I heard a breath-taking bird song. Then silence for a long pause, then the song again, repeated at regularly spaced intervals—always the same limpid melody. The beauty of its sound, intensified possibly by my lonely feelings, raised the hair on the back of my neck and ran chills down my spine. It left such an impression that ever since I have listened for that particular song and have heard it occasionally during the years. Now, strangely enough, for the past few springs I have been thrilled by the song near my studio in the country—the same haunting melody. An ageless continuity of tiny creatures singing the same God-given song, always the same perfect notes and beautiful variations, known only to its kind. From what far time, no one knows, nor to what distant end.

It is a long jump in years, feelings, and experiences from the time when I first heard that bird song to now. I can hardly believe I am the same being. Life has brought so many changes to the son of a roving builder of railroads, who has lived so much in other worlds, that the boy I was seems like another person who has told me the story of his pioneer youth.

their express commands that I have the honor to assure your Majesty of their unanimous disposition and desire to cultivate the most friendly and liberal intercourse between your Majesty's subjects and their citizens, and of their best wishes for your Majesty's health and happiness, and that of your royal family. The appointment of a Minister from the United States to your Majesty's Court, will form an epoch in the history of England and of America. I think myself more fortunate than all my fellow-citizens in having the distinguished honor to be the first to stand in your Majesty's royal presence in a diplomatic character, and shall esteem myself the happiest of men, if I can be instrumental in recommending my country more and more to your Majesty's royal benevolence, and of restoring an entire esteem, confidence and affection, or in better words, the old good nature and the old good humor, between people, who though separated by an ocean, and under different governments, have the same language, a similar religion, and kindred blood.

"I beg your Majesty's permission to add, that although I have some time before been intrusted by my country, it was never in my whole life in a manner so agreeable to myself."

The King listened to every word I said with dignity, but with an apparent emotion. Whether it was the nature of the interview, or whether it was my visible agitation, for I felt more than I did or could express, that touched him, I cannot say; but he was much affected, and answered me with more tremor than I had spoken with, and said:

"Sir,

"The circumstances of thy audience are so extraordinary, the language you have now held is so extremely proper, and the feelings you have discovered [*i.e.,* revealed] so justly adapted to the occasion, that I must say that I not only receive with pleasure the assurance of the friendly dispositions of the United States, but that I am very glad the choice has fallen upon you to be their Minister. I wish you, Sir, to believe, and that it may be understood in America, that I have done nothing in the late contest, but what I thought myself indispensably bound to do, by the duty which I owed to my people. I will be very frank with you. I was the last to consent to the separation; but the separation having been made, and having become inevitable, I have always said, as I say now, that I would be the first to meet the friendship of the United States as an independent power. The moment I see such sentiments and language as yours prevail, and a disposi-

tion to give to this country the preference, that moment I shall say, let the circumstances of language, religion and blood, have their natural and full effect."

I dare not say that these were the King's precise words, and it is even possible that I may have in some particular mistaken his meaning, for although his pronunciation is as distinct as I ever heard, he hesitated some time between his periods, and between the members of the same period. He was much affected, and I was not less so, and therefore, I cannot be certain that I was so attentive [but] . . . the foregoing is his Majesty's meaning as I then understood it, and his own words as nearly as I can recollect them. . . .

The conversation with the King, Congress will form their own judgment of. I may expect from it a residence less painful than I once expected, as so marked an attention from the King will silence many grumblers; but we can infer nothing from all this concerning the success of my mission.

With great respect, &c. JOHN ADAMS.

One of the most stubbornly contested issues of the peace negotiations had involved the northeastern boundary of the United States. The treaty referred to the "River St. Croix," whose location varied from map to map. There turned out to be two more or less parallel streams emptying into Passamaquoddy Bay, not far apart at their outlet but separated by some fifty miles at their respective sources. Believing that possession was nine tenths of the law, Loyalist exiles quickly crowded into the disputed area, to the consternation of the officials of Massachusetts (Maine, it must be remembered, was part of the Bay State until 1820). By itself Massachusetts could not settle the dispute, and it was one of the earliest to demand Jay's attention as Secretary for Foreign Affairs.

Jay's novel proposal for a settlement sprang from his own experience when, as a young man back in 1769, he had served as clerk of the New York-New Jersey Boundary Commission. From the successful, if protracted, settlement of that dispute Jay became familiar with the notion of a mixed commission, and it was this device that he now recommended to Congress. Although Jay's recommendation was not acted upon at this time, he later revived the notion and introduced it into the treaty of 1794 with England that bears his name. The mixed commission proved Jay's most original and durable contribution to the settlement of international disputes involving the United States.

Aside from the northeastern boundary, much other territory was in dispute with England: the northern and western frontier forts, principally those at Dutchman's Point, Oswego, Niagara, Erie, Detroit, and Fort Michilimackinac. These forts fell inside the territory ceded to the United States by the Treaty of 1783, and the British had agreed to evacuate them "with all convenient speed." But the day before George III officially proclaimed the ratification of the treaty, the British government, as a result of Canadian pressure, ordered that the posts be retained. With Spain pressing its claims to the lower Mississippi and the British refusing to budge from the northern and western border posts, the independence of the new nation was seriously threatened. One of Adams' first acts as minister to the Court of St. James's was to request the British to evacuate them. The British demurred, quite pertinently citing as justification the legal impediments put up by the states to collecting the debts owed by Americans to British merchants and the widspread refusal of the states to follow the treaty's recommendation that the confiscated property of American Loyalists be restored to them. In a long report to Congress, Jay confessed that he felt that the British had justice on their side.

On the issue of the return of Negroes carried away by the British troops, Jay held that humanitarian considerations supported a liberal interpretation of the treaty, and that compensation might properly be accepted in lieu of the Negroes themselves, who presumably had been freed by the British. Both these points were consistent with Jay's moral position regarding debts, which he felt should be paid, and slavery, which he abhorred. While he did not disclose to the British the details of this secret report to Congress, he was indiscreet enough to reveal its substance to Sir John Temple, the British consul in New York. Jay's indiscretion could have had no result other than to stiffen the British determination to hold the forts as hostage to treaty compliance by the Americans, for Temple promptly relayed the information to Lord Carmarthen, the Foreign Secretary.

New York, 7 December 1786.
. . . I am upon such a footing of Acquaintance with Mr. Jay as that the other evening, when by ourselves at his own House, I asked him what Question Congress had come to, if any, concerning the State of grievances drawn up and given to Mr. Adams, by My Lord Carmarthen? Then he frankly told me (but with desire that I would not mention it in this Country) that he had reported fully upon the matter, that his report . . . upon the whole was, a full acknowledgment that many of the most important Articles in your Lordships Statement were just. Must be admitted as fact—and consequently a violation of the subsisting Treaty. That His Majesty was every way justifiable in still holding the

Our Country, BY BENSON J. LOSSING, 1878

During Jay's term as Secretary for Foreign Affairs the trans-Allegheny frontier began filling up with settlers. Their dependence on the Mississippi as an avenue of trade forced Jay into negotiations with Spain, which controlled both the river and the Gulf.

Western Posts untill these States should Manifest a fair and honorable disposition to fulfill their part of the said Treaty. That he also in his report entered largely into the Complaint on the American side of the question, particularly of the Negroes being carried off contrary to an Article in the Treaty, and upon the whole, as far as I could judge from his verbal accot. of the Report, (which will doubtless be adopted by Congress) it seems, he has stated matters in such a light as will I trust be more pleasing to his Majesty and his Ministers than I expected it would be. The Report is I understand upon the Table of Congress, but nothing can be done concerning it till the beginning of next month, when they will meet, chuse a President, and then proceed to Business, soon after which, 'tis probable their Resolution and doings upon this Business will be transmitted to their self sufficient, wrong headed Minister in London [Adams], who by his Mulish disposition, has lost ground in every respect, with Congress as well as in the particular state he belongs to. It is more than probable that both himself and his useless Secretary [William Stephens Smith] will soon be called Home, at any Rate, that after the expiration of their three Years appointment (12 months hence) they never will be reappointed to the Court of London. It is now pretty generally thought that had a Man of a Modest conciliatory disposition been sent to London a much better understanding would have long before this have subsisted between His Majesty and these States.

Adams had indeed been experiencing difficulties at court. Within six months of his letter to Jay describing his cordial reception by the King, he had written another, in cipher, which told a far different, sadder story.

Grosvenor Square, Westminster, 3 December, 1785.
Dear Sir,—

I am anxious to convey to you, if I can, in as strong a light as that in which I see it myself, the impossibility of our doing any thing satisfactory with this nation, especially under this ministry. . . .

The King, I really think, is the most accomplished courtier in his dominions. With all the affability of Charles II., he has all the domestic virtues and regularity of conduct of Charles I. He is the greatest talker in the world, and has a tenacious memory, stored with resources of small talk concerning all the little things of life, which are inexhaustible. But so much of his time is, and has been consumed in this, that he is, in all the great affairs of society and government, as weak, as far as I can judge, as we ever understood him to be in America. He is also as obstinate. The unbounded popularity, acquired by his temperance and facetiousness, added to the splendor of his dignity, gives him such a continual feast of flattery, that he thinks all he does is right; and he pursues his own ideas with a firmness which would become the best system of action. . . .

[Prime Minister William Pitt] is very young. He has discovered abilities and firmness upon some occasions; but I have never seen in him any evidence of greater talents than I have seen in members of congress, and in other scenes of life in America, at his age. I have not yet seen any decided proofs of principle, or patriotism, or virtue; on the contrary, there are many symptoms of the want of these qualities, without which, no statesman ever yet appeared uniformly great, or wrought out any memorable salvation for any country. In American affairs he has oscillated like a pendulum, and no one can yet guess when he will be fixed. His attention appears to have been chiefly given to two objects,—preserving tranquillity and raising the stocks. . . . the stocks are at a great height, and the nation consequently in high spirits. As they have now evidence, as they think, that their commerce flourishes, and their credit is established, without a treaty with the United States, and without opening the West Indies or Canada, Nova Scotia and Newfoundland to us, without taking off the alien duty upon oil, or admitting our ready built ships for sale, they will not now think it necessary to do any of these things. . . .

The posts upon our frontier give me great uneasiness. The ministers and people are so assured of peace with all their neighbors in Europe, that they hold all we can do in indifference. . . . They rely upon it, that we shall not raise an army to take the posts. The expense and difficulty they know will be great, and, therefore, they think they may play with us as long as they please. . . . The resolutions of some of the United States, staying proceedings at law for old debts, and some other resolutions concerning the tories, represented to have been in some instances contrary to the treaty, will be the pretence.

In short, sir, I am like to be as insignificant here as you can imagine. I shall be treated, as I have been, with all the civility that is shown to other foreign ministers, but shall do nothing. I shall not even be answered.

. . . I find myself at the end of my tether; no step that I can take, no language I can hold, will do any good, or, indeed, much harm. It is congress and the legislatures of the States, who must deliberate and act at present. . . .

With great regard, &c.
JOHN ADAMS.

For its part, Britain refused even to appoint a minister to the United States, but used consuls and unofficial observers to keep informed about what was going on across the Atlantic. Discouraged, Adams early in 1788 closed up shop and came home. The matter of the frontier posts was settled by Jay's Treaty of 1794, but the other issues smouldered for two more generations; it took another Anglo-American war and some years after that before they were settled.

Meanwhile, as they no longer enjoyed the protection of the British Navy, American merchant ships in Mediterranean waters were constantly victimized by the various deys, emperors, beys, or pashas who governed the Barbary States of North Africa. Most bothersome of the piratical states was Algiers, whose ruler, an absolute monarch, based his power on a formidable Turkish military corps. With some discrimination Algerian corsairs staged piratical raids, seizing ships and cargo, and selling officers and crews into captivity. In seeking to put down this piracy the United States learned quickly that it could not count on aid from any European nation. It was a maxim among the English merchants that "if there were no Algiers, it would be worth England's while to build one." The English would make no move to give the United States a toehold in the lucrative Mediterranean carrying trade. Matters became critical when, as a result of a treaty concluded in June of 1785 between Spain and Algiers, the Algerians had access to the Atlantic. Within a few weeks their privateers captured two American vessels, taking the crews captive. Jay looked upon this turn of affairs as providential, a view which he expressed to the president of Congress, Richard Henry Lee.

Office for foreign Affairs
13th October 1785

Sir

. . . This War does not strike me as a great Evil. The more we are treated ill abroad, the more we shall unite and consolidate at Home. Besides, as it may become a Nursery for Seamen, and lay the Foundation for a respectable Navy, it may eventually prove more beneficial than otherwise. Portugal will doubtless unite with us in it, and that Circumstance may dispose that Kingdom to extend commercial Favors to us farther, than they might consent to do, if uninfluenced by such Inducements. For my own Part I think it may be demonstrated, that while we bend our Attention to the Sea, every *naval* War however long, which does not do us essential Injury, will do us essential Good. . . .

At a bargain price of $10,000 the United States bought a treaty with Morocco in 1787. There still remained Algiers, Tripoli, and Tunis, whose pirates continued their depredations on American shipping, to the delight of the English merchants. Blackmail dollars advanced by the administrations of George Washington and John Adams temporarily bought off these three vandal states. By heroic efforts the United States succeeded in extorting a treaty from Tripoli in 1805, and another—at the cannon's mouth—from Algiers at the close of the War of 1812.

Most inflammatory of all issues of foreign relations during the Confederation was the demand of the United States to have Spain agree on the Mississippi River as the western boundary of the new nation and on the free navigation of that river as laid down in the Treaty of 1783 with Great Britain. To Jay it was a familiar story: during his mission in Spain he had explored the same issues several times in face-to-face encounters with the Conde de Floridablanca, foreign minister to Charles III, and with the Conde's English-speaking deputy, Don Diego de Gardoqui. Now, to settle outstanding differences and arrange a commercial treaty, Spain dispatched to New York the same Gardoqui. He felt quite sure, he confided to his superiors in Madrid, that he could manage Jay, whom he believed to be "a very self-centered man" whose vanity his wife abetted. "This woman, whom he loves blindly," the Spaniard observed, "dominates him and nothing is done without her consent, so that her opinion prevails, though her husband at first may disagree." From this Gardoqui inferred that "a little management in dealing with her and a few timely gifts will secure the friendship of both, because I have reason to believe that they proceed resolved to make a fortune." No comment could prove further off target, for if Jay was vain, and Sally liked society, neither was in

the least concerned with building a personal fortune.

Gardoqui arrived in New York in July, 1785, was received by Congress, and proceeded to occupy the handsomest residence in town, the Archibald Kennedy house at 1 Broadway. Although he gave the Secretary a gift from Charles III of a stallion (which the scrupulous Jay accepted only after securing Congress's permission), Gardoqui made little headway. The Jay-Gardoqui negotiations gave promise of a stalemate, as had the talks in Spain several years earlier. The American West, which had been penetrated during the Revolution by "long hunters" and scouts, was now being inundated by settlers from the eastern states, and even easterners, much as they might have deplored this drain of cheap labor, realized that if the claims of these westerners were abandoned the Confederation might be split apart.

In his negotiations in Spain, Jay had revealed himself as a staunch defender of America's claims to the navigation of the Mississippi to the sea, but he now felt that, in view of Spain's obduracy and America's impotence, the United States could gain nothing by holding out for the impossible but at least might gain great commercial advantages by agreeing to forbear temporarily the use of the Mississippi within exclusively Spanish limits. In the midst of a furious debate in Congress over the proposal, Jay was summoned to appear before that body. At issue, in addition to the navigation of the Mississippi, was the settlement of the disputed boundary between Spanish West Florida and the American Southwest. On August 3, 1786, he argued in a carefully reasoned speech that it would be better "to yield a few acres than to part in ill-humour." After reviewing the commercial advantages that the proposed treaty held out to America, and they were manifold, Jay came to the heart of the controversy.

. . . My attention is chiefly fixed on two Obstacles which at present divide us Vizt. the Navigation of the Mississippi and the territorial Limits between them [the Spanish territories in America] and us. . . .

Mr. Gardoqui strongly insists on our relinquishing it. We have had many Conferences and much Reasoning on the Subject [navigation rights] . . . His

While Spain squeezed the new nation from the south, Britain —by retaining Great Lakes forts like Oswego (at left)— held the northern frontier.

LOSSING's *Field-Book of the Revolution,* 1860

concluding Answer to all my Arguments has steadily been, that the King will never yield that Point, nor consent to any Compromise about it—for that it always has been and continues to be one of their Maxims of Policy, to exclude all Mankind from their American Shores.—

I have often reminded him that the adjacent Country was filling fast with People, and that the Time must and would come, when they would not submit to seeing a fine River flow before their Doors without using it as a Highway to the Sea for the Transportation of their Productions—that it would therefore be wise to look forward to that Event and take care not to sow in the Treaty any Seeds of future Discord—He said that the Time we alluded to was far distant, and that Treaties were not to provide for contingencies so remote and future. . . . The Truth is, that Courts never admit the Force of any Reasoning or Arguments but such as apply in their Favor; and it is equally true, that even if our Right to that Navigation, or to any Thing else, was expressly declared in Holy Writ, we should be able to provide for the Enjoyment of it no otherwise than by being in capacity to repel force by force.—

Circumstanced as we are, I think it would be expedient to agree that the Treaty should be limited to twenty five or thirty Years, and that one of the Articles should stipulate that the United States would forbear to use the Navigation of that River below their Territories to the Ocean. . . .

Whether Mr. Gardoqui would be content with such an Article I cannot determine, my Instructions restraining me from even sounding him respecting it—I nevertheless think the Experiment worth trying for several reasons.—

1. Because unless that Matter can in some way or other be settled, the Treaty however advantageous will not be concluded.—

2. As that Navigation is not *at present* important, nor will probably become much so, in less than twenty five or thirty years, our Forbearance to use it while we do not *want* it, is no great sacrifice.

3. Spain now excludes us from that Navigation, and with a strong Hand holds it against us—she will not yield it peaceably, and therefore we can only acquire it by *War*—now as we are not prepared for a war with any Power, as many of the States would be little inclined to a war with Spain for that Object, at this Day; and as such a War would for those and a variety of obvious Reasons be inexpedient, it follows, that Spain will for a long Space of Time yet to come exclude us from that Navigation. Why . . . should we not (for a valuable Consideration too) consent to forbear to use, what we know is not in our Power to use.

4. If Spain and the United States should part on this Point—what are the latter to do? Will it after that be consistent with their Dignity to permit Spain forceably to exclude them from a Right, which at the Expence of a beneficial Treaty, they have asserted? They will find themselves obliged either to do this and be humiliated, or they must attack Spain. Are they ripe and prepared for this? I wish I could say they are. . . .

If such a Compromise should be attempted and not succeed, we shall lose nothing by it—for they who take a Lease admit the Right of the Lessor. . . .

With respect to territorial Limits, it is clear to me that Spain can justly claim nothing East of the Mississippi but what may be comprehended within the Bounds of the Floridas. How far those Bounds extend, or ought to extend, may prove a Question of more Difficulty to negociate than to decide. Pains I think should be taken to conciliate and settle all such Matters amicably, and it would be better even to yield a few Acres than to part in ill Humour. If their Demands when ascertained, should prove too extravagant, and too pertinaciously adhered to, one Mode of avoiding a Rupture will still be left Vizt. referring that Dispute to impartial Commissioners. . . .

It is much to be wished that all these Matters had lain dormant for Years yet to come—but such Wishes are vain—these Disputes are agitating—they press themselves upon us, and must terminate in Accommodation, or War, or Disgrace. The last is the worst that can happen, the second we are unprepared for, and therefore our Attention and Endeavours should be bent to the first. . . .

JOHN JAY

In Congress, the southerners—from whose home states most of the western settlers came—assailed Jay for abandoning the West; the fact is that Jay, Washington, and other statesmen failed to appreciate the speed with which the empty spaces of the West would be filled by American settlers, and assumed that it would take about a generation before the balance would turn so much in America's favor that either by diplomacy or force these concessions could then be wrested from Spain. What Jay saw was a nation, rushing headlong toward political anarchy, being forced to fight a foreign war for which it was unprepared. While Congress by a sectional vote authorized Jay to move ahead with the treaty as he had outlined it, he realized full well that under the Articles of Confederation any treaty that the Secretary for Foreign Affairs might sign had to receive the votes of two thirds of the thirteen states, and that, since five states had voted against liberalizing his instructions, the nine necessary for ratification were probably unobtainable. This lesson of the

Jay-Gardoqui treaty negotiations was not lost on those framers of the Constitution who hailed from the South. They made sure that the new national charter would require a two-thirds majority of senators present for the ratification of a treaty.

As Congress fell into desultory inactivity, the Jay-Gardoqui negotiations were dropped, not to be revived until 1795; then, as a result of the American rapprochment with England, as evidenced by Jay's Treaty, the Spaniards in alarm granted to Thomas Pinckney what they had long withheld from Mr. Jay.

*W*hile *negotiations with England dragged on and those with Spain came to a halt, Jay was charged with arranging a consular treaty with America's wartime allies, the French. He was not the ideal man to conduct the negotiations. The French foreign office was not likely to forget or forgive his part in the separate secret negotiations with England. In 1784, Benjamin Franklin had put his signature to a consular convention with France which not only departed materially from the plan drafted by Congress but contained certain features that seemed more appropriate to one of France's satellite powers, a Poland or a Turkey, than to a new, prideful nation demanding independence, equality, and complete reciprocity.*

Jay was suspicious of anything that the French foreign secretary, the Comte de Vergennes, might initiate, and he could be counted on to scrutinize this treaty for every misplaced comma. As a nationalist Jay found Franklin's convention repugnant; as a technical lawyer, he criticized its deficiencies at various and sundry points.

Jay spelled out his views to Congress in his report of July, 1785. His summation, herein excerpted, proved convincing to Congress.

. . . The Convention appears well calculated to answer several Purposes; but the most important of them are such as America has no Interest in promoting. They are these

1st. To provide against Infractions of the french American Laws of Trade.

2d. To prevent the People of our Country from migrating to another.

3d. To establish in each others Country an influential Corps of Officers, under one Chief, to promote mercantile and political Views. . . .

The *third* of these Objects as it respects *mercantile* Views is apparent from the general Tenor of the Convention, and it appears plain to your Secretary, that a Minister near Congress, Consuls so placed as to include every Part of the Country in one Consulate or other, Vice Consuls in the principal Ports, and Agents in the less important zones, constitute a Corps, so coherent, so capable of acting jointly and secretly and so ready to obey the Orders of their Chief, that it cannot fail of being influencial in two very important political Respects; *first* in acquiring and communicating Intelligence, and *secondly* in disseminating and impressing such Advices, Sentiments and Opinions, of Men or Measures, as it may be deemed expedient to diffuse and encourage.

These being the *three* great Purposes which the Convention is calculated to answer; the next Question which naturally occurs is, whether the United States have any such Purposes to answer by establishing such a Corps in France.

As to the 1st—We have no laws for the Regulation of our Commerce with France or any other Dominions, and consequently we want no Provisions or Guards against the Infraction of such Laws.

As to the 2nd—We have not the most distant Reason to apprehend or fear that our People will leave us, and migrate either to the Kingdom of France or to any of its Territories, and consequently every Restriction or Guard against it must be superfluous and useless.

As to the 3d—France being a Country in whose Government the People do not participate, where nothing can be printed without previous Licence, or said without being known, and if disliked followed with Inconveniences, such a Corps would there be very inefficient for political Purposes. Where the People are perfectly unimportant, every Measure to influence their Opinions must be equally so—For *political Purposes* therefore we do not want any such Corps in France.

As to assisting our Merchants, and such other Matters as properly belong to Consuls, they would answer all those Purposes just as well, without these extraordinary Powers as with them.

Hence it is clear to your Secretary that the *three* great purposes which the Convention is calculated to answer, are such as the United States have no interest in promoting. . . .

Your Secretary also considers this Convention as greatly deficient in Reciprocity, inasmuch as by it we are to admit french Consuls into all our Ports and Places without Exception, whereas no Provision is made for the Admission of ours into any of the Ports, Places and Dominions of his Most Christian Majesty except the Kingdom of France only. He also thinks that the Omission of the Article securing to Consuls the Right of worshipping in their own Way in Chapels in their Houses, is a Deviation from Reciprocity, especially as that Liberty is not only permitted but established here. . . .

As a result of Jay's report, opposition to the convention of 1784 mounted, and Congress dragged its feet about ratifying it. Finally, Congress dispatched new instructions to Franklin's successor in France, Thomas Jefferson. Jefferson proved a skillful compromiser and obtained a new and slightly less objectionable convention, whose advantages he succinctly summarized in a letter to Jay.

Paris, Nov. 14, 1788.

Sir

... The clauses of the Convention of 1784, cloathing Consuls with the privileges of the law of nations, are struck out, and they are expressly subjected, in their persons and property, to the laws of the land.

That giving the right of Sanctuary to their houses is reduced to a protection of their Chancery room and its papers.

Their coercive powers over passengers are taken away: and over those whom they might have termed deserters of their nation, are restrained to deserted seamen only.

The clause allowing them to arrest and send back vessels is struck out, and instead of it they are allowed to exercise a police over the ships of their nation generally. . . . And the Convention is limited to 12. years duration. . . .

With John Jay's endorsement, the revised consular convention would be ratified by the new federal Senate in 1789. It was the first treaty ratified by the Senate under the Constitution.

While a good part of his attention was quite naturally directed toward America's relations with the great powers of the world, John Jay never lost sight of the nation's domestic problems, especially the central one: the essential weakness of the Articles of Confederation as an instrument of stable self-government. In the year or two before the Constitutional Convention a sense of crisis gripped the country. Business had yet to rebound from the acute depression of the postwar years. Unemployed seamen haunted the dockyards of Boston seeking work; noisome jails in western Massachusetts were overcrowded with debtors; and farmers were being evicted by foreclosure proceedings. In the West, conspiracy and separatism were in the air. The frontier seemed ripe for Indian risings. England curtly rejected every American effort to settle outstanding differences; even lowly Algiers contemptuously disputed America's power on the seas. How could Congress deal with these threats to security if it was unable even to levy an impost?

From his central post in the Confederation, John Jay saw the issues in the large, and his correspondence with George Washington at Mount Vernon and with Jefferson and Lafayette in France discloses the concern of statesmen that events like Shays' Rebellion, which began in the late summer of 1786, might trigger a general movement of disruption and even anarchy. The solution: a federal convention. Jay's anxious letters to Mount Vernon clearly reflect the growing apprehension that gripped the nation's Founding Fathers. The General's replies contain ample evidence that he shared these concerns; from New York on March 16, 1786, Jay wrote to Washington.

Dear Sir

... Although you have wisely retired from public Employments, and calmly view from the Temple of Fame, the various Exertions of that Sovereignty and Independence which Providence has enabled you to be so greatly and gloriously instrumental in securing to your Country; yet I am persuaded you cannot view them with the Eye of an unconcerned Spectator.

Experience has pointed out Errors in our national Government, which call for Correction, and which threaten to blast the Fruit we expected from our "Tree of Liberty." ... An opinion begins to prevail that a general Convention for revising the articles of Confederation would be expedient. Whether the People are yet ripe for such a Measure, or whether the System proposed to be attained by it, is only to be expected from Calamity and Commotion, is difficult to ascertain. I think we are in a delicate Situation, and a Variety of Considerations and Circumstances give me uneasiness. It is in Contemplation to take Measures for forming a general Convention. The Plan is not matured; if it should be well concerted and take Effect,

Powerless in foreign relations, the Confederation was also weak at home. The need for reform was emphasized in 1786 by a revolt (above) of debt-ridden Massachusetts farmers under Daniel Shays. It made Jay "uneasy and apprehensive—more so than during the War."

Our First Century, BY R. M. DEVENS, 1879

I am fervent in my wishes, that it may comport with the Line of Life you have marked out for yourself, to favor your Country with your Counsels on such an important and *single* occasion. I suggest this merely as a Hint for Consideration, and am with the highest Respect and Esteem

Dear Sir, your most obedient and very humble Servant

JOHN JAY

On May 18 Washington answered:

Dear Sir,

. . . I coincide perfectly in sentiment with you, my dear Sir, that there are errors in our National Government which call for correction,—loudly I will add; but I shall find myself happily mistaken if the remedies are at hand. We are certainly in a delicate situation, but my fear is that the people are not yet sufficiently misled to retract from error! To be plainer, I think there is more wickedness than ignorance, mixed with our councils. Under this impression, I scarcely know what opinion to entertain of a general Convention. That it is necessary to revise and amend the articles of Confederation, I entertain *no* doubt; but what may be the consequences of such an attempt *is* doubtful. Yet, something must be done, or the fabrick must fall. It certainly is tottering! Ignorance and design are difficult to combat. Out of these proceed illiberallity, *improper* jealousies, and a train of evils which oftentimes, in republican governments, must be sorely felt before they can be removed. . . . I think often of our situation, and view it with concern. From the high ground on which we stood, from the plain path which invited our footsteps, to be so fallen! so lost! is really mortifying. But virtue, I fear, has, in a great degree, taken its departure from our Land, and the want of disposition to do justice is the source of the national embarrassments. . . .

From Philadelphia, where he had gone to attend a church convention, Jay replied on June 27.

. . . Our affairs seem to lead to some Crisis, some Revolution, something that I cannot foresee or Conjecture. I am uneasy and apprehensive—more so than during the War. Then we had a fixed Object, and tho the Means and Time of attaining it were often problematical, yet I did firmly believe we should ultimately succeed because I was convinced that Justice was with us. The case is now altered, we are going and doing wrong and therefore I look forward to Evils and Calamities, but without being able to guess at the Instrument Nature or Measure of them. . . .

That we shall again recover, and things again go well, I have no Doubt. Such a Variety of Circumstances would not almost miraculously have combined to liberate and make us a Nation, for transient and unimportant Purposes. I therefore believe we are yet to become a great and respectable People, but when or how, the Spirit of Prophecy only can discern.

There doubtless is much Reason to think and to say that we are woefully and in many Instances wickedly misled. Private Rage for Property suppresses public Considerations, and personal rather than national Interests have become the great objects of Attention. Representative Bodies will ever be faithful Copies of their originals, and generally exhibit a chequered assemblage of virtue and vice, of abilities and weakness. The Mass of Men are neither wise nor good (and the same may be said of their representative Bodies) and the Virtue like the other Resources of a Country, can only be drawn to a point and exerted by Strong circumstances ably managed or strong Government ably administered. . . .

What I most fear is that the better kind of People— by which I mean the People who are orderly, and industrious, who are content with their Situations and not uneasy in their Circumstances, will be led by the Insecurity of Property, . . . the Loss of Confidence in their Rulers, and the want of public Faith and Rectitude, to consider the Charms of Liberty as imaginary and delusive. A State of Fluctuation and Incertainty must disgust and alarm such Men, and prepare their minds for almost any Change that may promise them quiet and Security (Some already whisper that it was not so before the War, and that it is a pity Britain forced us to set up Independence. But my dear Sir, we may Reason and toil as we please, he who made the World governs it.) . . .

Mount Vernon, 15th Aug., 1786
Dear Sir

. . . Your sentiments, that our affairs are drawing rapidly to a crisis, accord with my own. What the event will be is also beyond the reach of my foresight. We have errors to correct. We have probably had too good an opinion of human nature in forming our confederation. Experience has taught us, that men will not adopt and carry into execution, measures the best calculated for their own good without the intervention of a coercive power. I do not conceive we can exist long as a Nation, without having lodged somewhere a power which will pervade the whole Union in as energetic a Manner, as the authority of the different State governments extends over the several States. To be fearful of vesting Congress, constituted as that body is, with ample authorities for national purposes, appears to me the very climax of popular absurdity and madness. Could Congress exert them for the detriment of the public without injuring themselves in an equal or greater proportion? Are not their interests inseparably connected with those of their constituents? By the rotation of appointment must they not mingle frequently with the mass of citizens? Is it not rather to be apprehended, if they were possessed of the powers before described, that the individual members would be induced to use them, on many occasions, very timidly and inefficaciously for fear of losing their popularity and future election? We must take human nature as we find it. Perfection falls not to the share of mortals. Many are of opinion that Congress have too frequently made use of the suppliant humble tone of requisition, in applications to the States, when they had a right to assume their imperial dignity, and command obedience. Be that as it may requisitions are a perfect nihility, where thirteen sovereign, independent, disunited States are in the habit of discussing and refusing compliance with them at their option. Requisitions are actually little better than a jest and a bye word throughout the Land. If you tell the Legislatures they have violated the treaty of peace and invaded the prerogatives of the confederacy they will laugh in your face. What then is to be done? Things cannot go on in the same train forever. It is much to be feared, as you observe, that the better kind of people being disgusted with the circumstances will have their minds prepared for any revolution whatever. We are apt to run from one extreme into another. . . .

What astonishing changes a few years are capable of producing! I am told that even respectable characters speak of a monarchical form of government without horror. From thinking proceeds speaking, thence to action is often but a single step. But how irrevocable and tremendous! What a triumph for the advocates of despotism to find that we are incapable of governing ourselves, and that systems founded on the basis of equal liberty are merely ideal and fallacious! Would to God that wise measures may be taken in time to avert the consequences we have but too much reason to apprehend.

Retired as I am from the world, I frankly acknowledge I cannot feel myself an unconcerned spectator. Yet, having happily assisted in bringing the ship into port, and having been fairly discharged, it is not my business to embark again on a sea of troubles. Nor could it be expected that my sentiments and opinions would have much weight on the minds of my Countrymen—they have been neglected, though given as a last legacy in the most solemn manner. I had then perhaps some claims to public attention. I consider myself as having none at present. With sentiments of sincere esteem and friendship,

I am, Dear Sir, Your most Obedient and Affectionate Humble Servant, GEO. WASHINGTON.

New York 7 January 1787

Dear Sir

They who regard the public good with more Attention and Attachment than they do mere personal Concerns, must feel and confess the Force of such Sentiments as are expressed in your Letter. . . . The Situation of our Affairs calls not only for Reflection and Prudence but for Exertion. What is to be done? is a common Question, but it is a Question not easy to answer.

Would the giving *any* further Degree of power to Congress do the Business? I am much inclined to think it would not for among other Reasons: It is natural to suppose there will always be Members who will find it convenient to make their *Seats* subservient to partial and personal Purposes; and they who may be *able* and *willing* to concert and promote useful and national Measures, will seldom be unembarrassed by the Ignorance, Prejudices, Fears, or interested Views of others.

In so large a Body Secrecy and Dispatch will be too uncommon; and foreign as well as local influence will frequently oppose, and sometimes frustrate the wisest Measures.

Large assemblies often misunderstand or neglect the Obligations of Character Honor and Dignity; and will collectively do or omit Things which individual Gen-

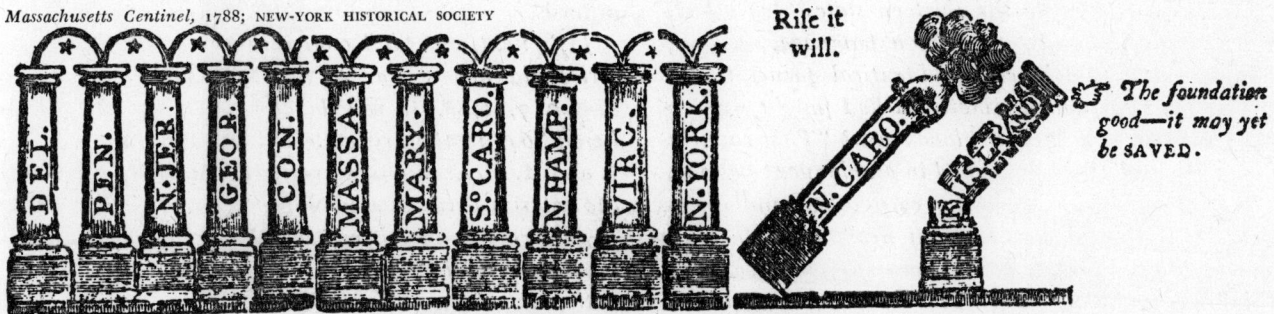

Rife it will.

The foundation good—it may yet be SAVED.

The FEDERAL EDIFICE.

Reform finally came, in the Constitution of 1787. Jay helped to get it adopted by writing some of The Federalist *papers and by influencing his native New York to ratify. North Carolina and Rhode Island were the last to enter "The Federal Edifice."*

tlemen in private Capacities would not approve. As the many divide Blame and also divide Credit, too little a Portion of either falls to each Mans Share to affect him strongly; even in Cases where the whole Blame or the whole Credit must be national. It is not easy for those to think and feel as Sovereigns who have always been accustomed to think and feel as Subjects.

The *executive* Business of Sovereignty depending on so many Wills, and those Wills moved by such a Variety of contradictory Motives and Inducements, will in general be but feebly done.

Such a Sovereign, however *theoretically* responsible, cannot be effectually so in its Departments and Officers, without adequate Judicatories.

I therefore promise myself Nothing very desireable from any Change which does not divide the Sovereignty into its proper Departments. Let Congress legislate, let others execute, let others judge. . . .

A Convention is in Contemplation, and I am glad to find your Name among those of its intended Members. . . .

No Alteration in the Government should I think be made, nor if attempted will easily take place, unless deduceable from the only Source of just authority— *The People. . . .*

*J*ay had made no secret of his Federalist views, and the Antifederalists of New York made sure that he was not a delegate to the Constitutional Convention. Like everyone else, he was kept in the dark about what was going on, since the convention strictly observed the rule of secrecy. But once the text of the Constitution was disclosed, Jay became one of its foremost champions. Collaborating with Hamilton and Madison, he wrote five of the famous Federalist letters that appeared in the New York press under the pseudonym of Publius.

Jay's first contribution appeared in print on October 31, 1787, four days after the initial essay, which was written by Hamilton. In Federalist No. 2 Jay diagnosed the weaknesses in the arguments of those Antifederalists who preferred a division of the states into distinct confederacies or sovereignties to a union of them all. Why ignore the geographical advantages which served to unite the thirteen states? Jay asked. Why deny the bonds of common language, religion, customs, and attachment to identical principles of government for which Americans had fought side by side through a long and bloody war? "This country and this people," he remarked in an eloquent passage, "seem to have been made for each other, and it appears as if it was the design of Providence, that an inheritance so proper and convenient for a band of brethren, united to each other by the strongest ties,

should never be split into a number of unsocial, jealous and alien sovereignties."

Four days later, on November 3, Publius once again appeared in the press as the author of the third Federalist letter. If peace and security were America's goal, then, Jay contended, a disunited America was more likely to provoke war than a united country. Indeed, military security depended on a strong and perpetual union.

Writing at a feverish pace, Jay rushed the fourth Federalist essay to the presses, and it appeared on November 7. Herein Jay turned from the problems of military security to the comparative commercial prospects of America under the Articles of Confederation and the Constitution. Reminding his readers that the Americans were the rivals of both the British and the French in the fisheries and of most European nations in the carrying trade, Jay showed how America challenged the trade monopolies that certain European powers sought to maintain in their commerce with China and India, and that it was to the interest of such powers (Britain and Holland were, of course, implied) to restrain American trade in these areas rather than to encourage it. Looking at the situation right on the American continent, Jay showed how Spain and Britain, in order to maintain their respective monopolies, continued to shut the Mississippi to American navigation and to exclude Americans from the St. Lawrence. Such grounds of friction might readily provide an envious foreign government with a pretext for war. Confronted by a united American government, however, a foreign power might have second thoughts about pursuing such a belligerent course.

Three days later, on November 10, Jay's fifth Federalist essay appeared in New York's Independent Journal; it was reprinted several days later in other New York papers, as the previous letters had been. Concentrating his fire on confederacies, Jay pointed to the small island of Britain which for centuries had been broken up and divided into three nations. Should the United States follow such a course and allow itself to be broken up into three or four confederacies, the most northern soon proving the most formidable and thereby provoking jealousy and animosity from the others?

Jay's next and final contribution to the Federalist series did not appear in the New York press until March 7, 1788. It was labelled No. 63, but numbered "64" in the first collected edition, published by J. and A. McLean and corrected by Hamilton. During the interim between mid-November and early March, Jay appears to have been painfully crippled by arthritis, which kept him from more active collaboration with Hamilton and Madison. There are but two

Federalist *papers known to be extant in draft form, and both are in Jay's hand. They are the fifth and the sixty-fourth. The original draft of the latter number, in a form considerably different from the published one, was uncovered by the Jay Papers researchers at the New-York Historical Society.*

Jay begins letter No. 64 by pointing out that the making of treaties is entrusted by the Constitution to the President, with the concurrence of two thirds of the Senate present, and that precautions are taken to guarantee that the men chosen for the respective elective posts are "the best qualified for the purpose." He feels that the choice of the President by the Electoral College and the selection of senators by state legislatures would ensure these results. In retrospect we may dispute Jay on both these points, for the Electoral College has proved a cumbersome and even fallible device, and the nation through the Seventeenth Amendment has long since stripped state legislatures of the power of designating United States senators.

What gives special pertinence to No. 64 is its comment on the need for secrecy and timing in treaty-making, and its stress—echoed ever more loudly in our subsequent history—on the key role of the President to negotiate a treaty with dispatch.

... They who have turned their attention to the affairs of men, must have perceived that there are tides in them. Tides, very irregular in their duration, strength and direction, and seldom found to run twice exactly in the same manner or measure. To discern and to profit by these tides in national affairs, is the business of those who preside over them; and they who have had much experience on this head inform us, that there frequently are occasions when days, nay even when hours are precious. The loss of a battle, the death of a Prince, the removal of a minister, or other circumstances intervening to change the present posture and aspect of affairs, may turn the most favorable tide into a course opposite to our wishes. As in the field, so in the cabinet, there are moments to be seized as they pass, and they who preside in either, should be left in capacity to improve them. So often and so essentially have we heretofore suffered from the want of secrecy and dispatch, that the Constitution would have been inexcusably defective if no attention had been paid to those objects. Those matters which in negociations usually require the most secrecy and the most dispatch, are those preparatory and auxiliary measures which are no[t] otherwise important in a national view, than as they tend to facilitate the attainment of the objects of the negociation. For these the president will find no difficulty to provide, and should any circumstance occur which requires the advice and con-

For Jay and other backers of a strong central government, triumph came with the inauguration of President-elect Washington at New York's Federal Hall on April 30, 1789.

sent of the senate, he may at any time convene them. Thus we see that the constitution provides that our negociations for treaties shall have every advantage which can be derived from talents, information, integrity, and deliberate investigations on the one hand, and from secrecy and dispatch on the other. ...

Fateful for the success of the great experiment was the fight to win New York over to the pro-Constitution camp, and in that fight Jay played a leading role. New York was sharply divided into pro- and anti-Federalist camps. At the very end of May, Jay drafted a letter to Washington in which he expressed regret that the election of delegates to the state's ratifying convention had not been delayed, because as things stood, the majority of the convention would be "composed of anti-foederal characters." As Jay saw it, and probably correctly, the tide of public opinion was running in favor of the Constitution. To him, all that was needed to counter the propaganda of the antis was the passage of time.

Jay's forebodings were borne out. When the ratifying convention met at Poughkeepsie on June 17 the Antifederalist delegates were the overwhelming majority. Jay shrewdly distinguished between Antifederalists like Governor George Clinton, who hoped for a quick vote rejecting the Constitution with "as little debate and as much speed as may be," and "their followers," many of whom he considered more disinterested.

Jay, along with Hamilton and Robert R. Livingston, the undisputed leaders of the pro-Constitution faction, quickly saw the advantage in driving a wedge between the Antifederalist leaders and their followers. As early as May 30 he let word drop to Washington that the notion was being bruited about that, should the Antifederalists prove obdurate, the southern part of the state would separate and adhere to the Union, leaving the upstate fragment a landlocked republic.

On July 4, Jay reported to Washington that the

issue had boiled down to whether the Constitution would be ratified in New York with prior or with subsequent amendments. As yet the antis were not agreed among themselves on the formula. It was Jay who cut the Gordian knot. On July 11 he moved both the unconditional ratification of the Constitution and the recommendation of such amendments as might be deemed expedient: "Let us agree and be unanimous. . . . We will have our Constitution; you will have your Amendments." It was largely through Jay's efforts that the convention, by a close vote (30 to 27), ratified the Constitution. The convention adopted a compromise plan, resolving unanimously to prepare a circular letter to the state legislature recommending a general convention to consider amendments. The first ten amendments (the Bill of Rights) were proposed by Congress and ratified by the states, making such a general convention unnecessary. Up to now, no such general convention has ever assembled, although there is much agitation for one at the present time.

*W*ith the Confederation drawing to a close, Jay sought to defer decisions on foreign affairs until the new government was formally installed. One problem could not be put off, however. In 1787 the Comte de Moustier was named France's minister to the United States, succeeding the chargé d'affaires, Louis-Guillaume Otto, whom Jay disliked intensely. The Comte was accompanied to New York by his sister-in-law, Madame la Marquise de Bréhan, who travelled with him ostensibly for reasons of health. The Comte had never been known for his tact, and, save perhaps for "Copenhagen" Jackson, the offensive British envoy to the United States on the eve of the War of 1812, it is hard to think of a diplomat better calculated to arouse the most hostile feelings in his host nation than was Moustier. The Comte presented his credentials to Congress in February, 1788, and settled down with the Madame la Marquise in a splendid town house. He quickly rubbed everyone the wrong way by his unadulterated snobbery and his outrageously bad manners. He showed his contempt for Americans by various calculated insults: he called Cyrus Griffin, the Virginia lawyer and President of Congress, "a tavern-keeper"; and he took along his own chef when he went out to dine. Apart from his hauteur and his notorious stinginess, Moustier shocked American society, above all the very proper John Jay, by giving credence to the growing scandal that he was living in sin with his very odd sister-in-law, who held him captive to her caprices. Jay put the matter to Jefferson in Paris in a letter he entrusted to Gouverneur Morris, who was about to sail for France. The request for Moustier's recall, it must be remembered, was from Jay, not from Congress.*

Private
N York 25 Novr. 1788

Dear Sir

. . . The Count de Moustier found in this Country the best Dispositions to make it agreable to him, but it seems he expected more particular and flattering Marks of minute Respect than our People in general entertain ideas of, or are either accustomed or inclined to pay to anybody. This added as I suspect and believe to Insinuations from persons who have no Desire that he should be very agreable to us, or we to him, have led him into Errors relative to men and things which naturally dispose him to give and receive Disgust. Appearances (whether well or ill founded is not important) have created and diffused an opinion that an improper Connection subsists between him and the Marchioness. You can easily conceive the Influence of such an opinion on the Minds and Feelings of such a People as ours. For my part I regret it; she seems to be an amiable woman; and I think if left to the Operation of his own judgment and Disposition his Conduct relative to this Country would be friendly and useful. These are things that I have not said or written to any other person. Nor is it pleasant to say or write them, but in the situation you are in, Information of this Kind may have its uses. With great Esteem and Regard I am Dear Sir Your most Obt. & Hble. Servt.,

JOHN JAY

On prodding from Jefferson, France's foreign secretary, the Comte de Montmorin, Vergennes's successor, granted Moustier a "leave of absence." In October of 1789 Moustier sailed for home, the first foreign diplomat to be the victim of an American foreign secretary's notions of propriety.

In the spring of 1789, meanwhile, Jay had seen his efforts rewarded when a strong central government under the leadership of President Washington took up its task. The President-elect was met by cheering crowds on his journey from Mount Vernon to New York to assume his post as the nation's first Chief Executive under the Constitution. A barge especially constructed for the occasion conveyed him from Elizabeth, New Jersey, to New York Harbor. He was greeted by a tumultuous welcome, and on April 30 he was inaugurated at Federal Hall. Jay saw his fondest hopes fulfilled. In the years to come he was to continue to play a leading role in the great federal drama.

Mr. Morris, Gouverneur Morris Professor of History at Columbia University, is one of the nation's leading authorities on the American Revolution and its aftermath. This is the second excerpt we have presented from the Jay Papers, which he is preparing for publication by Harper & Row.

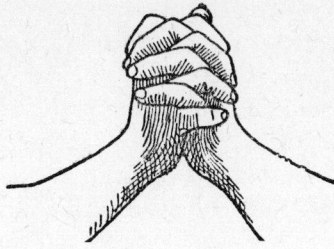

The Flowering of the Speaker's Art

Well down on the title page of *The Speaker's Ideal Entertainments; for Home, Church and School* comes the promise of "Hints upon Gesture and Dramatic Poses." Hints is far too modest a word, for this primer on elocution all but demands that the public declamation of words and evocation of moods be accompanied by precisely appropriate and intricate sets of gesticulation and posturing. The book was published in the 1890's, at the end of a golden century of freewheeling rhetoric—the eras of Clay and Calhoun, of Webster and Sumner, of Lincoln and Douglas—and doubtless was intended to set in order the house of oratory. The book's strength and appeal lay in its rigid formulas for conveying thought and emotion; conformity to its rules offered comfort and confidence to the speaker and, supposedly, instantaneous comprehension to his listeners. Take, for example, the four figures in our frontispiece; they appear, along with several others, in *The Speaker's Ideal*. Their gesticulation being perfectly wedded to the words they are uttering, the proper pairings of captions and photographs should be child's play. The captions are: "Hence! horrible shadow, Unreal mockery, hence!" "Nathan said unto David, 'Thou art the man.'" "Fly, fly, beloved mistress, the devils of the mountains are upon us!" and "Blessed mother, save my brain!"

In its ministrations to "the amateur, as well as the elocutionist," *The Speaker's Ideal* leaves little to chance. Introductory sections discuss such matters as carriage ("Dignity and grace should characterize the walk as the performer approaches the front. The limbs . . . while being flexible and elastic, should not have a looseness or shambling action"); the need to analyze a given piece and to express its meaning exactly ("It is a heinous sin to commit intellectual murder . . ."); various vocal tones—guttural, pectoral, aspirate, falsetto—and their appropriate employment; and the choice of material itself ("In cases of uncertainty, it is well to consult the committee, and if they sanction, all responsibility will be removed from the performer"). Ah, but it is gesture—"without which, there can be neither natural, oratorical, nor dramatical delivery" —that comes in for the most detailed examination. "As a tree without leaves," contend the authors, "so is recitation without gesture," thereby forever denying the possibility of beauty in a winterscape. The would-be Cicero is told that "a thorough . . . drill upon the mechanical formation and elements of action is indispensable"; he is warned that "no one should depend upon the inspiration of the moment." The book then takes him through the Positions of the Feet (Retired, below), tells him what to do with his Hands (Supine, at the left; Vertical, above; Clasped, top), and, finally, illustrates a staggering multiplicity of windmillings for hand and arm. *The Speaker's Ideal* then thoughtfully provides a glossary on gesture (page 103), which is a table of reference for the footnotes accompanying many of the recitative selections that comprise the remainder of the book. Except for one item in the glossary, "Sp.—Special," there are no chinks in the armor that protects the speaker from his own inventiveness. The instructional section concludes with line drawings (examples, overleaf) of the proper, and presumably only, attitudes for expressing almost every passion, emotion, and sentiment. The poem on the next two pages typifies the book's taste and its approach to oratory. As you try it out before a mirror, you will have to decide who the victim of your intellectual murder will be —the happily forgotten author of "A Woman's Vengeance" or Hamlet, who tells you not to "saw the air too much with your hand, thus. . . ."

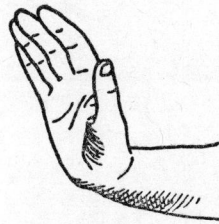

—*John L. Phillips*

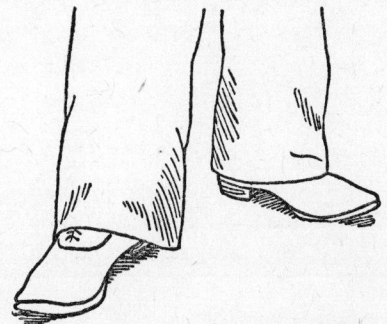

EXPECTATION.

DISCERNING.

GREETING.

MISCHIEF.

REPULSION.

BASHFULNESS.

TRIUMPH.

RIDICULE.

MADNESS.

A Woman's Vengeance

I thank[1] you for your sympathy,
But help! No,[2] there is none for me.
For what I've done I feel no sting
Of penitence, nor can time bring
One pang of sorrow. You may think
Me hard, unfeeling, and may shrink[3]
From me with loathing when I say,
I'm glad my bullet found the way
Into his heart; and I would do
The same again, and glory,[4] too,
In having done it. Penalty!
For what they now may do with me
I care but little.[5] He is dead,
And that ends all.
What made me do the deed? The old,
Old[6] time-worn story of man's cold
And heartless cruelty; of wrongs
Heaped on her head,[7] to whom belongs
At least respect,[8] if nothing more.
I met him—him, my husband—just
Five years ago. My God! what trust
I placed in his fair words, so soft,
So sweet, so full of love. But love is blind,
And I was madly so. The first two years
Were full[9] of joy—joy without tears.
My life was of peaceful love.
But ah! the change came sudden, fast;
My summer sun was overcast.[10]
The godlike being that I thought
Of all mankind[11] the most perfect wrought,
Tore off[12] the mask that hid his face,
And, to my horror,[13] in his place
Revealed a demon,[14] blackest-hued,
Remorseless, pitiless, imbued
With all the wickedness that heart
Can hold, or shameless sin[15] impart....
Then came at last the final blow—
The worst that love can contemplate,
And which can turn that love to hate.[16]
One night, when he had gone from me,
I found a letter which he carelessly
Had overlooked. The script[17] was small
And neat—a woman's hand! A wall
Of fire outstretched[18] before my eyes;
A nameless horror seemed to rise.

GESTURES. 1. Bow head. 2. V. Con. 3. B.V. to right. 4. A.O. 5. Shrug shoulders. 6. H.B. 7. P.H.O. 8. H.O. 9. B.H.O. 10. V.A.O. 11. B.H.O. 12. V. Sp. 13. B.V. to R. 14. Ind. D.O. 15. P.D.O. 16. P.D.O. 17. Look in left hand. 18. V.H. Sw. 19. Clasp to breast. 20. To head. 21. B.P.D. 22. B.Cl. D. 23. Sp. 24. Trace on left hand. 25. Hand to head. 26. H.O. 27. To self. 28. Left Sp. 29. H.F. 30. B. sp. 31. Lis. 32. To self. 33. H.O. 34. Lean to R. and raise hand. 35. To head. 36. B.V.Sp. 37. H.F. 38. Look to left. 39. B.D.F. 40. Left H.O. 41-42. B.Sp. 43. Start back. 44. R. hand to heart. 45. Left V. Sw. 46. Sp. 47. Ind. H.F. 48. B.V.H.F. 49. B.H.O. 50. A.O. 51. To self.

No, no! this could not be. He might
Be bad, be dead to sense of right,
But false! O Heaven![19] The dreadful thought
Surged in my brain.[20] I crushed[21] it, fought[22]
It down with frenzied eagerness.
The note was open; chilled, nerveless,
I drew it[23] from its fold and read,
[24]"This night to meet him," so it said.
This night! how throbbed[25] my aching head!
Her house it gave—the place, the hour—
I seemed renewed with sudden power.
He[26] would be there, and so would I.[27]
I cast[28] the hated letter by;
My child from off the floor I clasped,
And from the bureau drawer I grasped
A loaded pistol that would right
My wrong. So out[29] into the night,
Into the raging storm, I fled,
My babe clasped[30] in my arms. . . .
So through the night I sped along
Until I reached her house.
And then I heard[31]
A voice within—his voice! Each word
In sweet and loving tenderness,
And accents that my[32] heart should bless
Were lavished on her[33] listening ears.
I listened, listened,[34] all unseen,
Until I thought I should go wild.[35]
Then, with a desperate hand, flung wide[36]
The casement. With a bound, beside
The two[37] I stood. She started—screamed;
He turned[38] and saw me, and then seemed
A moment as if turned to stone;
And as his baseness I made known,
She—poor thing—with a long, low cry,
Sank[39] to the floor despairingly.
Then, like a fiend let loose from hell,
He toward[40] me leaped with one fierce yell,
And grasping[41] quick a heavy chair
Cried, "Curse you!" whirled it high[42] in air.
I sprang aside[43] in sudden dread;
The blow fell full upon the head
Of my sweet child, that lifeless dropped
Back in my arms. My heart throbs[44] stopped;
A red mist swam[45] before my sight;
I could not scream, try as I might.
I grasped the pistol[46] from my breast,
And then I killed[47] him! All the rest
For days to me was blank;[48] and when—
O Heaven! why did I not die then?
At last my sense came back. I would
Have taken my own life if I could.
But it perhaps was better[49] so;
God will not judge me hard, I know.
And when, in answer to His call,
I stand within the heavenly hall,[50]
And the Blessed One
Says, "Why hast thou transgressed my laws?"
My babe shall plead its mother's[51] cause.

SURPRISE.   APPEAL.   ENTREATY.

NOTATIONS OF GESTURE

Front, Oblique, Lateral, and Backward are relative
directions for the hand and arm. The Supine hand is
used unless there is a specific indication to the contrary.

D.F.—Descending Front	V.—Vertical hand
D.O.—Descending Oblique	Ind.—Index finger supine
D.L.—Descending Lateral	Ind. P.—Index finger prone
D.B.—Descending Backward	Cl.—Clinched hand
H.F.—Horizontal Front	Cla.—Clasped hands
H.O.—Horizontal Oblique	Ap.—Hands applied
H.L.—Horizontal Lateral	Sp.—Special
H.B.—Horizontal Backward	Sw.—Sweep from shoulder
A.F.—Ascending Front	Sust.—Sustained gesture
A.O.—Ascending Oblique	Lis.—Hand to ear
A.L.—Ascending Lateral	Par.—Arms parallel
A.B.—Ascending Backward	L.—Use left hand
B.—Both hands to be used	Imp.—Impulse or repetition
P.—Prone hand	Con.—Movement from elbow

DEFIANCE.   WOE.   MOURNING.

"Take the hatred away..." CONTINUED FROM PAGE 80

Sweet, who had admitted firing his gun, as the best candidate. If Henry was acquitted, the weaker cases against the other defendants would collapse.

The second trial, begun in April, 1926, followed a pattern similar to the first. Darrow spent a week selecting the jury, working his way through some 165 talesmen. The same number of witnesses paraded to the stand for the prosecution and stubbornly told the same story. Darrow was able to dig a little deeper into their testimony. He got one man to admit that at the July 12 meeting of the Water Works Park Improvement Association a representative of the nearby Tireman Avenue Improvement Association had risen and recommended driving out the Sweets with violence, and he had received a rousing round of applause. Very much perturbed, District Attorney Toms rose to ask if the Tireman Avenue delegate had *advocated* violence. After a pause, the witness answered, lamely, "Yes."

Darrow also managed to produce an additional white witness, a Mrs. Hinteys, who lived on the block and said she had seen at least five hundred people swarming there on the murder night. Dr. Ossian Sweet gave his version of the fatal uproar, and Henry Sweet, too, took the stand in his own defense. He "made an excellent appearance in the witness chair," Darrow said later. "He was frank and open-mannered and made no attempt to conceal his part in the tragedy."

The mood of this second trial was harsher and angrier than the first. The prosecution made a serious attempt to make a martyr out of the late Leon Breiner. They pictured him as a peaceful, law-abiding citizen, minding his own business on his neighbor's lawn. Assistant prosecutor Moll in his summation said that Henry Sweet was a coward who had shot Breiner in the back as he leaned forward to light his pipe. Moll also stated that race had nothing to do with the case. It was a murder case, not a race case, he insisted.

When Darrow rose to make his final summation, he was angry. This time he read no poems, and he made very little effort to create sympathy for Henry Sweet. When he talked about race, he did it in hard, gutty terms, bluntly telling the jury, "I say you are prejudiced," and insisting "there isn't a man in Detroit who doesn't know that the defendant did his duty, and that this case is an attempt to send him and his companions to prison because they defended their constitutional rights.

. . . Now that is this case, gentlemen, and that is all there is to this case. Take the hatred away, and you have nothing left."

Then Darrow tore into the late Leon Breiner. "Mr. Moll says that this is a case between Breiner and Henry Sweet."

"No, I did not say such a thing," Moll snapped.

"Well, let me correct it. He says that he holds a brief for Breiner. That is right; isn't it?"

"That is right."

". . . If he holds a brief for Breiner he should throw it in the stove. It has no place in a court of justice. . . . It isn't easy to talk about the dead, unless you 'slobber' over them and I am not going to 'slobber' over Breiner. . . . Who was he? He was a conspirator in as foul a conspiracy as was ever hatched in a community; in a conspiracy to drive from their homes a little family of black people. Not only that, but to destroy these blacks and their home. . . . Why was he there? He was there just the same as the Roman populace were wont to gather at the Colosseum where they brought out the slaves and the gladiators and waited for the lions to be unloosed. . . . He was there waiting to see these black men driven from their homes, and you know it; peacefully smoking his pipe, and as innocent a man as ever scuttled a ship."

He went on to skewer the police. Of one policeman who claimed only four people had been in the school yard, he snarled, "I wouldn't say this man lied. It takes some mentality to lie. An idiot can't lie."

The residents of Charlevoix Avenue received equally rough handling. Most of them were of immigrant stock, with far less education than the Sweets. They regularly mispronounced nearby Goethe Street. Darrow selected one, a schoolteacher named Miss Stowell; "fifteen years a high school teacher and in common with all the other people in the community she called it Gother Street," he sneered. ". . . If they had one colored family up there, some of the neighbors might learn how to pronounce Goethe."

He castigated the Water Works Park Improvement Association, and scorched both its members and the police for their conduct on July 12. The police had admitted that two plainclothesmen had been at the meeting. "They heard a man make a speech that would have sent any colored man or political crusader to jail. Advocating violence! Why

104

wasn't he arrested? A man haranguing a crowd to violence and crime in the presence of officers! And the crowd applauded this mad and criminal speech."

Darrow talked for almost eight hours, mostly in the same tough, no-nonsense vein. Only at the close did he return to a plea for sympathy and understanding. "Let me say just a parting word for Henry Sweet, who has well nigh been forgotten. I am serious, but it seems almost like a reflection upon this jury to talk as if I doubted your verdict. What has this boy done?"

Deftly Darrow summed up Henry's motives for going to the house of his brother. "[Ossian] had helped Henry through school. He loved him. He had taken him into his home. Henry had lived with him and his wife; he had fondled his baby. . . . Should this boy have gone along and helped his brother? Or should he have stayed away? What would you have done?"

Darrow paused; he could have ended here. But as one reporter wrote, "Some deep instinct warned him that he had not yet said quite all," and he returned again to what he believed was the heart of the case:

. . . the life of the Negro race has been a life of tragedy, of injustice, of oppression. The law has made him equal, but man has not. And, after all, the last analysis is, What has man done?—and not, What has the law done? I know there is a long road ahead of him, before he can take the place which I believe he should take. I know that before him there is suffering, sorrow, tribulation and death among the blacks and perhaps the whites. I am sorry. I would do what I could to avert it. I would advise patience; I would advise toleration; I would advise understanding; I would advise all of those things which are necessary for men who live together.

Gentlemen, what do you think is your duty in this case? I have watched day after day these black tense faces that have crowded this court. These black faces that now are looking to you twelve whites, feeling that the hopes and fears of a race are in your keeping.

This case is about to end, gentlemen. To them it is life. Not one of their color sits on this jury. Their fate is in the hands of twelve whites. Their eyes are fixed on you, their hearts go out to you, and their hopes hang on your verdict.

This is all. I ask you, on behalf of this defendant, on behalf of these helpless ones who turn to you, and more than that, —on behalf of this great state, and this great city which must face this problem, and face it fairly—I ask you in the name of progress and of the human race, to return a verdict of Not Guilty in this case!

A friend who met Judge Murphy inside the door of his chambers immediately after Darrow finished speaking said, "I had never seen [Murphy] so moved. He took my hand and said, 'This is the greatest experience of my life. That was Clarence Darrow at his best. I will never hear anything like it again. He is the most Christlike man I have ever known.'"

The jury deliberated only three hours. As they filed in to give the verdict, another eyewitness described Darrow "seated with his hands grasping the arms of the chair, his great body stooped over, his head leaning forward." When the foreman of the jury, in response to the Judge's question, said, "Not guilty," Darrow sank down in his chair, and Toms, afraid that his opponent was about to faint, stepped to his side. Darrow gave him a weary smile. "I'm all right," he murmured to the District Attorney. "I've heard that verdict before."

The state dropped the charges against the other defendants, and Dr. Ossian Sweet eventually moved into his house and lived there for a number of years. But the rest of his life was marked by a series of personal tragedies. His daughter died in childhood, and his wife succumbed to tuberculosis after a long struggle. On March 19, 1960, after years of ill health, Ossian Sweet was found dead, a bullet through his head and a revolver in his hand. Henry Sweet became a lawyer and practiced in Detroit until his death in 1940. Of the other principals, only Otis Sweet, the dentist, is still alive. Interviewed by Detroit news reporters on the fortieth anniversary of the case, Otis recalled his arrival by taxicab that evening. "The street was a sea of humanity," he said. "The crowd was so thick you couldn't see the street or the sidewalk. Just getting to the front door was like running the gantlet. I was hit by a rock before I got inside."

The Sweet house still stands on the corner of Garland and Charlevoix. The neighborhood is still composed of middle-class families in similar houses on small, city-size plots. But now it is predominantly Negro. It was untouched by the rioting that burned down dozens of square blocks of Detroit in the summer of 1967. But Dr. Otis Sweet's dental office on the second floor of 9300 Mack Avenue on the east side was destroyed when looters sacked and burned the shoe store on the street level.

In his final comment on the case, Clarence Darrow, in a more philosophic mood, wrote that he felt the white people who tried to drive the Sweets out of their home were not really responsible for their actions. They were only "a product of the bitterness bred through race prejudice." To this he added a last sentence that rings with harsh reality for both white and black citizens in Detroit and the nation today. "As long as this feeling lives, tragedies will result."

Mr. Fleming is a frequent contributor to our pages. His tenth book, West Point: The Men and Times of the U.S. Military Academy, *will be published next month by Morrow.*

build the dam and would not know until they had completed their surveys. Assuming that the engineers would keep them informed, the Indians once more let them make their studies.

The members of the Seneca Nation by this time numbered approximately 4,300, of whom perhaps 1,800 lived on the Allegany Reservation, 2,200 on the Cattaraugus Reservation thirty miles away, and the rest off the reservations. The Allegany Reservation, on which the engineers were focusing their attention, totalled 30,469 acres in a slender, forty-two-mile-long strip, averaging a mile wide, on both sides of the Allegheny River as it wound through a valley to the Pennsylvania border. Some 12,000 acres of the reservation were occupied by Salamanca and the other white towns or were taken by rights of way for roads and railroads, and much of the rest of the land was steep, rocky, forested hillside and therefore uninhabitable. Most of the Indians lived in frame houses or hemlock-board shanties strung out in a long line in clearings and wooded areas on the lower hills and bottomlands along the river. The average annual income of a family was about $3,000 (as against $5,000 for a white family in Salamanca), but the Indians, generally, lived in contentment, with fish, game, and firewood close at hand, and with a privacy and a closeness to nature that many a white visitor envied. South of the Pennsylvania line and separated from the reservation by three miles, about fifteen of Cornplanter's descendants still lived on his grant, close to the cemetery where his monument stood.

The engineers made their surveys and left, and in 1956 the Senecas were startled to learn that Congress had appropriated funds for plans for Kinzua Dam. Hearings had been held in Washington, and the engineers had testified, but the Indians had neither been invited to the hearings nor been informed that they were occurring. Now thoroughly alarmed, the Senecas and their tribal attorney moved quickly on two fronts. First they sought an injunction to keep the engineers off their land. Next, recognizing the need for flood control, they hired two eminent private engineers, Dr. Arthur E. Morgan, a former chairman of the Tennessee Valley Authority, and Barton M. Jones, who had built the T.V.A.'s Norris Dam, to make an independent study of the need for Kinzua Dam and, if possible, to propose an alternative dam site that would not involve the flooding of their lands.

The cat was now out of the bag. Newspapers began to publicize the Senecas' plight, and angry congressmen claimed that the engineers had misled them, that

they had not been informed about the treaty. But if the engineers were chagrined, they failed to show it. Ignoring their critics, they got federal courts, early in 1957, to uphold their right to continue to make surveys on the reservation. And that same year, when Morgan and Jones presented an alternative plan for diverting Allegheny flood waters into Lake Erie at what they claimed was a cheaper cost than the Kinzua project, and without inundating reservation land, the engineers testified successfully against it in Congress (with "explicit misstatements and misrepresentations," according to Dr. Morgan) and won another one-million-dollar appropriation to complete the planning and begin the construction of Kinzua Dam.

The Indians had friends, in and out of Congress, but not enough of them. Dr. Morgan produced still another alternative proposal—a dam site that would not involve any Indian lands—but a study sponsored by the engineers concluded that Dr. Morgan's dam would cost more money and take longer to build. Morgan and the Senecas did not agree, and sought an independent comparison, but the engineers prevailed on the Senate to turn aside this request. Treaty or no treaty, the engineers were not going to risk a reversal of their plan, which now, it was revealed, would necessitate the condemnation of slightly more than 10,000 acres of the Indians' habitable land (leaving them only 2,300 on which they could live); the moving of 134 families, or about 700 people, more than one third of the population of the reservation; the relocation of about 3,000 Seneca graves; and the inundation of the Cornplanter grant in Pennsylvania.

Falling back on the 1794 treaty, which promised that the United States would never claim the Senecas' land and guaranteed that it should be theirs until they chose to sell it, the Indians, in a case against the Secretary of the Army, now sought to halt construction of the Kinzua project, hoping to force the adoption, instead, of the Morgan plan. On April 14, 1958, the U.S. District Court for the District of Columbia ruled that the engineers could take reservation land, the same as any other, by the right of eminent domain, implying, in effect (although the court did not condone it), that the government of the United States, which could make a treaty, could also break it if it wished to do so. The case went on to the U.S. Court of Appeals for the District of Columbia and to the Supreme Court, but the judgment stood. Whether by their own ignorance or by the withholding of information from Congress, the engineers had maneuvered Congress into a position of voting, in the 1950's, to break still another Indian treaty, which it had the constitutional, if not the moral, right to do. By the time Congress realized what it had done, it was too late. The engineers had too many friends on Capitol Hill, and there was no one strong enough to induce the bureaucratic wheels within the corps to reverse themselves.

That this was true became painfully clear to the Senecas when, as a last desperate measure, they appealed to President Kennedy in 1961, hoping that he would use his prerogative to withhold funds appropriated for the dam. On August 9, 1961, Kennedy replied to Basil Williams, the president of the Seneca Nation: "I have now had an opportunity to review the subject and have concluded that it is not possible to halt the construction of Kinzua Dam. . . . Impounding of the funds appropriated by the Congress after long and exhaustive congressional review, and after resolution by our judicial process of the legal right of the Federal Government to acquire the property necessary to the construction of the reservoir, would not be proper."

And so the dam was built. In his letter to Williams, President Kennedy had added that he would direct federal agencies to assist the Senecas by considering the possibility of finding new land to exchange with the Nation for the area it would lose; by reviewing the recreational potential of the reservoir and methods by which the Senecas could share in that potential; by determining the special damages suffered by the Nation's loss of so much of its land; by aiding those Senecas who had to give up their homes; and by preparing recommendations for whatever legislation might be required to achieve those ends. The White House sent a copy of the letter two days later with a covering memorandum to Major General William F. Cassidy, director of civil works, Corps of Engineers, ordering the corps to "look into these questions without delay."

The letter was bucked down through the corps, and although meetings, begun two months later, were held with other government agencies such as the Bureau of Indian Affairs, as well as with representatives of the Senecas, the corps behaved as if it were thoroughly irritated with the Indians and had no intention of doing anything for them. The corps did pay the salary of an able and dedicated representative of the B.I.A., Sidney Carney, a Choctaw Indian who was sent to work among the Senecas. But except for that, two full years later, with the dam nearing completion and the

At a council meeting, two members consider plans for Seneca-run tourist concessions.

Indians still living in their old homes that were threatened by the reservoir, so little had been done by Cassidy and the engineers to carry out Kennedy's order that some congressmen, moved to anger, introduced bills authorizing payments for the relocation and rehabilitation of the Indians. "Apparently you don't want to try to do anything for this Indian tribe," Congressman John P. Saylor of Pennsylvania berated a stony-faced corps witness. "Apparently you have become so calloused and so crass that the breaking of the oldest treaty that the United States has is a matter of little concern to you. . . . the Corps of Engineers has never intended to do anything whatsoever with regard to the Seneca Indians, and they have intended from the very beginning to treat this as just any other dam and leave the Indians only their recourse in the courts."

On August 31, 1964, after months of disagreement between the House and Senate over how much to pay the Senecas—a disagreement caused to some extent by the corps's influence in urging the Senate to cut down the original House figures and not pay the Indians except via the usual court proceedings—Congress passed a $15,000,573 reparations bill for the Senecas. But added to the bill was a disturbing amendment requiring the Secretary of the Interior to present to Congress within three years a plan for the termination of the Senecas' relations with the federal government—in effect bringing to an end such things as the tax-exempt status of the reservation and federal approval of leases and trusteeship of Seneca land. (The plan was submitted at the end of the three-year period. That was in 1967, and although Congress has so far failed to act on the Senecas' termination, it may do so at any time.)

Meanwhile, shortly after President Kennedy had shut the final door on them, the Senecas, who had fought hard to save their land, set about determinedly to prepare for the coming disruption. Under the leadership of George Heron, a past president of the Nation, they set up committees to pick relocation areas for new homes and cemeteries, to plan housing and new community centers, and to propose economic

development projects that would aid the people in their new situation. When Congress's appropriation became available in September, 1964, the Senecas were ready to move quickly. New ranch-type homes of varying designs were built during the wet and wintry months, in two tightly compressed areas that totalled 500 acres. One of them, named Jimersontown, near Salamanca, was laid out in 145 one-acre plots; the other, Steamburg, near the southern end of the reservation, had 160 plots of the same size. The Corps of Engineers built the streets in both of the new settlements. A family could own as many as three plots, but even so, the shift to suburban-type living, with houses close to each other, was a sharp change for people who had been used to privacy and a closeness to the woods and wild game. Other money was used to move 3,000 Seneca graves to two new cemeteries; to build a community center and tribal council headquarters on each reservation; to develop a sixty-acre industrial park on the Cattaraugus Reservation for industry that hopefully would employ Indians; and to set up a 1.8-million-dollar educational fund for college and business and vocational school scholarships for young Senecas. In addition, twenty-five public housing rental units on the Allegany Reservation and thirty-five at Cattaraugus were erected with other federal funds.

The hubbub of moving was accentuated by a constant harassment from the engineers, whose plans called for completion of the dam in 1965 and who kept posting deadlines for the Indians to get out of the condemned area. In working with the leadership of the Senecas, the engineers behaved properly and according to orders and regulations, but many Senecas today remember only their cold and officious manner and recall them as the Sioux recall Custer.

It was traditional in the nineteenth century for the government, when it wanted something from the Indians, to promise them anything and then let someone else worry about carrying out the promise—which, more often than not, was never done. In the case of the Senecas, the government revived the tradition. By 1968, with the dam built and the engineers gone from the scene, the Senecas were well on their way to adjustment to a new life on their smaller reservation. But in scores of ways, hopes that the Indians had once held high were still unrealized. Complaints ranged from new homes left unfinished (front steps not provided from the porch to the ground) or already showing signs of shoddy construction, to frustrated attempts to bring revenue to the Nation through use of the area's new recreational potential. Although the engineers, in response to President Kennedy's letter, had led the Senecas to believe that they could profit from concessions on the reservoir, the Indians were indefinitely stalled:

the water level at their end of the reservoir, the upper portion, rises and falls the most, and through much of the year contains great mud flats. Solving the problem by channelling or other means would have cost much more than the Indians could afford, especially since their concessions would be competing economically with other facilities (some of them free to the public) prepared by the engineers at the taxpayers' expense lower down on the lake, where the water level is more constant.*

The owners and residents of the Cornplanter grant, across the state line in Pennsylvania, were treated even more highhandedly by the engineers. Acquiring that plot, sacred to the chief's descendants and to the followers of the Handsome Lake religion, required delicate treatment by the engineers; instead, its owners were treated like any other citizens being ousted from their property. As early as February, 1961, the Cornplanter heirs, organized as the Cornplanter Indian Landowners Corporation, accepted the fact that most of the grant would have to be given up to the reservoir and that The Cornplanter's grave and monument would have to be moved. As a means of persuading the Senecas to accept this decision quickly and without a legal contest, the engineers promised Merrill W. Bowen, president of the Cornplanter group, that the cemetery would be moved to a place of the Indians' choice.

The Senecas first selected a site on the highest part of the grant, which would not be flooded, but the engineers turned it down with the argument that they could not build an access road to it. Then, on August 23, 1963, the Senecas were given a sixty-five-acre tract above the level of the reservoir by the family of Latham B. Weber, publisher of the Salamanca *Republican-Press*. The site was ideal. It was on the west side of the river, close to the old grant and contiguous to the southern boundary of the Allegany Reservation. But no sooner had the newspaper announced the gift than the engineers informed both Bowen and the Webers that they needed that tract too, not for the reservoir but for public recreation purposes! "It is essential to the needs of the project," the engineers wrote.

There then began a protracted attempt by the Senecas to change the engineers' mind, an attempt that floundered in a sea of deafness, evasions, and red tape. On October 1, 1963, despite their original promise to relocate Cornplanter's grave in a place of the Indians' choice, the engineers announced in a newspaper re-

* One way in which the Senecas hoped to profit from the expected flow of visitors was to create a multimillion-dollar tourist attraction called Iroquoia, which would project the Indians' history and culture in a Williamsburg-like re-creation of Iroquois settlements of the past. The Senecas have not yet decided whether the plan is economically feasible.

lease that all the graves on the grant would be moved to a new cemetery on a hill across the river, which the Indians would share with whites who were losing their cemetery too. More than 150 Cornplanter heirs signed a petition in protest, but the engineers were unmoved and on March 31, 1964, received authority from a federal court in Erie, Pennsylvania, to relocate the Indian graves wherever they wished. The relocation to the site across the river, which began on August 26, was attended by threats, rumors, and charges. Fearful of trouble (one Indian, it was claimed, did try to stop the work), the engineers were overly secretive about the matter, and on the day that the monument was to be moved and Cornplanter's grave opened, only two heirs were notified to be present as witnesses. Two others showed up, however, and charges later appeared in newspapers and were filed with the engineers and with the office of Senator Joseph S. Clark of Pennsylvania, claiming rough and irreverent handling of the remains, mixing of the bones, and other misdeeds by those carrying out the work. The engineers went to great length to deny the charges, though they did not take affidavits from those who made them. True or not, the charges reflected the state of tension and hostility between the Cornplanter heirs and the engineers.

The conflict was not over, for the Cornplanters still had no land for a memorial and meeting grounds to take the place of the old grant. In December, 1964, Senator Clark made a personal appeal to Colonel James C. Hammer, the district engineer in Pittsburgh, to allow the Indians to keep the Weber tract. Hammer first told Clark's office that the Webers had given the land to the Senecas only after they had known it was to be condemned, which was totally untrue and which the Webers and Bowen were quick to deny. Hammer then replied formally on January 27, 1965, suggesting that the corps meet with the Indians to try to help them find a suitable site, but implying that they

Presiding at the meeting was Calvin "Kelly" John, just completing a two-year term as the Senecas' president.

could not have the Weber tract, which provided "a prime location for recreational facilities." In February, Curtis F. Hunter, a corps representative in Warren, Pennsylvania, near the dam site, met with Bowen and the Webers' attorney in Salamanca, proposed certain alternative possibilities, including the Indians' use of the Weber tract by license rather than ownership, and suggested that they all meet with Colonel Hammer the next time that officer was in the area. On March 14 Hunter called for a meeting on the following day. Hammer did not show up, and instead of talking about the Weber tract, Hunter seemed anxious to pressure the Indians into acceptance of the use of an alternative site across the river. When an impasse was reached, he promised to write Colonel Hammer a letter explaining the Indians' reasons for wanting to retain the Weber tract and told Bowen he would send him a copy. He failed to do this; instead, on April 1, one of his colleagues in Warren, a real-estate official named Stanley O'Hopp, asked the Senecas for another meeting on April 5. At that conference, O'Hopp told them that they could not keep the Weber property, but he offered them three alternative sites, the biggest of which, across the river, totalled about sixty-three acres. When the Indians again argued for the Weber tract, he told them to state their position on paper and submit it to the corps for consideration.

On April 21, Bowen followed up the suggestion and wrote to Colonel Hammer, telling him that O'Hopp's alternative proposals did not reflect a "clear understanding" of the needs and desires of the Cornplanter descendants, and then explaining in detail why the Indians wished to retain the Weber tract. On receipt of the letter, Hammer decided that nothing more could come of further discussions with the Cornplanter heirs, and he ordered condemnation proceedings to be started against the Weber property. Withholding this information from the Cornplanters, Hammer wrote Bowen on May 13 a curt note stating, "I have carefully considered the contents of your letter, but I am unable to find a valid basis for changing the determination . . . that the Weber tract in its entirety is essential to the needs of the Project."

When Bowen got the letter, he telegraphed Hammer, asking for a meeting with him personally. On May 21 Hammer's deputy, Lieutenant Colonel Bruce W. Jamison, replied evasively in a letter that "the Corps" would be pleased to be "represented at such conference as you may arrange," and also notified the Seneca, almost as an afterthought, that "in line with" Colonel Hammer's letter of May 13, the corps was commencing eminent domain proceedings for the acquisition of the Weber tract. "As you know," Jamison concluded, "the negotiations for acquisition by purchase were not productive of a mutually agreeable price." The Indians could not have known such a thing, because there had never been any negotiations with them over a price.

Meanwhile, the Quaker representative living among the Senecas had written President Johnson an appeal for his assistance in behalf of the Cornplanters, who were still being pushed around. The letter was referred by the White House to Lieutenant General W. K. Wilson, Jr., chief of engineers, in Washington, who sent it to Colonel Hammer in Pittsburgh for his comments. On May 27 General Wilson replied to the Quaker representative, passing on several pieces of misinformation supplied him by Hammer, among them that Hammer "had met with Mr. Bowen on several occasions to negotiate the acquisition of the land for the project" (they had not met face-to-face once, despite Bowen's request for such a meeting), and that when the Webers had given the land to the Indians, "it was well known that the 'Weber' tract was scheduled for acquisition by the Corps" (an untruth that Bowen and the Webers had already set straight). "The entire 'Weber' tract is essential to the needs of the project and must be acquired," General Wilson concluded, employing the same words that Hammer had used in his note of May 13 to Bowen.

The Army had its back up, and neither General Wilson nor anyone else in the corps could see the silliness of their bureaucratic rigidity. Insisting that a small, sixty-five-acre tract for recreation was essential to the success of the Kinzua Dam project would have been farcical had it not been so unhappy for the Indians. Nor did the Army stop there. From its point of view, the Quaker representative had made a grievous mistake in appealing to the President, and now the Senecas would pay for it.

On May 28, in reply to another telegraphed appeal from Bowen, Colonel Hammer let the Cornplanter leader know that there was nothing more to discuss about the Weber property and that the Army had already instituted eminent-domain proceedings. Recognizing that the engineers could not be stopped, the Cornplanter heirs finally surrendered on June 15, writing Colonel Hammer that they would give up the Weber land but wished to discuss use of the sixty-three acres across the river that Hunter and O'Hopp had mentioned the previous March and April. Hammer replied, asking Bowen to set up the meeting, but shortly afterward Bowen's wife died, and the conference did not occur until September 16. It proved to be the last straw. Hunter and O'Hopp appeared for the engineers and announced that, because of the Indians' "procrastination," the offer of sixty-three acres had been reduced to 8.42 acres, almost entirely hillside,

covered with trees and brush. The Indians were shocked, but they could get nowhere with the corps's negotiators. In a last pitiful appeal, Bowen asked if Hunter could get the engineers to tack on another two acres at the bottom of the hill where the ground was level and the Cornplanters could hold their picnics without danger of sliding. Hunter said he would try, but the next day he called back and reported that the answer was No. Some day, he said, there might be a ski development "back in that direction," and the level land would be needed for a road on which to get in.

So the Cornplanters, in the end, accepted an exclusive but revocable license to use the 8.42 isolated acres of steep land. They have not used it yet, and probably will never use it. On September 24, 1965, Bowen wrote a final letter to Senator Clark, who, although an insistent advocate of the building of Kinzua Dam, had also tried to help the Cornplanters. Telling the Pennsylvania Senator of the outcome of their struggle, Bowen urged him to make no further effort in their behalf. "We have been informed," he said, "that our prior efforts to obtain your assistance and that of President Johnson have merely irritated the Corps of Engineers and possibly damaged our case. Your intervention now might only bring about some excuse to take away the few crumbs still offered to us."

His reason for writing the Senator, Bowen went on, was "to give you the benefit of our sad experience as you may find legislative opportunities to improve the approach of the Corps of Engineers to other people in the future—people who may be as inexperienced, poor, and lacking in shrewdness and legal services as we have been."

Kinzua Dam was formally dedicated on September 16, 1966. Two hundred and eighty-three years after William Penn had signed his famous treaty, Pennsylvania lost the last of its Indians. At a gala luncheon in the local high school after the ceremonies at the dam, a quartet of girls known as The Kinzua Damsels entertained Governor William Scranton and the other guests with the song "This Is My Country." And in California, Montana, Alaska, and elsewhere, the Army Corps of Engineers was already threatening other Indian tribes with plans for more Kinzuas.

Mr. Josephy, editor of the American Heritage general books division, is the author of The Patriot Chiefs *(Viking, 1961),* The Nez Perce Indians and the Opening of the Northwest *(Yale, 1965), and* The Indian Heritage of America, *just published by Alfred A. Knopf. In 1966–67 he held a Guggenheim fellowship for a study of the present status of the Indian; the results will also be published by Knopf.*

To make his drawings, Mr. Silverman visited the Allegany Reservation and attended a Seneca council meeting.

110

How Harding Saved the Versailles Treaty

CONTINUED FROM PAGE 67

tions about the treaty with sufficient nonchalance. There was, reported the *New York Times* the next day, "no mystery as to the whereabouts of the officially certified copy." Still, the *Times* added, with a slightly puzzled air, the President "will not come out flatly and tell just where the treaty is deposited."

The aftermath is largely told in an exchange of notes between Harding and Hughes after the news conference was over on July 15. From Harding:

My dear Mr. Secretary:

I have your note of this date enclosing a copy of the letter of Ex-President Wilson with which he sent to you the official copy of the Versailles Treaty. I did not have the information when the newspaper correspondents queried me on this subject and I made reply to them along the lines of our conversation at noon today. If mysterious publicity results I think perhaps it would be well for you to say at your next newspaper conference that you have the Treaty in the files of the Department of State, and let it go at that without further explanation or elaboration. If I had had the information I might have very easily answered the inquiry and disposed of the question.

Very truly yours,
WARREN G. HARDING

From Hughes:

My dear Mr. President:

I should have added to my note referring to the return of the Versailles Treaty by Mr. Wilson, that I received it from Mr. Wilson's messenger while you were holding your Press Conference, and at once telephoned to Mr. Christian so that word could in some way reach you during the Conference in case any question were asked. Mr. Suydam of this Department [Henry W. Suydam, chief of the Division of Current Information], who was in attendance at the Conference, of course knew nothing about the return of the Treaty as it was received after he had left the Department.

Faithfully yours,
CHARLES E. HUGHES

The treaty document was promptly and carefully filed in the Department of State's archives. Newspapermen were assured in a matter-of-fact way that the treaty was where it ought to be and that any press speculation regarding its possible loss was unfounded. The incident was thereafter soon forgotten and a public joke at the government's expense was prevented—or at least postponed until the relevant notes turned up, when the Harding Papers were made available by the Harding Memorial Association in 1964. It was then revealed how the Harding administration had "saved" the Treaty of Versailles.

Mr. Murray is the head of the history department at Pennsylvania State University. He is the author of Public Opinion and the American Red Cross (1950) *and of* Red Scare: A Study in National Hysteria (1955).

Statement of Ownership, Management and Circulation (Act of October 23, 1962; Section 4369, Title 39, United States Code)

1. Date of Filing: October 1, 1968
2. Title of Publication: AMERICAN HERITAGE
3. Frequency of Issue: Bi-Monthly
4. Location of known office of publication: 551 Fifth Ave., City, County, and State of New York, 10017.
5. Location of the headquarters or general business offices of the publishers: 551 Fifth Ave., N.Y., N.Y. 10017.
6. Names and addresses of publisher, editor, and managing editor: Publisher, Darby Perry, 551 Fifth Ave., N.Y., N.Y. 10017; Editor, Oliver O. Jensen, 551 Fifth Ave., N.Y., N.Y. 10017; Managing Editor, Robert L. Reynolds, 551 Fifth Ave., N.Y., N.Y. 10017.
7. Owner, American Heritage Publishing Co., Inc., 551 Fifth Ave., N.Y., N.Y. 10017. The names and addresses of stockholders owning or holding 1 percent or more of total amount of stock of American Heritage Publishing Co., Inc.: American Association for State and Local History, Nashville, Tenn.; The Society of American Historians, Inc., c/o Prof. Eric F. Goldman, Dept. of History, Princeton University, Princeton, N.J.; Charles Bruce Catton, Irwin Glusker, Oliver O. Jensen, Richard M. Ketchum, James Parton, individually and as Trustee under Declarations of Trust for James Parton III, for Dana Parton, for Nike Parton, and for Agnes L. Parton and a Child of the Grantor, Joseph J. Thorndike, all of 551 Fifth Ave., N.Y., N.Y.; Virginia L. Thorndike, 520 E. 77th St., N.Y., N.Y.; Gerald P. Rosen, 3307 N.E. 16th St., Fort Lauderdale, Fla.; Merrill, Lynch, Pierce, Fenner & Smith, Inc.,* 70 Pine St., N.Y., N.Y.; Alexander Hehmeyer, 401 North Wabash Ave., Chicago, Ill.; Roger S. Phillips, P.O. Box 11, Rowayton, Conn.; Shearson, Hammill & Co.,* 14 Wall St., N.Y., N.Y.; Barbara Joan Straus, c/o Irving Trust Co., 1 Wall St., N.Y., N.Y.; John Thorndike and Alan Thorndike, 11 Owenoke, Westport, Conn.; Evans & Co., Inc.,* 60 Wall St., N.Y., N.Y.; Clark Dodge & Co., Inc.,* 61 Wall Street, N.Y., N.Y.; Gale & Co.,* c/o Harris Trust & Savings Bank, 111 West Monroe St., Chicago, Ill.
8. Known bondholders, mortgagees, and other security holders owning or holding 1 percent or more of total amount of bonds, mortgages, or other securities: None.
9. For completion by nonprofit organizations authorized to mail at special rates (Section 132.122, Postal Manual): The purpose, function, and nonprofit status of this organization and the exempt status for Federal income tax purposes (check one)
☐ Have not changed during preceding 12 months
☐ Have changed during preceding 12 months
10. Extent and nature of circulation:

* Held for accounts of clients.

	AVERAGE NO. COPIES EACH ISSUE DURING PRECEDING 12 MONTHS	ACTUAL NO. COPIES SINGLE ISSUE NEAREST TO FILING DATE
A. Total No. Copies Printed (Net Press Run)	335,900	302,000
B. Paid Circulation		
1. Sales through dealers and carriers, street vendors and counter sales	800	800
2. Mail Subscriptions	319,400	293,800
C. Total Paid Circulation	320,200	294,600
D. Free Distribution (including samples) by Mail, Carrier, or other means	3,400	3,400
E. Total Distribution (Sum of C and D)	323,600	298,000
F. Office Use, Left-over, Unaccounted, Spoiled after Printing	12,300	4,000
G. Total (Sum of E and F —should equal net press run shown in A)	335,900	302,000

I certify that the statements made by me above are correct and complete.

Darby Perry
Publisher

A Note to Hippies & Flower People

DRAWN FOR AMERICAN HERITAGE BY GERRY GERSTEN

"We have reached an age, those of us to whom fortune has assigned a post in life's struggle, when, beaten and smashed and biffed by the lashings of the dragon's tail, we begin to appreciate that the old man was not such a damned fool after all. We saw our parents wrestling with that same dragon, and we thought, though we never spoke the thought aloud, 'Why don't he hit him on the head?' Alas, comrades, we know now. We have hit the dragon on the head and we have seen the dragon smile."

—ERNEST LAWRENCE THAYER, *Harvard '85 at his class's tenth reunion*

This quotation appeared in The Annotated Casey at the Bat, *a book about Mr. Thayer's famous poem, edited by Martin Gardner (Clarkson N. Potter, 1967).*

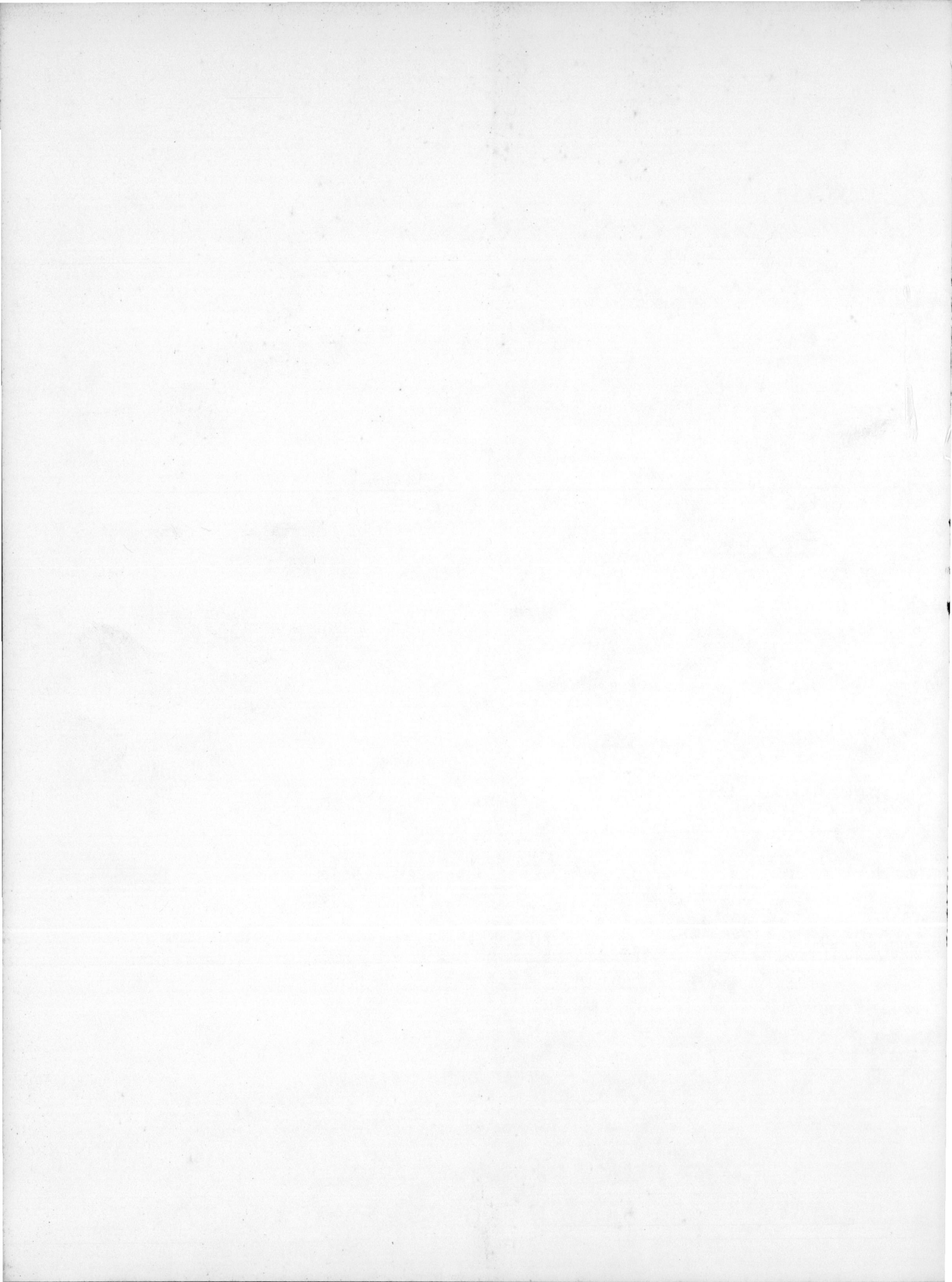